The

Erotic Phenomenon

Jean-Luc Marion

TRANSLATED BY *Stephen E. Lewis*

THE UNIVERSITY *of* CHICAGO PRESS

CHICAGO & LONDON

Originally published as Le phénomène érotique, © Éditions Grasset & Fasquelle, 2003.

The University of Chicago Press, Chicago 60637
The University of Chicago Press, Ltd., London
© 2007 by The University of Chicago
All rights reserved. Published 2007
Paperback edition 2008
Printed in the United States of America

17 16 15 14 13 12 11 10 09 08   2 3 4 5 6
ISBN-13: 978-0-226-50536-7 (cloth)
ISBN-13: 978-0-226-50537-4 (paper)
ISBN-10: 0-226-50536-7 (cloth)
ISBN-10: 0-226-50537-5 (paper)

Library of Congress Cataloging-in-Publication Data

Marion, Jean-Luc, 1946–
   [Phénomène érotique. English]
   The erotic phenomenon / Jean-Luc Marion ; translated by Stephen E. Lewis.
        p.   cm.
   Includes index.
   ISBN-13: 978-0-226-50536-7 (cloth : alk. paper)
   ISBN-10: 0-226-50536-7 (cloth : alk. paper)
   1. Love. I. Title.
   B2430.M283P4413 2007
   128'.46—dc22   2006011176

⊚ The paper used in this publication meets the minimum requirements of the American National Standard for Information Sciences—Permanence of Paper for Printed Library Materials, ANSI Z39.48-1992.

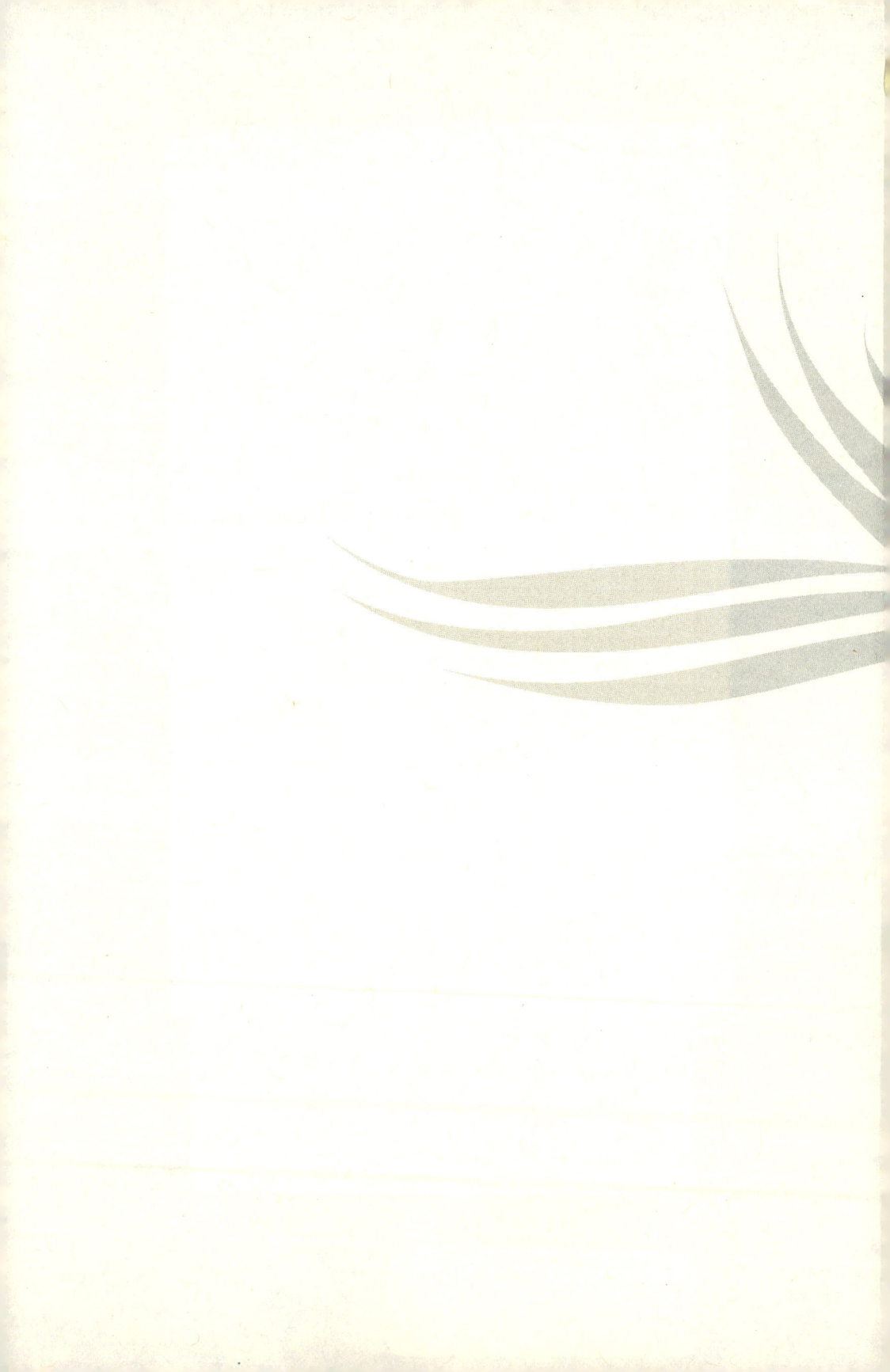

L'ardent désir du haut bien désiré.

SCÈVE

Nemo est qui non amet.

SAINT AUGUSTINE

CONTENTS

TRANSLATOR'S ACKNOWLEDGMENTS

*T*he task of the translator is made many times easier when the previous works of a writer have been well translated. Such is the case with English translations of Jean-Luc Marion's books, and I have had the happy occasion to refer often to the English renderings of Marion by Thomas A. Carlson, Jeffrey L. Kosky, and Robyn Horner and Vincent Berraud, respectively, as I worked upon this translation. Throughout, I have endeavored to translate key words from the Marion lexicon in a manner consistent with previous renderings, though here and there slight departures may be noted. Translation decisions that seem to require explanation are treated in the occasional translator's footnote.

I would like to thank Jeffrey Kosky for his comments on and corrections to the final manuscript of this translation; his help was much appreciated and highly valued. I would also like to thank Darren E. Dahl and Claude Romano for a variety of helpful suggestions, and Jean-Luc Marion for his patient answers to numerous questions, rendered always in a manner at once enlightening and reassuring.

I would like to dedicate my work on this translation to my parents, Stephen and Elaine Lewis, to my wife, Suzanne M. Lewis, and to the memory of Msgr. Luigi Giussani, † February 22, 2005. Each exemplifies for me the generative power of love.

The Silence of Love

*P*hilosophy today no longer says anything about love, or at best very little. And this silence is for the better, because when philosophy does venture to speak of love it mistreats it or betrays it. One would almost doubt whether philosophers experience love, if one didn't instead guess that they fear saying anything about it. And for good reason, for they know, better than anyone, that we no longer have the words to speak of it, nor the concepts to think about it, nor the strength to celebrate it.

Philosophers have in fact forsaken love, dismissed it without a concept and finally thrown it to the dark and worried margins of their sufficient reason—along with the repressed, the unsaid, and the unmentionable. Doubtless other forms of discourse claim to recover from this escheat, and, in their own way, they have sometimes succeeded. Poetry can tell me about the experience I have not known how to articulate, and thus liberate me from my erotic aphasia—but it will never make me understand love conceptually. The novel succeeds in breaking the autism of my amorous crises because it reinscribes them in a sociable, plural, and public narrativity—but it does not explain what really and truly happens to me. Theology knows what love is all about; but it knows it too well ever to avoid imposing upon me an interpretation that comes so directly through the Passion that it annuls my passions—without taking the time to render justice to their phenomenality, or to give a meaning to their immanence. Psychoanalysis is able to resist these rash movements and knows to remain among my lived experiences of consciousness and, especially, unconsciousness—but it does so precisely to verify more thoroughly that I suffer from a lack of words to tell of them, or indeed that psychoanalysis itself lacks concepts for thinking them. The result of all of these failed efforts is that ordinary people, or, put another way, all those who love without knowing what love wants to say, or what it wants of them, or above all how to survive it—that is to say, you and I first and foremost—believe themselves condemned to feed on scraps: the desperate sentimentalism of popular prose, the frustrated pornography of the idol industry, or the shapeless ideology of that boastful asphyxiation known as "self-actualization." Thus philosophy keeps quiet, and in this silence love fades away.

Such a desertion of the question of love by the concept ought to scandalize, all the more since philosophy takes its origin from "that great god" love and from it alone. Nothing less than the name "philosophy" bears witness: "*love* of wisdom" (which remains a proper translation of φιλοσοφία, however badly suited it has at times been). How should we understand this name? The most widely received meaning—it is necessary to search for the wisdom that one does not yet possess, precisely because it eludes us—results only in a banality, or a truism. But it masks another, more radical meaning: philosophy defines itself as the "love of wisdom" because it must in effect begin by loving before claiming to know. In order to comprehend, it is first necessary to desire to comprehend; put another way, one must be astonished at not comprehending (and this astonishment thus offers a beginning to wisdom); or one must suffer at not comprehending, indeed fear not comprehending (and this fear opens onto wisdom). Philosophy comprehends only to the extent that it loves—I love to comprehend, therefore I love in order to comprehend. I do not, as one might prefer to believe, end up by comprehending enough to dispense forever with loving. It in no way simply follows that, as paradoxical as this may seem to us today, philosophy has first and foremost to do with science, as if the project of knowing simply imposed itself as necessary, without any mediation or presupposition. Instead it may be that in order to attain the truth, it is necessary, in *every* case, first to desire it, and therefore to love it. And the contemporary experience of ideology, this knowledge that sacrifices everything to power, has demonstrated in actual events that man does not spontaneously love the truth, and that he often sacrifices it for a lie, provided that this lie assures him power. To the degree that philosophy ceases to comprehend itself first as a love and starting from love, to the degree that it lays claim immediately to a knowledge and hoards it, not only does it contradict its original determination, but it flees from truth, which it exchanges for the science of objects—that pottage of lentils. We know that, little by little, in an evolution at first stubborn, then accelerated and irrepressible, philosophy in the end renounced its first name, "love of wisdom," for that of metaphysics, as late in coming (in the middle of the Middle Ages) as it was problematic from the outset (in the classical period). This radical mutation not only definitively consecrated the primacy of beings as universal object of knowledge, and thus opened the way to the project of science and, indissolubly, to technology's hold upon the world, but above all it censured the erotic origin of "*philo*-sophy." Thus it may be that the forgetting of being masks and is the result of a more radical forgetting—the forgetting of the erotics of wisdom. At the completion of this history (today, in other words), after having degraded beings to the dishonorable rank of objects and forgotten being in its complete retreat, philosophy, henceforth nearly silent, even lost that to which it had sacrificed the erotic: its rank as science, and eventually its dignity as knowledge. As for love, the forgetting of which has doubtless decided everything, philosophy has forgotten its forgetting to the point of denial; it has lost even the desire for love; indeed, sometimes one would almost believe that philosophy hates love. Philosophy does not love love, which reminds her of her origin and her dignity, her powerlessness and their divorce. She therefore silently ignores it, when she does not hate it outright.

I will put forth a hypothesis: this hatred remains nevertheless an amorous hatred. I want to believe—and to show—that out of philosophy's amorous disaster we can reconstruct an inquiry on love. Doesn't the history of philosophy's divorce from the love within it merit at least as much attention and effort as the history of being and of its retreat? Obviously, this history remains almost entirely to be written—and we will not even sketch it here. But given the immediate need, we will hold to an initial inventory of the situation: not only do we no longer have a concept of love, but we do not even have a word to say it. "Love"? It resonates as the most prostituted word there is—strictly speaking, the word for prostitution; let's rehearse spontaneously its lexicon: one "makes" love like one makes war or makes deals, and all that remains to be determined is with which "partners," at what price, for what profit, at what interval, and for how long. As far as telling it, thinking about it, or celebrating it: silence in the ranks. A silence saturated with pain, which pierces through the political, economic, and medical chitchat that smothers it in an attempt to reassure us. In this great erotic cemetery, the air is close, its vibrations allowing a single phrase to resonate. To declare "I love you" sounds, in the best of cases, like an obscenity or a derision, to the point where, in polite society (that of the educated), no one dares *seriously* to utter such nonsense. Nor to hope for any substitute for this bankruptcy, not even the least note of credit. Thus the word "charity" itself is found to be, if possible, even more neglected: one "does" charity, too—or rather, in order to avoid its having to ask for alms and reduce itself to begging, even charity's magnificent name is snatched away, and it is covered by rags deemed more acceptable, such as "fellowship," "solidarity," "humanitarian aid"; at least, that is, as long as one does not amuse oneself with watching it play at out-of-date flights of "grace," in order to enjoy with nostalgia the "soul" that one no longer has. Of love (or charity) we have nothing to say—and we will not expect the least bit of help from philosophy as it now stands.

And yet, it again falls to philosophy to carry out the diagnosis of this powerlessness. For there is a single, simple reason that explains why we can say nothing of love or of charity: we have no concept whatsoever of love. Without a concept, each time that we pronounce the word "love" or reel off "words of love" we literally no longer know what we are saying and, in fact, we say nothing. Without a concept, we can of course feel violently such or such erotic disposition, but we can neither describe it, nor distinguish it from other erotic dispositions, nor even from nonerotic dispositions, much less articulate them in a right and sensible act. Without a concept, we can even make for ourselves a very clear idea of a love we have experienced, but never an idea the least bit distinct—one that would allow recognition of when it is and is not the case, which behaviors arise from it and which in no way concern it, what logic necessarily binds them or not, what possibilities are opened or closed to action, etc. At this stage, multiplying the historical inquiries or the literary evocations (which it will certainly be necessary to undertake later, but which we will abstain from here) would do us no good, because we still wouldn't know what we are looking for. Nothing, then, releases us from attempting, even if only in a sketch, to fix with preliminary outlines and framework a concept of love.

Where is our point of departure? For the beginning always determines the whole and, more than in other cases, the erotic disaster makes the beginning dangerous here. But this disaster, if it no longer offers any path, still retains the trace of one. In principle, it would be enough to guess at it, to identify the decisions that forbade philosophy to think about the love within it, and then to invert them. And these decisions are located fairly quickly: the concept of love succumbed because philosophy simultaneously refused love's unity, its rationality, and its primacy (and to begin with, its primacy over being).

In the first place: every concept of love is weakened and compromised as soon as one allows oneself to distinguish competing divergent, or indeed irreconcilable, meanings—for example, by opposing from the outset, as if it were an unquestionable evidence, love and charity (ἔρως and ἀγάπη), supposedly possessive desire and supposedly gratuitous benevolence, rational love (of the moral law) and irrational passion. A serious concept of love distinguishes itself by its unity, or rather by its power to keep together significations that nonerotic thought cuts apart, stretches, and tears according to the measure of its prejudices. The entire effort consists in maintaining for as long a time as possible the indivisibility of the single garment of love. The search will thus unfold, so far as we are capable, without the analysis at any moment forcing a choice of one pole rather than another (sexual difference rather than filial affection, the human rather than God, ἔρως rather than ἀγάπη). Univocal, love is only told in *one way*.

Next, a concept of love must be able to give a rationality to all that nonerotic thought disqualifies as irrational and degrades to madness: certainly desire and oaths, abandonment and promises, sexual enjoyment and its suspension, jealousy and lies, children and death, all of these events escape a certain definition of rationality—one that fits with the things of the world, objects of order and of measure, and with their calculation and their production. But this clean getaway surely does not imply that these events lie in exile outside all rationality; it suggests rather that they fall under another figure of reason, a "greater rationality"—that which does not limit itself to the world of things nor to the production of objects, but which instead rules our hearts, our individuality, our life and our death, in short that which defines us deep down in all that concerns us in the final instance. The concept of love is distinguished exactly by its aptitude to think about that which philosophy takes for madness—an aptitude that does not always disqualify, but often gives reason to amorous events as such, according to a rationality that proceeds from love itself. Love falls under an *erotic* rationality.

Finally, a concept of love must reach the experience of erotic phenomena starting from themselves, without inscribing them from the outset and by force within a foreign horizon. Philosophy, in particular in its metaphysical guise, considers first and last the question of being or not being, or the question that asks what beings are, which is to say, what οὐσία (essentiality) is; within this horizon, the quest to know if I am loved or if I love clearly receives only secondary attention, at best; and the presupposition is that in order to love or to make oneself loved, one must first be. But the slightest experience of the erotic phenomenon attests to the contrary—I can perfectly well love what is not or is no longer, just as I can make myself loved by what is no longer, by what is not yet, or by something the being of which remains undecided; and reciprocally, that a being indeed is does not qualify it further as something I love or that loves me, any more than the uncertainty of its being renders me erotically indifferent. The search for a concept must therefore describe the erotic phenomenon in its own proper horizon—that of a *love without being*.

Will we be able to bring about these three inversions? One can answer no without any other form of trial, as both good sense (the least shared thing in the world) and metaphysics (sparkling with all its erotic incompetence) suggest. Nevertheless, one might ask oneself if the three prohibitions that offend the concept of love are not rooted in a single decision. Why is love thrown to the wind, why is it refused an erotic rationality, why is it framed by the horizon of being? The answer is not hidden far away: because love is defined as a passion, and therefore as a derivative modality, indeed as optional to the "subject," who is defined by exercise of the rationality exclusively appropriate to objects and to beings, and who, by thinking, is originarily. *Ego cogito, ego sum*—put another way: since I am as an *ego*, an *ego* essentially *cogitans* and principally thinking through the ordering and the measuring of objects, therefore the erotic event will never come upon me except as a second derivation, indeed as a regrettable perturbation. And in fact, we think of ourselves most of the time as just such an *ego*, a being who cogitates orderable and measurable objects, so that we no longer look upon our erotic events except as incalculable and disordered accidents, happily marginalized, indeed optional, so much do they do damage to the clear exercise of *this* figure of thought. Our denials of the *ego cogito*—those rehearsed by so much recent metaphysics—do not prove the contrary; they simply betray our difficulty in tearing ourselves away from this paradigm, disgraced because it still obsesses us. Let us therefore conclude, instead, that beginning with this *ego cogito,* the event of love has no more reason than does the erotic disposition have legitimacy; or again, that the *ego cogitans* establishes itself only in opposition to and by repressing the erotic instance.

The proof of this repression is written out plainly in the definition Descartes assigns to the *ego*: "Ego sum res cogitans, id est dubitans, affirmans, negans, pauca intelligens, multa ignorans, volens, nolens, imaginans quoque et sentiens" (A.T. [Adam and Tannery, ed., *Oeuvres de Descartes*] VII, p. 34, lines 18–21); otherwise said: I am a thinking thing, that is to say one which doubts, which affirms, which denies, which understands few things, which is ignorant of many, which wills, which does not will, which imagines, too, and which even feels. Fine, except that it follows by omission that I am no longer supposed to love, nor to hate; or better: I am of such a sort that I have neither to love, nor to hate, at least in the first instance. To love would not belong to the first modes of thought and, therefore, would not determine the most original essence of the *ego*. Man, as *ego cogito,* thinks, but he does not love, at least from the outset. Yet the most incontestable evidence—that which includes all other evidence, governs our time and our life from beginning to end and penetrates us in every intervening instant—attests that, on the contrary, we are, insofar as we come to know ourselves, always already caught within the tonality of an erotic disposition—love or hate, unhappiness or happiness, enjoyment or suffering, hope or despair, solitude or communion—and that we can never, without lying to ourselves, claim to arrive at a fundamental erotic neutrality. Besides, who would strive for inaccessible ataraxy, who would demand it and boast of it, if he did not feel himself precisely to be, from the outset and forever, wrought, paralyzed, and obsessed by amorous tonalities? Man is revealed to himself by the originary and radical modality of the erotic. Man loves—which is what distinguishes him from all other finite beings, if not the angels. Man is defined neither by the *logos,* nor by the being within him, but by this fact that he loves (or hates), whether he wants to or not. In this world, only man loves, for animals and computers, in their own way, think just as well as he, indeed better than he; but one cannot affirm that they love. But man does—the loving animal. What is omitted by the Cartesian definition of the *ego* ought to shock us as a monstrously mistaken description of the phenomenon that is nonetheless the closest and most accessible—the phenomenon that I am to myself. Moreover, the fact that, of all the supposed errors for which Descartes has been taken to task, this one alone—doubtless his only error—has remained unnoticed for nearly four centuries, says much more than anything else about the erotic blindness of metaphysics.

For the honor of philosophy, however, it is necessary to point out that at least one reader must have been surprised by Descartes' definition; in fact, his first French translator, the Duc de Luynes, took it upon himself to correct it by adding to the *ego:* "I know that I am a thing which thinks, that is to say which doubts, which affirms, which denies, which knows few things, which is ignorant of many, *which loves, which hates,* which wills, which does not will, which imagines, too, and which feels" (A.T. IX-1, p. 27, lines 7–10). What remarkable lucidity; but this judicious rectification underscores all the more the size of the difficulty: if the concept of love became impossible because the *ego* excluded love (and hate) from its original modalities (in order subsequently to submit it, arbitrarily and not without danger, to the will), could one reestablish a radical concept of love without destroying this very definition of the *ego*? We will see later that in fact it is necessary to pay this price by redefining the *ego,* insofar as the *ego* thinks, exactly through the modality of love that metaphysics omitted and repressed—as the one that loves and hates preeminently, as the *cogitans* that thinks insofar as it first loves, in short as the *lover* (*ego amans*). It will therefore be necessary to take up once more the entire description of the *ego* and redeploy all its figures according to the order of reasons, but this time complying with the Duc de Luynes's addition, against the omission in the Latin text of the *Meditationes*—substituting for the *ego cogito,* which does not love, the originally loving *ego*. It will be necessary, then, to take up the *Meditationes* from the starting point of the fact that I love even before being, because I am not, except insofar as I experience love, and experience it as a logic. In short, it will be necessary to substitute erotic meditations for metaphysical ones.

It goes without saying that this effort, which absolutely must be attempted, passes far beyond anything I might be able to accomplish. This is owing, certainly, to the limits of my talent and power, but above all to the difficulty of the thing itself, imposed upon whomsoever were to approach it.

First off, we shall not be able to lean on the attainments of the tradition, but will have to beware of them, because each step will involve "destroying" the tradition in order to free a path toward that which metaphysics, with somnambulant stubbornness, has missed. This constant piercing through traditional aporiae will necessitate the introduction of the clearest possible, and therefore initially disconcerting, paradoxes. Thus we will have to take our distance from the figures of subjectivity (transcendental, but also empirical), the empire of being, the marvels of objectivization, the easy answers offered by psychologism, and above all the various attempts at a "metaphysics of love"—that contradiction in terms. An initial precaution, as insufficient as it is obligatory, will consist in avoiding scrupulously the citation of any author at all; not because I owe nothing to anyone and claim originality at any price (connoisseurs will hardly have any trouble adding from time to time a likely reference in a virtual footnote); nor because I hold to an overly radical easing of the reader's task (it may be that these slow, often repetitive conquests will cost the reader as much as they do me). No, the only concern is to make imperative the effort to return to things in themselves, or at least, since one can never guarantee the fulfillment of this program, not to turn away from them at the outset, by assuming theories as facts. We shall also strive not to presuppose any sort of lexicon, and to construct each concept out of phenomena, without skipping any step, indeed from time to time moving backward in order to assure each advance; thus, in principle, the reader should be able to see everything played out in front of him or her, to verify everything and, whether the reader approves or disapproves, to know why. In short, the point will not be to tell stories, nor to tell ourselves stories, but to allow that which is the point to appear—the erotic phenomenon itself.

As a result we must attempt the impossible: to produce what we will show starting from itself. To be sure, anyone who writes, especially conceptually, must, to one degree or another, assume this responsibility. But here, when one tackles the erotic phenomenon, this assumption imposes itself without the least restriction. For one must speak of love in the same way as one must love—in the first person. Indeed, loving is only properly spoken of and made in its own right—first and foremost, without any possible substitution. Loving puts in play my identity, my ipseity, those resources of mine that are more inward to me than myself. In love I put myself on stage and implicate myself, because in loving I make a decision about myself like nowhere else. Each act of love is inscribed forever in me and outlines me definitively. I do not love by proxy, nor through a go-between, but in the flesh, and this flesh is one only with me. The fact that I love cannot be distinguished from me, any more than I would want, in love, to distinguish myself from that which I love. To love—this verb is conjugated, in all its tenses and modes, always and by definition first in the first person. Thus, because one must speak of love as one must love, I will say *I*. And I will not be able to hide myself behind the *I* of philosophers, that *I* who is supposed to be universal, a disengaged spectator or a transcendental subject, a spokesman for each and everyone because he thinks exclusively what anyone can by right know in the place of anyone else (being, science, objects): that which concerns no one personally. In contrast, I am going to speak of that which affects each of us as such; I will therefore think about what affects me as such and constitutes me as this particular person, whom no other can replace and from whom no other can exempt me. I will say *I* starting from and in view of the erotic phenomenon within me and for me—*my own*. I would thus be lying in claiming a surface neutrality: it will be necessary that I and no other speak of this erotic phenomenon that I know, and as I know it. And obviously, I will do it badly; I will do this phenomenon ill, but that will do me good—if only because it will make me feel my incapacity to say it, just as it will make me take note of my powerlessness to make it. I will therefore say *I* at my own risk and peril. But, dear reader, know this: I will say *I* in your name. Do not pretend to be unaware of the erotic phenomenon, or to know more about it than I. We don't know the same thing about the erotic phenomenon, yet we know as much; we remain in front of it with an equality that is as perfect as our solitude. Thus you are going to allow me to speak in your name, because I am paying the price here of speaking in my own name.

Of course, I am going to speak of that which I barely understand—the erotic phenomenon—starting from that which I know badly—my own amorous history. May it disappear most of the time within the rigor of the concept. Nevertheless I will keep within me the memory, new at each instant, of those who have loved me, who still love me, and whom I would like to be able to love, one day, as they should be loved—without measure. They will recognize themselves in my grateful recognition of them.

This book has obsessed me since the publication of *The Idol and Distance* in 1977. All the books I have published since then bear the mark, explicit or hidden, of this concern. In particular, *Prolegomena to Charity* was published in 1986 only to give witness to the fact that I had not given up on this project, despite the delay in completing it. All of my books, above all the last three, have been just so many steps toward the question of the erotic phenomenon. Today, as I finish this last essay, I want to express my gratitude to Françoise Verny, who, as soon as the first book appeared, bound me by contract to this one: after twenty-five years of patience and reminders, she is finally able to see it appear.

J.-L. M.

Chicago, April 1998—Lods, September 2002

Concerning a Radical Reduction

§ 1. Doubting Certainty

Every man desires to know, and no man desires not to know. Between not knowing and knowing, no one hesitates to prefer knowing. But why? After all, the conquest of knowledge—or more modestly, of a body of knowledge—requires attention, labor, and time, to the point that one would often like, voluptuously, to do without it. But in fact, we do not do without it. Why then do we prefer, even at the price of restraint, to know rather than not to know?

A first response suggests that we desire to know for the simple pleasure of knowing—perhaps the most exciting, the most durable, and the purest of the pleasures that it is possible for us to experience in this life. To the point that one could see in it the only possible natural beatitude, the rival of the other, the unconditioned. But how do we fail to see that, in this case, we do not desire to know simply in order to know, but in order to experience the pleasure of knowing—we know in order to enjoy knowledge, in order to enjoy the act of knowing, and thus, finally, in order to enjoy ourselves through the process of knowing. Thus we do not desire to know, except for the sake of self-enjoyment. Knowledge becomes the simple means, albeit the most efficacious and economical, to such an enjoyment of self. Desire itself, more essential than the desire to know, springs forth—desire, which, even in knowledge, only desires self-enjoyment.

To this primacy of the desire to enjoy knowledge over knowledge itself, one could immediately object with the following: even if knowledge sometimes fulfills us to the point of pleasure, it nevertheless does not always work this way. First of all, this is because knowledge can fail to discover the true or, worse, can leave us with the delusion of having discovered it. Next, because, once averred, it sometimes happens that this knowledge wounds and worries us all the more. One will admit that, in this case, we do not know for the pleasure of knowing, and even less for the sake of self-enjoyment in this act of knowing—since on the contrary we suffer from it. But does it follow that, when we know even that which wounds or worries us, we desire to know for the sake of knowing? Nothing is less sure: for why do we admit that it is better to run the risk of knowing the truth, even when it is unwelcome, than not to know it at all? For an obvious reason: knowing a fact that is potentially damaging to me allows me either to guard myself against it, or at least to foresee it; knowing, especially knowing that which threatens, contributes to the security of the one who knows, which is to say to his safeguarding of self. Certainly, the desire to know is directed upon the known or the knowable—but above all and finally to the benefit of the knower. Confirmed as more essential than the desire to know is the desire to safeguard oneself, that is to say, to enjoy oneself.

We thus very much desire to know rather than not to know, and yet this desire does not bear upon what we know, but rather upon us, we who know. And there is here only the appearance of a paradox, since we find it in the most classical definition of science—we call science a certain knowledge. The irruption of certainty indicates here that it is not enough just to know in order to know at the level of reason, in conformity with a science: science attains its certainty only by distinguishing in things what can be reduced to permanence (by models and parameters, reproduction and production) and what cannot. From this distinction there results, on the one hand, the object—the known insofar as certified, insofar as certain for the one who knows; on the other, the unobjectifiable—that within the thing that remains in itself and does not satisfy the conditions of knowledge, in short the doubtful. Who traces the frontier between the certain and the doubtful, between the object and the unobjectifiable? The one who knows, the *ego*—the *I* who separates that which will become for him an object from that which will not, and which will escape him. Certainty thus indicates the placing of the known (and, negatively, of the unknowable) upon the *ego,* such that, in the knowledge of the object, it is the *ego* more than this object who objectifies it, constitutes it, and literally certifies it. Yes, the object shines with certainty, but this certainty would have no meaning if it did not refer to the *ego,* who alone sees and above all founds it. The object owes its certainty—its certificate—to the *ego* that certifies it. In the certain object there is shown first of all, in fact and by right, its certifier. Even with certain knowledge of the object, even under the rules of certainty, the desire to know still comes under self-enjoyment. Constituting the object gives me enjoyment, through it, of myself. Thus the determination of the truth by certainty confirms what the desire to know already allowed to appear: in all knowledge, in the end, there is self-enjoyment. It should therefore follow that every desire to know makes the one who knows better known than what he knows; or that all certain knowledge of an object assures for us the certitude of the certifying *ego*.

Nevertheless, we must put this evidence of certainty into doubt. Or rather, we must doubt that the certainty of certified objects can flow back, in the same way, upon the *ego* who certifies them. The univocality of certainty is in no way certain. For, even if a single certainty governed the *ego* and its objects, the *ego* would still escape if it had to confront an entirely other doubt than that which certainty annuls. This is established by several arguments.

First, one can question the extent of the field of certainty. To certify means to maintain an object with perfect mastery under the guard of one's watching regard or gaze (*re-garder, in-tueri*). To hold it under this guard means to be able to constitute and reconstitute it, after having analyzed it into parts, each part being clear and distinct enough that the gaze [*le regard*] takes possession of it without blurriness, or residue. Only thus reduced to its atoms of evidence does the object offer itself to certainty. And so it is necessary to begin with the simplest objects—those that mathematics deals with (which ask for nothing more than the intuition of pure space), or logic (which require nothing but noncontradiction). The same goes for the objects that technology produces serially (the formal identity of which requires only an abstract form, a plan or "concept," and a material become homogeneous). Such objects—an equation, a logical proposition, and an industrial product—do indeed offer a "total quality" and merit the qualification of *certain*. But only phenomena so poor in intuition can be averred so rich in certainty.

Indeed, what does this certainty matter to me? Why would I hold it in such high esteem? Does it go without saying that my need for assurance can satisfy itself with the certainty of poor phenomena? For in the end such a certainty only concerns *objects,* which relate to me precisely as not being me, and not being like me. So how am I, exactly? I am according to my *flesh.* Contrary to the formal abstraction that makes objects, my flesh allows itself to be affected without end by the things of the world; and it can do so only because it reveals itself to be affectable in itself, and thus affectable first off by itself and in itself. It thus offers me to myself as a phenomenon, in which the flux of intuitions always, and by far, exceeds the safety of the forms that I could ever assign to them, as does the intelligibility of the intentionalities that I could ever read there. There lies a definitive caesura between this saturated phenomenon (my flesh) and the poor phenomena of objectness. Paradoxically, the certainty of these poor phenomena, at the very moment in which I master it, no longer interests me: it concerns only the usage of phenomena of a type other than mine, and in no way my own manner of behaving, nor the unique ipseity of my invisible and uncertifiable flesh.

Second, one might ask *a contrario*: what would this *ego* gain if one were to concede without discussion the certainty of certified objects? Suppose we grant the canonical argument: the *ego* attains a certainty, indeed the greatest certainty, for, as is known, even and above all if it mistakes the most obvious evidence, for example its own existence or its own thought, it is still necessary that it be, even if only thus to make mistakes. And the more that I make mistakes (or am deceived), the more I am, because, in order to make a mistake (or be deceived), it is necessary first and foremost to think—and thinking implies the performing of an act, an act that attests to being. Without any doubt the *ego* thus attains *a* certainty. Sure, but which one? That is our question. The *ego* has a certainty, one only—that of remaining present for as long as, and for each time that, it thinks. Thinks what? That, in order to make a mistake or be deceived, it is necessary to think, and thus to be. Thus I will be in the exact measure wherein I perform an act—in effect, an act of thought, for at this moment I have no other act at my disposal—and I will of course perform it in the present, from moment to moment, for as long as I think (myself). Surely, here is a real certainty. Nevertheless the same question returns: in what way does this certainty assure me according to another mode than that of the objects that I myself certify? Can certainty, which I share with the objects that I certify, in turn certify me as such, that is to say, as the condition of the possibility of objects? And if I am only certain after the manner of objects, have I become an object, or does certainty split in two?

By reversing the question, we might ask: what can I no longer doubt? I can no longer doubt only this—that I am in the instant wherein I think that I am, and that I am for as long as I repeat this instant. But as it happens, the same is true of a certified object: I can no longer doubt that it is each time and for as long as I think it: if I succeed in thinking it, it is, at least as a thought object (if not as an autonomous being). I am thus only certain in the same way as my objects: in the present instant, blow by blow, without any future guarantee. One will object that there nevertheless remains a difference: the object may not offer itself all the time to thinking, while I will always be able to think myself, since it depends only upon me to think. This objection is worthless, because death will end up by suspending my faculty to think myself, just as the contingency of things will end up by annihilating the object. Thus I therefore am only certain of myself in the same way that I am certain of an object: I do not doubt that I subsist and, for all of that, that I am. There remains no more than one alternative. Either I am certain of myself, because I think myself; but then I make myself the object of myself and I receive only a certainty of an object. Thus I miss myself as *ego*. Or I admit that *I* am certain of the object of myself, and thus that this very *I* is already no longer the object of which it is certain, simply because certainty always receives its certification from an other; this *I,* who certifies for himself the existence of a me become an object, is other than this me. *I* is other than me, and the certainty of the me-object does not attain the *I* that I am.

Whence there comes a third argument: once I am certain to exist, then I can truly doubt myself. In effect, I, who am certain of being, have never stopped doubting myself. What have I doubted? Clearly not my actuality, nor my subsistence in presence, nor even my enjoyment of myself in the instant—these have always seemed to me to be established until proven otherwise, placed level and in the light without my having to worry about them. I doubted elsewhere, and otherwise—about my possibility and my future. Thus I learned to doubt my talents and the strength of my desires. For a long time I believed I would become a great soccer player, and then, even more seriously, a very good runner of the 1,500-meter race. As a child, I believed for a long time that I was not happy, even though I was; then, as a semi-grown-up, that I would be, when I was doing everything not to be. I believed later that success would make me sure of myself, and then, as I collected successes, I saw their insignificance and I returned to my initial uncertainty. I spontaneously believed all of the promises and all of the avowals that told me to love myself, and even today when I think back on them, I believe them all over again; but the usual ruptures, my failures, and my lassitude have in the end taught me to doubt myself anyway. Without any satisfaction, especially that of having grown in wisdom or in character, I see the proof of my lack of faith, and of my stupidity. The retrospective shipwreck of my lost possibilities has taught me skepticism. But all of this compelled skepticism hardly dazzles me, any more than it does others: to admit it requires no force of mind, just weakness and a touch of lucidity; and there is no reason to brag about one's helplessness or one's defeats. But such skepticism—that into which each destiny, weighted down by its own gravity, sinks—nevertheless instructs us with a piece of evidence: we can still doubt, radically and for a long time, even if the known objects are already certain for us, and even if the *ego,* which in us knows them, is certain, too.

How can I doubt myself, if I am certain to exist? From where does this doubt about myself come, if my certainty of existing is not enough to stop it? How far does my doubt stretch when, without a glance, it overtakes my certainty to exist? Could it be that the doubt about me unfolds itself beyond the closed field of certain existence? Perhaps doubt does not work, in the final instance, to produce certainty, but rather to go beyond it.

§ 2. "What's the Use?"

Metaphysical thought considers itself to have filled all of its speculative duties in furnishing us with a certainty, or indeed in promising us every thinkable certainty. Metaphysics imagines itself accomplishing an incomparable exploit in attaining the certainty of the object, and then extending it even to the *ego.* But this accomplishment only attests to its blindness.

In fact, metaphysics does not keep its promise, because it delivers, in the guise of certainty and in the best of cases, only the certainty of objects (or even that of only certain objects), a certainty that concerns us not at all (in every case not I, who am not an object), because it is silent about the certainty that would matter to me—the certainty which concerns exactly that which matters to *me* first and foremost: *me.* The products of technology and the objects of the sciences, the propositions of logic and the truths of philosophy can very well enjoy all the certainty of the world, but what have I to do with it—*I* who am neither a product of technology, nor an object of science, nor a proposition of logic, nor a truth of philosophy? The only inquiry whose result would truly matter to *me* would tackle the possibility of establishing some sort of certainty about my identity, my status, my history, my destiny, my death, my birth, and my flesh, in short about my irreducible ipseity. One should not reproach metaphysics or the sciences that descend from it for ending up with more uncertainties than certainties—after all, they did what they could, and deplore more than anyone the ambiguity of their results. One cannot even hold it against them for having limited the quest for wisdom to the inquiry into the truth, and the inquiry into the truth to the conquest of certainty—after all, nothing has produced as many objective results as this double restriction; and one easily understands that their prestige is seductive. But we must legitimately reproach them for only ever having aimed at a secondary and derivative certainty, foreign and in the end futile (the certainty of objects, of their knowledge, production, and handling), while neglecting or being unaware of the only certainty that concerns me, the certainty of me.

For certainty, even certainty reduced to the objects that I am not, does not even then remain undamaged by every suspicion: it is exposed to a counter-proof that can disqualify it all the more radically in that its validity is not contested in the first degree. It is enough for me to address a simple question to this certainty: "What's the use?" Logical calculation, mathematical operations, models of the object and its technologies of production offer a perfect certainty, a "total quality"—but so what? How exactly does that concern me, if not for as much as I am engaged in their world and I inscribe myself within their space? As I nevertheless remain other, otherwise and elsewhere than they, a porous frontier controls our exchanges: I intervene in the world of certain objects, but I am not there to stay, because I have the terrible privilege of opening for them a world that, without me, they would not obtain on their own. Their certainty does not matter to me, because I only inhabit their world momentarily, from time to time making the owner's rounds—but living elsewhere. Thus, I can—or better, I cannot not—feel when faced with this certainty of another world (in fact of the world of which I am not) the irrepressible tonality of its vanity: this vain certainty, supposing that it can be obtained, doesn't matter to me, does not concern me, does not reach me, who am not . . . of their world. In everyday language, one could say that technological progress makes better neither my life, nor my capacity to live well, nor my knowledge of myself. In conceptual language, one could think that intramundane certainty in no way decides the *ego,* which alone opens this world to objects, to beings, and to phenomena. The certainty of the world of beings works like the "call of being"—they touch me only if I want them to; and, since they do not at all reach me in fact and by right in my vitals, since they mean nothing to me (nothing of me), I have no motive to be interested in them, nor to put myself among them. Thus I leave them to themselves and they succumb to indifference, to the verdict of vanity. Vanity disqualifies the certainty of objects, which, of course, remain sure and certain. But this surety does nothing to reassure me about me, it certifies nothing for me. A useless and certain certainty.

But, one might reply, metaphysics has understood this very well: it has succeeded in extending the certainty of things of the world to the *ego,* which only opens that certainty because it is itself excepted from it. Nothing is more certain than my existence, provided that and as often as I pronounce and think it. The certainty of the world can very well founder; the more it collapses, the more I, who challenge it, think and thus am, with certainty. This response certainly demonstrates the certainty of the *ego,* but all the while in full vanity, since it is limited to extending to the *ego,* which is nevertheless stranger to their world, the same type of certainty as that which befits objects and intramundane beings. For, what at heart does it matter to me if I am certain like they are, or indeed more than they are? This certainty of persisting in existence, when and for as long as I want, only comes upon me as an effect of my thought, like one of my products, like my first *artifact*—the *artifact* par excellence, since it mobilizes my most original art, my *cogitatio;* it is thus not original to me, but derives from my *cogitatio,* which alone assures that I am when I want to be assured of it. Everything thus depends on what I cogitate—on my thinking will. I am because I can doubt objects and because I am still thinking while willing to doubt; in short, I am certain because I am quite willing. But can't I also not will it? And am I certain always to will it again? Seeing as it comes down to a pure decision of the *cogitatio,* could I not always retort, "What's the use?" in front of the possibility of producing my own certainty of being? What certain reason assures me of willing this very certainty without flaw or reserve? What absolutely unshakable motive do I have to produce myself in certainty, rather than not? After all, why not will not to be rather than to be? Today, when nihilism marks our age, no one takes this question as folly. Behind the evidence of the *cogitatio* of self there thus emerges the shadow of a decision— that of producing, or not, my certainty. Here the question "What's the use?" is exercised without resistance. The certainty of the *cogitatio* does not go back to the origin, which is occupied only by a more primitive decision; and this decision offers only a certainty that vanity can always disqualify.

Moreover, doesn't a certainty that I can (or cannot) produce at will remain essentially contingent, derived and thus still foreign to me? If my certainty depends on me, this very surety, that I must decide about, can in no way reassure me, since, even fully accomplished, it only has me as its origin—this me that it is in turn necessary to secure. Either it is a matter of an auto-foundation, and thus of a logical circle condemned to mime without success the supposedly divine *causa sui* (itself already untenable); or it is a matter of a demi-foundation, of an empirical event with a transcendental claim, that temporality always leads back to its irremediable contingency. This supposedly first certainty, on the contrary, marks an insurmountable gap between, on the one hand, that which remains of my domain, me without any other assurance than myself, and, on the other hand, that which alone could reassure me of myself—that is to say a certainty that comes upon me from elsewhere, prior to me.* Either I am through myself only, but my certainty is not originary; or my certainty is quite originary, but it does not come from me. The certainty of self can proclaim itself as loudly and strongly as it wants, but it finally avers itself to be always provisional, waiting in delusion on another principle, which would finally truly assure it. Such a metaphysical recourse avows the insufficiency of every autarkic certainty to assure itself completely.

Thus nothing exposes me more to the attack of vanity than the metaphysical demonstration of the existence of the *ego,* or of my claim to be certain in my capacity as *ego.* Certainty attests its failure in the very instant of its success: I indeed acquire a certainty, but, like that of beings of the world certified by my efforts, it sends me back to my initiative, and thus to me, the arbitrary operative of every certainty, even my own. To produce my certainty myself does not reassure me at all, but rather maddens me in front of vanity in person. What is the good of my certainty, if it still depends on me, if I only am through myself?

§ 3. The Erotic Reduction

Vanity thus disqualifies every certainty, whether it bears upon the world or upon myself. Must we then for all of that give up on assuring ourselves, or reassuring ourselves against every assault from vanity? The powerlessness to respond to the question "What's the use?" or even the powerlessness to endure it, illustrates the supremely ruthless vanity of vanity, does it not? Nothing resists vanity, since it can still skirt and annul all evidence, all certainty, all resistance.

At least in order truly to assure the *ego* of itself, it is necessary to renounce the paradigm of certainty, which comes from the world and bears

---

*The French *d'ailleurs* will be rendered sometimes as "from elsewhere" and at other times as "from out there."—Trans.

upon it, and to abandon, to the absurd ambition to guarantee myself, the poor certitude of a conditioned existence, at the same rank as an object or a being of the world. In my case, in my case alone, assurance demands much more than an existence that is certain, or indeed, than a certainty in general. It asks that I might consider myself, in this existence, as freed from vanity, released from the suspicion of inanity, indemnified against the question "What's the use?" In order to confront this demand, it is no longer a question of obtaining a certainty of being, but instead the response to another question—"Does anybody love me?"

Certainty befits objects and, more generally, beings of the world, because being, for them, is equivalent to subsisting in actual presence—and actuality can be certified. But this manner of being does not suit me. First of all, it does not suit me because I am not according to the measure of my actuality, but rather of my possibility; if I had to remain in the actual state in which I am for a long time, I would of course be what I am, but it would be right to consider me as "dead"; in order to be the one that I am, it is instead necessary for me to open a possibility to become other than I am, to postpone myself into the future, *not* to persist in my present state of being, but to alter myself into another state of being; in short, in order to be the one that I am (and not an object or a being of the world), I must be as possibility, and thus as the possibility of being *otherwise*. Now, no possibility whatsoever falls within the hold of certainty—possibility is defined by its very irreducibility to certainty. Thus, by my mode of being according to possibility, I do not come under certainty.

But certifiable actuality does not suit me for another, more radical reason: because I do not reduce myself to a mode of *being*, even that of possibility. In effect, it is not enough for me to be in order to remain the one that I am: it is also, first and foremost, necessary for me that someone love me—the erotic possibility. A counter-proof verifies this: let us suppose that we were to propose to someone, anyone, to be with certainty (actuality) for an open-ended amount of time, with, as sole condition, the definitive renunciation of the possibility (not even the actuality) of someone ever loving that person—who would accept? No *I,* no *ego,* in fact no man, above all not the greatest cynic in the world (who thinks only of someone loving him). For to give up on even the possibility that someone loves me would be like operating a transcendental castration upon myself, and would bring me down to the rank of an artificial intelligence, a mechanical calculator or a demon, in short, very likely lower than an animal, who can still mimic love, at least to our eyes. And in fact, those of my likeness who have given up—in part and only in a certain respect, it is true—on the possibility that someone loves them have, in proportion, lost their humanity. To give up on asking (oneself) the question "Does anybody love me?" or above all to give up on the possibility of a positive response implies nothing less than giving up on the human itself.

An objection, powerful in appearance, could arise: does not the demand that someone love me presuppose that I first be? Put otherwise: in order to be loved, in order to be well, it is first necessary, quite simply, to be. Or: to be loved or lovable would remain the simple ontic corrective of a more original ontological character; the being that I am counts, among its other existential characters, that of the ability to make one's self love. In short, the question of love would have all the correctness and pertinence that one could wish, but it would remain no less secondary, the business at best of a philosophy second to others (such as ethics, politics, etc.). But this is pure sophism, which holds as already established precisely what needs to be shown—that the *ego*'s mode of being (or not being) can be reduced to the mode of the being of objects and of beings of the world, and be understood beginning from there. Now, only these objects and these beings, in order to be well or to be loved, must first of all be, just as in order to be they must, first of all, subsist. On the contrary *I* myself can only be, from the very first, according to possibility, and thus according to radical possibility—the possibility that someone loves me or could love me. In every other case than my own, "to be loved" is understood as a synthetic statement, where "loved" is added from the outside to its presupposition, "to be." But, in *my* very own case, the *I*, "to be loved" becomes an analytic statement, for I could not be, nor accept to endure being, without at least the open possibility that at one moment or another someone is loving me. For me, to be signifies nothing less than to be-loved (English appears to suggest this in its own way: "to be loved" can be said in one word, "beloved"). Why can't I accept being except on the express condition that someone loves me? Because in my being I only resist the assault of vanity under the protection of this love, or at least its possibility.

Thus it is necessary to have done with that which produces the certainty of objects of the world—the *epistemic reduction,* which keeps in a thing only that which stays repeatable, permanent and as if permanently under the mind's regard or gaze (I, insofar as object or as subject). It is necessary to put aside the *ontological reduction* too, which only keeps in a thing its status as being in order to lead it back to its being, or indeed, eventually, to track it to the point of catching a glimpse of being itself (I as *Dasein,* the being in which what is at stake is being). There remains, then, the attempt at a third reduction: in order for me to appear as a full-fledged phenomenon, it is not enough that I recognize myself as a certified object, nor as a certifying *ego,* nor even as a properly being being; I must discover myself as a given (and gifted) phenomenon, assured as a given that is free from vanity. What instance could give such assurance? At this point on the path, we know neither *what* it is, nor if it *is,* nor if it even has *to be.* Nevertheless we can at least sketch the signal function: it is a question of assuring me against the vanity of my own given (and gifted) phenomenon by responding to a new question: no longer "Am I certain?" but "Am I not, despite my certainty, in vain?" Now, asking to assure my own certainty of being against the dark assault of vanity comes down to asking nothing less than, "Does anybody love me?" So there we are: the assurance appropriate to the given (and gifted) *ego* puts into motion an *erotic reduction.*

I am: this eventual certainty, even when assumed to be unshakable, even when set up as the first principle by metaphysics, which envisages nothing higher, is nonetheless worthless if it does not go to the point of assuring me against vanity by assuring me that I am loved. For I can always and more often than not completely make fun of being, to the point of becoming indifferent to my fact of being, or avoid dealing with it, or, indeed, even hate it. It is not enough that I know myself to be, certainly and without restriction, in order to put up with, accept, and love being. The certainty of being can even on the contrary suffocate me like a yoke, bog me down like mud, imprison me like a jail cell. For every *ego,* to be or not to be can become the stake in a free choice, without the positive response necessarily assumed. And the question here is not necessarily that of suicide, but first and always that of the empire of vanity; for under the rule of vanity, I can very certainly recognize "I think, therefore I am"—only immediately to annul this certainty by asking myself, "What's the use?" The certainty of my existence is never enough to make it just, or good, or beautiful, or desirable—in short, it is never enough to assure it. The certainty of my existence simply demonstrates my solitary effort to establish myself in being by my own decision and on my own account; of course a certainty produced by my own act of thinking remains my initiative, my work, and my business—the autistic certainty and narcissistic assurance of a mirror always mirroring only another mirror, a repeated void. I only obtain an existence, and the most barren one at that—the pure product of hyperbolic doubt, without intuition, without concept and without a name: a desert, the poorest phenomenon, which only delivers its own inanity. I am—a doubtless certainty, but at the price of the absence of every given. I am—less the first truth than the final fruit of doubt itself. I doubt, and this doubt at least is certain. Yes, I am certain, but with a certainty such that it appears immediately impossible that it matters to me and does not collapse in front of vanity, which asks, "What's the use?" As the minimalist mime of the self-cause, certainty nails the *ego* to just enough existence to receive, without any defense, the shock of vanity. It is thus necessary, in order for me to be not only certainly, but with a certainty that matters to me, that I be more and otherwise than what I can guarantee to myself, that is to say, be with a being that assures me *from elsewhere* than from me. I can of course produce and reproduce for myself my certainty of being, but I cannot assure it against vanity. Only an other than me could assure me of it, like a guide in the mountains assures his client. For assurance is not to be confused with certainty.

Certainty results from the epistemic reduction (or indeed from the ontological reduction) and plays out between the *ego,* who is master, and its object, the mastered; even if the *ego* becomes certain of its existence, above all if it remains the first master before God, it still knows its existence as its own object, a derived product, entirely exposed to vanity. In contrast, assurance results from the erotic reduction; it plays out on the one hand between the *ego,* its existence, its certainty, and its objects, and, on the other hand, a still indeterminate yet sovereign instance, provided that assurance responds to the question "Does anyone love me?" and allows one to hold out against the objection "What's the use?" The *ego* produces certainty, while assurance radically goes beyond it, because assurance comes to the *ego* from elsewhere, and delivers it from the crushing burden of auto-certification, which is perfectly useless and defenseless in front of the question "What's the use?" Certifying my existence myself depends upon my thought, and thus upon me. Receiving assurance against the vanity of my certain existence does not depend upon me, but requires that I learn from elsewhere that I am and above all if I have to be. Holding out when faced with vanity, which is to say obtaining the justification to be from elsewhere, means that I am, not by being (even through myself, even as a privileged being), but insofar as I am loved (and thus chosen from elsewhere).

Of what elsewhere are we speaking? I do not yet have the means to respond to this question. But neither do I yet have need to decide it here. For the erotic reduction to be accomplished, it is enough to understand what I am asking (myself) for: not a certainty of self by the self, but an assurance that comes from elsewhere. This "elsewhere" begins as soon as the oneiric closure of self upon self gives way and there pierces through an instance that is irreducible to me and from which, according to variable and still undefined modalities, I receive myself. Thus it does not matter if this elsewhere identifies itself as a neutral other (life, nature, the world), or as the other in general (such and such a group or society), or even as such and such an other (man or woman, the divine, or even God).* It only matters that it come upon me from elsewhere, so cleanly that it could not fail to matter to me, since it matters within me. Far from weakening the impact, its anonymity instead reinforces it: in effect, if it remains anonymous, elsewhere will come upon me without announcing itself or giving warning, and thus without allowing me to foresee anything; and if it takes me unawares, it will surprise me, and strike me all the more at heart; in short, it will matter to me deep down. In mattering to me deep down, the anonymous somewhere else will occur as an event. Only a radical event can dissipate the indifference of the vanity of being and disrupt the question "What's the use?" The lethargy insinuated by the question "What does it matter?" is dissipated when the elsewhere matters within me and thus matters to me. The anonymous event thus gives me an assurance about me (that I am, from elsewhere) in the very proportion that it denies to me every certainty about it (about its identity). Thus it is not initially necessary to seek the identity of the elsewhere, since its very anonymity makes it matter all the more. Regarding the elsewhere, it is suitable just to understand how it comes to matter to me, that is, to replace the interrogation "Am I?" with the question "Does anybody love me?"—in short, it is suitable just to understand how it accomplishes the erotic reduction.

In a first approximation, we will say that since the anonymous elsewhere assures me in coming upon me, since it breaks the autism of the certainty of self by self alone, then it exposes me to itself, and determines originarily *that which* I am by *that for whom* (or for which) I am. Being signifies from this point forward for me being according to the advent from else-

---

Autrui, the other, is always masculine in French, yet it is used, as in this sentence, in association with masculine and feminine nouns and third-person pronouns alike. At times, a referential ambiguity exists in the original that is impossible to reproduce in English. Thus the gendering of *autrui* in this translation attempts to follow context, sometimes referring to he or him, sometimes to she or her, and sometimes to he or she or him or her. Clearly, with such decisions the translator's interpretation of the text becomes rather visible. A guiding principle in my interpretive decisions surrounding the translation of *autrui* has been the belief that sexual difference is to be taken seriously in this text, a belief based upon the author's statement, in the introduction, that when he writes "I" in this book, he does so "starting from and in view of the erotic phenomenon within me."—Trans.

where, being toward and for that which I am not—whatever it may be. No longer am I because I will it (or think it, or perform it), but because someone wills me from elsewhere. What could someone from elsewhere will for me? Good or ill, in the strictest sense, by female to male, by man to man, by group to group; and also, or even to begin with, in the extra-moral sense, in the way that even inanimate things can deploy good or ill against me (for the world can become for me hospitable or inhospitable, the landscape unattractive or pleasant, the city open or closed, the company of the living welcoming or hostile, etc.). Thus I am insofar as someone wills me good or ill, insofar as I can experience myself as received or not, loved or hated. I am insofar as I ask myself, "What is wanted of me (*was mögen sie*)?"; I am insofar as I am susceptible to a decision, which does not belong to me and which determines me in advance, because it comes to me from elsewhere, from the decision which renders me likeable or not. Thus, beyond certainty (which thus originarily becomes me nonoriginarily), assurance decides that I could only be insofar as I am loved or not. Insofar as loved through elsewhere—not insofar as thinking myself, by myself, as a being. For me, being is always determined by a sole tonality that alone is originary—being insofar as loved or hated, through elsewhere.

Couldn't one object that this figure of the *ego* in the situation of the erotic reduction sanctions an unreservedly radical, and thus unjust, selfishness or "egoism"? No, for if one understands this "egoism" correctly, it is right to praise it. Unlike the self-certainty that comes to the *ego* from the self, assurance can never come to the *ego* from itself, but rather always from elsewhere: whence an alteration, or indeed a radical alterity of the *ego* to itself, originarily. In this strict sense, the "egoism" of an erotically reduced *ego* thus acquires an ethical privilege, that of an egoism altered from elsewhere, and opened by it.

Egoism, then? Yes, egoism, but on the condition of having the means and the resolve. For this disarmed and learned egoism has the audacity not to hide itself in transcendental neutrality, where the "I think" deludes itself about its certainty, as if that certainty assured it, as if it owed itself nothing more, as if it could owe nothing to no one—out there. The egoism of the erotic reduction has the courage not to hide the terror that threatens every *ego,* as soon as it confronts the suspicion of its own vanity, and not to turn its gaze away from the silent dread cast by the simple question "What's the use?" For in fact, if the *ego* were only what it flatters itself with being—the existence about which it wants to be so poorly certain—from whence would it draw the obstinate and unacknowledged strength to remain itself, where would it get the legitimacy thus to endure its un-assured penury? Who, without panic, would resign himself to the limitation of being a thinking *ego,* restricted to its alleged transcendental neutrality, when the dark hour comes, no longer of doubt about certainty, but instead of vanity without assurance? Not I, not anyone—except if we hypocritically claim unconsciousness of this trial—could act as if it made no difference if someone loves me or not, as if the erotic reduction did not open up a cardinal difference, as if this difference did not make more difference than every other, and did not render them all indifferent. Who can hold seriously that the possibility of finding oneself loved or hated does not concern him at all? One has only to try it: the moment he walks this line, the greatest philosopher in the world yields to dizziness. And besides, where is the coherence in humbly claiming oneself unselfish in front of the erotic reduction, while at the same time taking pride without hesitation or fear in exercising the imperial function of a transcendental *ego*? Inversely, by what right do we accuse the *ego* of egoism when it honestly admits to lacking assurance and, without holding anything back, exposes itself to an elsewhere that it cannot know and, in any case, must not master?

Thus it is time to be done with the second-degree vanity of claiming not to feel touched at heart by the vanity of every certainty, above all of this arid certainty, which I confer upon myself in thinking myself. Taking everything into account, what injustice is there in wanting someone out there to love me? Don't the justice and the exactness of reason require, on the contrary, that I assure myself—I, without whom nothing in the world could give itself or show itself? And who, then, more than me has the duty to worry himself about my erotic assurance—the only one possible—I, who am the first to carry the burden of responsibility for myself? And above all, without the rational egoism and courage to accomplish the erotic reduction, I would allow the *ego* in me to give way. There is no ethical obligation, no altruism, no substitution that could impose itself upon me if my *ego* did not first itself resist vanity and its "What's the use?"—and thus if I did not first and without condition ask for an assurance from "out there" for myself. In the light of the erotic reduction, even egoism allows for an originary alterity, and thus alone renders possible, eventually, the trial of the other.

§ 4. The World according to Vanity

The world cannot be phenomenalized except by giving itself to me and by making me its gifted. My place in the sun—in the erotic sun which assures me as someone who is loved or hated—has nothing about it that is unjust, or tyrannical, or hateful: laying claim to it is imperative, like my first duty.

Another objection, however, could stop me. Substituting the loved or hated *ego* for the thinking *ego* could in fact weaken it, for two reasons. First of all, because it lies with the *ego cogitans* to think itself by itself alone and thus to produce its certainty in perfect autonomy, whereas when I envisage myself according to the erotic reduction, I only pose the question "Does anyone love me?" still without any response. This question makes me depend upon an anonymous elsewhere that I cannot, by definition, master; it thus exposes me to the radical uncertainty of an always problematical and perhaps impossible answer. Henceforward, I must give up autonomy, that uninterrogated obsession, as lost. Next, the ego could be weakened because, even if an eventual erotic confirmation came upon me from elsewhere, I would still stagnate in a definitive uncertainty. Indeed, assurance from elsewhere would not come to add itself to self-certainty in order to confirm it, but, at best, would compensate the failure, after having itself provoked it by wounding the *ego* with an alterity that is more originary to it than itself. By entering into the erotic reduction, I would thus lose myself, for my heretofore determinate characteristic—loved or hated—will no longer ever belong to me in its own right (like it previously belonged to me in thought); it will no longer confer me upon myself, but will instead send me out of myself toward an undecided stake, which nevertheless will decide everything—and first of all me. In short, the *ego* is weakened by a double heteronomy: *de jure,* and then *de facto.* And this double weakening cannot be contested: the objection carries full weight.

Indeed, it is necessary to admit that the erotic reduction reaches the *ego* in its most inward part, by definitively rendering it destitute of all self-production in certainty and in existence. If, by chance, a response to the question "Does anybody love me?" must be offered, it will always be inscribed within this dependence as its ultimate horizon, without ever reestablishing—even in a desired sketch or in an ideal of reason—the autonomy of certainty through the *cogitatio.* But this destitutive result is not so much a total loss as it is a still-obscure attainment. If, under the blow of the erotic reduction, I cannot receive myself with certainty except insofar as I am loved or hated, and thus only as potentially loved (a beloved), I enter into an absolutely new terrain. It is no longer an issue even of being as someone loved, or of making oneself loved or hated with the goal of succeeding in being or not being, but instead of appearing to myself directly, beyond every status as an eventual being, as potentially loved and as lovable. Henceforward "loved" no longer plays the role of an adjective quali-

fying a being by its mode of being, since under the rules of the erotic reduction confronting vanity, one can no longer assume without precaution,
as in metaphysics, that "to be or not to be, that is the question." The question "Does anyone out there love me?" which is definitively substituted,
no longer aims at being and no longer concerns itself with existence. It introduces me into a horizon in which my status as loved or hated, or in short
my status as lovable, no longer refers to anything but itself. In asking if
someone out there loves me, I do not even any longer have first to inquire
about my assurance: I enter into the reign of love, where I immediately receive the role of he who can love, and whom one can love, and who believes that someone must love him—the *lover.*

The lover is thus opposed to the cogitant. First of all because he renders destitute the quest for certainty and replaces it with the quest for assurance; because he substitutes the reduced query "Does anyone love
me?" for certainty's question "Am I?" (and thus also for its variant, "Am I
loved?"); because he is not insofar as he thinks, but, supposing that he still
must be, is only insofar as someone loves him. Above all, while the cogitant only cogitates in order to be and only exerts his thought as a means to
certify his being, the lover loves not so much in order to be as in order to
resist what annuls being—vanity, which asks, "What's the use?" The lover
sets his heart on surpassing being, in order not to succumb with it to that
which renders it destitute. From the point of view of the lover, or in fact
from the point of view of the erotic reduction, being and its beings appear
as contaminated and untouchable, irradiated by the black sun of vanity.
The point is to love, because under the rules of the erotic reduction, nothing unloved or unloving holds. In passing from the cogitant (and thus also
from he who doubts, knows not, and comprehends, wills and does not will,
imagines and feels) to the lover, the erotic reduction does not modify the
figure of the *ego* in order to attain, by other means, the same goal—to certify its being. The erotic reduction renders destitute the question "To be or
not to be?"; it deposes the question of being from its imperial responsibility by exposing it to the question "What's the use?"; it considers it seriously
from the point of view of vanity. In the erotic reduction, wherein the lover
is at stake, the question "What are beings (in their being)?" loses its privilege as the oldest question, forever sought and forever missed. The aporia
of the question of being does not consist in one's forever missing it, but
rather in one's persistence in always posing it first, when it remains—in the
best of cases—derived or conditional. Neither first nor last, it only comes
under a second philosophy, or at least as soon as another question—

"What's the use?"—troubles it and a more radical philosophy asks, "Does anyone out there love me?" This reversal of the natural attitude—naturally ontological, and thus naturally metaphysical (here at least)—alone can accomplish a reduction of a new style, which we have identified as the erotic reduction. But how is the erotic reduction accomplished? How does it differ from other reductions or from the natural attitude? In short, how does it put the things of the world on stage? To respond to this question, it is necessary to go back to the lover—he who asks himself, "Does anyone love me?" According to the natural attitude, he would simply consider all the beings and being [*l'étant*] in general. But, under the rules of the erotic reduction, he notices that no being, and no *alter ego,* not even he himself, can furnish himself with the least assurance before the question "Does anyone love me?" Any old being assures the lover all the less, because he himself is exposed entirely to vanity. No *alter ego* can assure him either, because it would first be necessary to be able to distinguish it from a being in the world, which, at this moment in the investigation, remains impossible. As for the *ego,* it cannot of itself furnish the least assurance when confronted with the query "Does anyone *out there* love me?" On principle, vanity thus extends universally. Effectively, it accomplishes the erotic reduction upon all the regions of the world and their borders. It thus remains to describe briefly vanity and the erotic reduction, following their three privileged moments: space, time, and the self's identity.

§ 5. Space

The erotic reduction renders destitute the homogeneity of space. According to the natural attitude (and thus, here, metaphysics), space is defined as the order of compossibles, of all the beings that can exist together and at the same time, without rendering each other mutually impossible. Whence its homogeneity, which is noted through the first property of beings in space: they can—by right, if not always in fact (but the problem is only that of the power of the technological means)—move about, pass from one place to another, and exchange their positions. Every *here* can become an *over there,* and every *over there* can once again become a *here.* Spatial beings are thus characterized by the paradoxical property of not holding to any proper place, or of not having any fixed home. One constantly replacing the other, they ceaselessly circulate within an indifferent space. Thus it has been possible to thematize, quite rightly, this exchange as a circle (a "whirlwind")—the merry-go-round of beings in movement, from the accidental place of one to another accidental place, which another used to occupy and could return to occupy, endlessly. In space, no being possesses a proper or natural place.

Let us move now to the rule of the erotic reduction. I am in the lover's situation, determined from top to bottom by the question "Does anyone love me?" As such, where am I? I am there in space exactly where the question "Does anyone love me?" situates me. In order to define this place, it is necessary to describe a situation that is exemplary, yet known to all, real or at least imaginable: I have just left my accustomed home, I have traveled thousands of miles, I find myself in a land that is foreign in terms of language, surroundings, ways and customs, and it is in this land that, whether once and for all or for some specified interval, I am going to live. On site, my contacts of course remain at first quite limited (the institution or power that has invited me, a few professional relations, some vague friendships, a functioning domestic environment). On site, then, where am I? As a subsistent being, I am at the intersection of a latitude and a longitude; as a being who uses tools ("functioning," working, online, etc.), I am at the center of a network of economic and social exchanges. But as a lover, where am I? I find myself there where (or alongside whom) I can ask (myself), "Does anyone love me?" Why do I persist in naming once again *there* this place that actually offers a *here*? How do we define this *there*? Clearly, by the elsewhere that renders it thinkable, or put another way, by the one who I would like to love me, the one upon whom alone depends not only the response to my question "Does anyone love me?" but also the very fact that this question occurs to me as an obsession, which strikes with vanity all that which does not correspond to it, stands in its way, or, quite simply, does not hear it. In these facts, the question is decided by the choice that I will soon make—that of identifying this elsewhere, as a geographically factual elsewhere, perhaps frustrating because far away, or even inaccessible. But how will I identify it?

We know only too well—in the desert that vanity extends around me and around my new localization, I will identify this elsewhere simply by the telephone number (or fax number, or e-mail address) that I enter, or by the address to which I will write. The first number or the first address that, consciously or voluntarily, or as is more often the case, impulsively and automatically, I select with confidence or with anguish, with hope or at random, will designate—even if only provisionally and superficially—the elsewhere that concerns me, because it responds or at least appears to be able to respond to the question "Does anyone love me?" This elsewhere (and no other) is important to me, because it and only it renders me capable of overcoming the vanity that strikes with "What's the use?" all the beings that closely surround me with their incontestable material weight and which, nevertheless, concern me not at all as a lover. But why then does *this* particular elsewhere and no other deliver me from the vanity of my new world (and not only from the anguish of the absence of this elsewhere)? Because this vanity (and this eventual anguish) arises uniquely from *this* particular elsewhere, since it alone has authority to make me become, under the erotic reduction, the lover—to wit, the one who asks (himself) the question "Does anyone love me?" The horrors of settling in a foreign country are well known: upon entering a new apartment, one first looks for the telephone (or equivalent device); the first concern is to inquire how to work it (the dial tone, the number, the telephone company, the calling plan); the first freedom consists in finally using it. It is necessary to take these trivial details seriously (and each of us can correct or complete them in accord with his or her own personal experience), because they describe the incontestable day-to-day experience of a place that is neither interchangeable nor commutable, a place whose *over there* will never reduce to a *here,* because my physical transport, bag and baggage, from one *here* to another *here,* not only retains in this latter *here* the status of *over there,* but reinforces it. For henceforward, I know that this *over there*—where I am—does not stay as such (*over there*) for geographical or circumstantial motives, but instead refers back to a more radical *here,* which plays the role of elsewhere, in relation to which I allow myself to be taken, in the erotic reduction, by the question "Does anyone love me?"

At once, I discover that, even and above all when I was still staying *over there,* this elsewhere did not constitute a *here* any more than it becomes one today now that I passed on to a new *here;* as close as it remained then, it was already showing itself, as it is here and now, as elsewhere, as the *over there* that makes me a lover. Once again, let us underscore that the identity of the bearer of the telephone line or of the address is unimportant: in no way does it matter whether we are talking about the president of my institution, my banker, a longtime friend, a woman, my child, my mother, a brother, or an old, nearly dormant acquaintance, or even my professional rival or my best enemy. None of these would intervene as the one that I must at any cost urgently call or call again, if he or she was not exerting, in whatever way that might be, the function of the elsewhere, who *over there* arouses in me the question "Does anyone love me?" Space thus appears, under the rule of the erotic reduction, as essentially heterogeneous; all the *over there*s can no longer be exchanged for so many *here*s; a place becomes for me unsubstitutable for the first time, fixed and natural, if you like—not the *here* wherein, like a subsistent being in the world, I find myself, and which does not cease to be displaced, but the precise *over there* stuck in me, where I receive the elsewhere, that is to say, the *over there* from whence I receive finding myself riveted into myself, the elsewhere itself. Thus I do not live where I am, *here,* but rather there whence there comes over me the elsewhere that alone concerns me, and without which nothing, of the beings of the world, would concern me: thus *over there.* I do not live there where the beings that the unreduced world delegates to me in such and such a circumstance are deployed and piled up, because, in passing into another environment, eventually totally different, I would refer myself to the same elsewhere (the same address, the same name, etc.) as in the preceding ontic environment. The world of beings close to me can very well hem me in, and then transform itself completely, but the elsewhere that exerts the function of my center will not vary, ever: it will thus always define the unique and natural place from whence the question "Does anyone love me?" reaches me. This place defines space according to the erotic reduction.

Here and *over there* are no longer exchanged in a neutral space; they change places according to whether or not I find myself in the situation of the erotic reduction. Without the erotic reduction, I am *here* (at home) everywhere I go, and the domicile left behind immediately becomes an *over there.* Within the erotic reduction, where I go will remain an *over there* for as long as the former *here,* though left behind and geographically far away, still defines for me the elsewhere, from whence the question "Does anyone love me?" is posed.

§ 6. Time

The erotic reduction likewise renders destitute the succession of time. According to the natural attitude (here according to metaphysics), time is defined as the order of successives, of all the beings that cannot exist together without rendering one another mutually impossible. Whence their succession, which is noted by the order of beings in space: they must be replaced in the same place, passing from one instant to another and exchanging their instants. Every *now* comes from a completed *before* and is destined right away to become an *after.* Like beings in space, they exchange themselves, but, unlike them, they exchange themselves by changing themselves, modifying themselves irreversibly, each passing into the other. Whence their property of not holding fast to any proper moment, of not having any fixed duration, of having, at each instant, to repeat themselves in order to remain what they already no longer are. One always replacing the other, they circulate unceasingly in an indifferent succession. The procession of temporal beings transposes them without end, in each of three temporal postures, without any *present* ever being established, if not in the passage of the instant. Time never passes, but, in its present, nothing finds the time to happen. Strictly speaking, nothing stays put in time, which thus offers no center.

Let us enter into the erotic reduction, where the event from elsewhere reigns. According to what moment of time does this elsewhere temporalize itself, and according to what ecstasy of time? It is temporalized in its coming about as event. Now it is proper to the event not to be foreseeable, or to be produced or even less to be reproduced at will. The event thus compels me to await it, subject to its initiative. I can decide to continue to love and to make myself loved, but I cannot decide the moment in which I will begin one or the other, because I cannot decide, by an act of will proportionate to a light in the understanding, if and when I will face the question "Does anyone love me?" Elsewhere, as event, compels me to the posture of expectation. The temporality of such an expectation remains to be determined. Paradoxically, while the time of the action, of the occupation and of the handling of beings, does not cease to flow, by immediately transforming the *not yet* into a *now* and the *now* into an *already passed,* or in short while time does not cease to pass and to pass away, by contrast, for as long as I wait, time does not pass. Erotic time does not pass as long as I wait, for a very clear reason: while I am waiting, still nothing happens; I am waiting precisely because still nothing happens, and, precisely, I am waiting for something finally to happen. The time of expectation does not pass, for nothing is happening. Only my expectation lasts: it suspends the flux of time, because it still finds nothing in time that arises and, thus, that can disappear. In the world's time, that which passes does not last. In the erotic reduction's time, only the expectation for which nothing happens lasts.

This evidence is surprising: in the time in which I wait for something to happen, and in which nothing happens, a whole host of things nevertheless happen—even if they are only the activities I undertake to pass the time during which nothing happens (vague reading, frenetic tidying, compulsive consultation of my watch, bored walking, the coveted tiredness resulting from athletic activity, absentminded conversation, etc.). Nevertheless, nothing happens so long as and insofar as I wait, because nothing occurs—at least, nothing that I am *precisely and particularly* waiting for. So long as what stands in for elsewhere in this occurrence has not called me, has not sent his letter, has not issued her message, has not come, in short has not entered into my field of vision, or in a word, and exactly, for so long as she has not *arrived* from her elsewhere to me, nothing will have *happened* here and now. Nothing will have *happened,* so long as it has not *happened* here, and in this way transformed where I am (*over there*) into a full-fledged *here* (its own). And paradoxically, in this case, space commands time, external meaning governs internal meaning, because the external meaning—space, or rather the nonspatial *here/over there* of the erotic reduction—decides in the final instance the internal meaning—time, or better, the *now* of the erotic reduction. For the temporality of expectation is only accomplished by an event, and this event only arrives to an addressee, from elsewhere to a *here*. From that point forward, time is no longer defined as the extension of the mind, but as the extension of the event, of the elsewhere arising from outside the mind and suddenly coming upon it.

A situation results, that, while quite banal, we have all nevertheless lived through. Nothing happens for as long as I wait; at each instant, I can tell myself: "Still nothing, always nothing." Which means that all the facts and beings visibly present, which have no compunction about swarming all around me, nevertheless receive none of my attention, and find themselves rendered destitute, struck with vanity by the erotic reduction. Suddenly, something happens ("There it is!"); but this something no longer has anything of a thing about it, or of a simple being subjected to vanity; it comes forward like an event, surviving the erotic reduction, eroticized, so to speak: expected but unforeseen, actual but without assignable cause, provocative but nonreproducible, unique but immemorial. The present at last is accomplished, not as an enduring permanence, but as a present that is given, in short as a present that is received, not as a presence subsisting in itself. It can at last deliver me from the indefinite and dolorous future of expectation, because it truly arrives from elsewhere, instead of provisionally occupying a lapse of time in the present that it would rent without inhabiting. The present that is given accomplishes the present instant, precisely because it overflows presence. What is more: the arrival from elsewhere is not only accomplished in the present, it gives me my first present. With its passage, at last something—once again—happens. This gift of the precise present results from the arrival of an elsewhere within the indefinite future of my expectation.

As a consequence, this present only comes forward for the one or those who share the same expectation—that of a given arrival, of a specific passage, of an elsewhere that is not mixed up with any other. Thus an absence orders the coming forward of present time, but an absence that is sufficiently precise and identifiable, not to be confused with any other absence (and *a fortiori* with any occupation, which holds the attention of those who expect nothing). Whether I expect the results of a competitive exam or the publication of a book, the judgment of a trial or the result of a political election, the final goal of a soccer match or the finish of a race, the birth of a child or the death of a parent, the message of a woman or something purely unexpected, each time, the expectation bears upon nothing that is present (nothing that has yet happened for the moment), and instead upon an elsewhere so precise that it distinguishes itself by its very unreality from so many other present things, real or possible, which do not matter to me. Each expectation selects, so to speak, a population that is invisibly separated from the rest of its counterparts by the very identity of the absent that is to come, which is sufficient to bring it together and fascinate it; a family or a whole people, an individual or a couple, a business, a union, or a collective, a group of fans or a regiment, it makes no difference. In each of these cases, I distinguish myself (or we distinguish ourselves) not so much by what we are and do in permanent presence ("everyday"), as by what we expect, indeed by that which can come upon us without our expecting it consciously. The expectation of the absent, which still must happen, delineates the border between all those who do not expect or expect something else and those who stay awake in order to await *that* particular elsewhere over there and no other—a border that is traced each time by the erotic reduction, an erotic border. The expectation of *this* elsewhere thus does not only temporalize me; it identifies me by assigning me to my own—that which must happen for me (or us) tells me who I am (or who we are). The temporality of the expectation of an elsewhere defines originary individuality and, eventually, originary community. That is because for myself alone the elsewhere that I await makes the difference—not only between the time in which nothing happens and the present where the elsewhere happens, then passes, but also between me (or us), who await *this* befalling, *this* passage, *this* elsewhere, and all the others, who can't make any sense of it. I alone await *this* precise absentee (this face, this news, this letter); for the others, who do not await the same absentee or who await nothing at all, the very absentee of my expectation remains effectively absent; the expectation collapses when the erotic reduction fades away. The others miss what is happening—which is to say that what I await is not yet happening and thus that nothing is happening for me—because they busy themselves with all the available presence of beings, which they have to manage without losing any time. They thus lose the passage of the elsewhere, which only ever arrives in expectation. In order not to lose time, in order not to lose what does not happen, they prefer the illusion of stability to what passes, the permanent to the event.

The expectation of the elsewhere that must happen thus determines, starting from the future of its advent, the only present that the erotic reduction will tolerate: the given that takes over from the permanent present, the awaited and unforeseen moment, where the call sent forth by the elsewhere happens, is given and thus makes the present of itself. The expectation of the elsewhere that just passed, and thus that just made the present of its advent, determines a past that conforms to the erotic reduction: belonging to the past are the moments in which the call from elsewhere has already resounded and already made the present of its gift, and yet has already passed on—the past begins as soon as what happens has passed beyond it. Whence comes the possibility of a definitive past: not the expectation of that which no longer can or no longer must come about (for, by definition, I can expect everything always), but the definitive widowhood of every elsewhere, the renunciation of expectation as such ("to expect nothing more out of life"). The past, in the erotic reduction, does not assemble the former present moments in memory; rather it sanctions the closure of expectation. It does not hoard the already given, but mourns every possibility of a new advent, of the possibility of expecting anew. In short, it does not conserve the completed present moments, but closes up the future. The past becomes the over and done with, no longer the management of absence (which belongs properly to expectation and to the future), but its censure—the recording that expectation is henceforth over with. In the erotic reduction, the past does not conserve the present under the form of the past, like a patrimony; it sanctions the very absence of true absence—the absence of expectation, the erotic absence. For a love is not over with when the beloved vanishes, but when the need and the very absence of the beloved vanish—when the lack itself goes lacking. The past buries the dead, dead of no longer expecting. This past will remain definitively over if elsewhere can no longer be expected, if it can no longer happen; by contrast, it will remain eventually provisional for as long as a new expectation can hope for the return of an absence still to come. Nostalgia opens possibility, recollection can nourish expectation, what has been passed over can give rise to a new passage of what happens. In the erotic reduction, history lasts for as long as I expect.

Thus, according to the erotic reduction, the future is defined as the time of the expectation of an elsewhere, in which nothing happens; the present, as the time in which elsewhere comes to pass and makes the present of its passage; the past, as the time in which elsewhere has passed beyond the moment of its present and abandons our time to the side of the road, where it withdraws. In every case, time essentially unfolds itself according to the mode of an event, like the unpredictable arrival of an elsewhere, of which no one knows the day nor the hour, and of which the present can only be given as an unexpected and unmerited gift. According to its character as advent, elsewhere is never constituted as a common phenomenon, arranged according to the supposedly dominant point of view of a transcendental *ego,* but instead gives itself by anamorphosis—by imposing upon he who expects it the particular point from which its arrival can be seen and its present received; it is necessary to find oneself here and now, which is to say *there* where and when it decides to arrive. Thus I can never escape the necessary contingency of the advent of the elsewhere: not only might it or might it not come forward (logical contingency at the literal level), but, even if it comes forward and after the fact seems necessarily to have come forward ("it had to end up this way"), this very necessity will happen according to the mode of advent, and thus according to a necessary contingency (second-degree contingency). When I am expecting, I inhabit that which can come upon me from elsewhere and without which no present or past would matter to me.

§ 7. Ipseity

The erotic reduction renders destitute all identity of self to self, which would found itself upon the thought of the self. But when I find myself in the situation of asking, "Am I loved?" what am I? I am no longer this being who is insofar as he performs, in speech or in thought, his existence; for it is precisely this very certainty that will not deliver me from vanity, which demands not certainty, but an assurance, an assurance that can only come upon me from elsewhere (§ 3). By saying, "Does anyone love me?" I thus do not know who I am, but I do know at least *where* I am: I find myself *here,* which is to say there where the question that I pose (to myself) finds me, there where I experience the vanity that this question attempts to ward off, there where the call that has come from elsewhere will (or will not) come upon me. I am there where what touches me affects me, and thus first of all there where I affect myself. I am not first of all there where I touch some thing other than me (where I think it, aim at it, and constitute it), but rather there where I experience myself touched, affected, and reached. In posing *myself* (in and as) the question "Does anyone love me?" I discover myself preeminently in the situation of that which is exposed to the touch of an affection: in effect, either this question admits a positive response—an other loves me—and the advent of that response affects me at the deepest level; or it remains without a positive response—no other loves me, as far as I know—and this denial affects me at the deepest level. The question "Does anyone love me?" thus designates the point at which I discover myself affected as such, as unsubstitutable. I cannot abandon this point, this *here* that comes to me from *over there,* nor go away from it; for wherever I may go, I will find myself there again, and always. In the erotic reduction, I am not the being that I make myself to be by thought, but I am there where I find myself, there where a possible elsewhere affects me—I am the *there,* where the question "Does anyone love me?" finds me and comes to drive me out. I am a *there*—not a being-*there* (a *Da-sein*), but a *there* where someone can love me or not love me. The *there* that receives me and confines me does not first of all come under being ("to be or not to be" is decidedly not the question), but instead comes under a possible love ("Does someone love me, or not?"—that is the question).

It remains to define more exactly this *there* where the elsewhere reaches me. We can identify this target with a privileged phenomenon, known by the name *flesh.* The flesh is opposed to the extended bodies of the physical world, not only because it touches and feels bodies, while bodies do not feel, even if a sense of touch feels them; but above all because it only touches bodies in feeling itself touch them, as much as, or indeed more than it feels them. The flesh can feel nothing without feeling itself, and feeling itself feeling (touched, or indeed wounded, by what it touches); it can even happen that it feels by not only feeling itself feeling, but also feeling itself felt (for example, if an organ of my flesh touches another organ of my own flesh). In the flesh, the interior (what feels) no longer is distinguished from the exterior (what is felt); they merge in a unique sentiment—feeling oneself feeling. Thus I can never put myself at a distance from my flesh, or distinguish or remove myself from it, or even less, absent myself from it. Every attempt to draw back from it (with the hypocritical intention of taking leave of it) would amount, if I dared to carry it out, to killing myself, for I would remove myself, take leave and undo myself. Thus by taking flesh, I take hold of myself. I do not take flesh as if I already had at my disposition a *here* from which I could come toward it and make it mine. I only take flesh in the way that cement "takes" or sets: by solidifying myself, so to speak, in and as myself. By "taking" or setting as flesh, I reach, for the first time, the place that I am—the *here* where it will be possible, from this point forward, always and for every being of the world, to reach me. I am there where one may reach me—and I am only reachable there where I have taken flesh, where I am taken as flesh. There where my flesh exposes me, I am; which is to say, I am there where the question "Does anyone love me?" assigns me. Only my taking flesh assigns me my ipseity.

With this flesh of mine, it is of course still a matter of a modality of thought: I still think myself when I take flesh, even if I no longer think myself according to representation, or understanding. I think myself in feeling myself, and according to the modality of feeling, in an immediacy that abolishes the separation that is proper to representation; contrary, then, to thought under the modality of understanding. Thought according to understanding in effect proceeds according to the universal, works upon the universalizable, and operates by universalizing. Thus, understanding always supposes that its reasons or its arguments can be comprehended by their receptor as well as by their emitter; such that the roles can—and, in the rational dialogue, must—be exchanged; the same reasoning, if it wants to deserve its claim to truth, must be able to find itself repeated and thereby validated for all and sundry, and thus for anyone. Whence comes the privilege of the understanding in rational discussion: only this form of rationality can convince without violence, because each argument belongs as much to the one who comprehends it as to the one who devises it. As a consequence, thought as understanding is deployed only on the express condition that it not include persons and that it not be singularized (which is what distinguishes scientific and juridical discourse from the words of poets, writers, and theologians, and sometimes even philosophers). Properly speaking, thought as understanding is addressed to all, because it belongs to no one and designates no author, but instead offers itself to the appropriation of all those who reason by understanding. It thus owes its perfection to its refusal to be individualized.

The taking of flesh, by contrast, assigns me to a *here* (in fact to a *there*) that is irreducible, and only permits me a word that individualizes me as far as the final ipseity. I cannot and must not at first pronounce this word of ipseity—for couldn't it be that everything I will say might have already been said by an other, or an infinity of others, such that I would dissolve myself at once into a common discourse? If I cannot say it by uttering it, doubtless all that remains for me is to receive it in hearing it—or at least to wait to hear it. Not that I produce it, because I let it be, and let it be in me—an interior word. In the erotic reduction, I do not say the words "Does anyone love me?" as a question that I could choose to say among a thousand others ("Who am I?" "What can I know?" "What ought I to do?" "What may I hope?" "What is man?" or indeed, "How will I make my living?" "How can I live happily?" and so on), but instead as the question that delivers me to myself, and in which I experience to the depths my taking flesh, in short as the question that says me to myself, before and without my responding—because it gives me my *here*—or rather, from its point of view, my *there*.

I had acknowledged the necessity of doubting (§§ 1–2). Upon entering into the erotic reduction, I recognized that doubt did not have to do first of all with the certainty of objects or of beings in the world (as the theory of science would have it), nor even the certainty of my own existence (as metaphysics would have it), because each of these still fell to the blow of vanity, which always retorts victoriously, "What's the use?" I discovered that doubt in the end demands nothing less than the assurance of me, in my originary passivity; and that this assurance could only be received from elsewhere than me (§ 3). I thus had to admit that no question reached me more radically than that which asked me not, "Am I in thinking?" but, "Does anyone out there love me?" In short, "to be or not to be," that is no longer the question, but only "Does anyone out there love me?" (§ 4). It is important not to attempt to respond to this question too quickly. I cannot respond to this question, precisely because it puts me in question. I thus can only expect from it a response which, as a pure event, would impose itself—if it ever arrives—upon me as an unforeseeable advent, which would only make me the present of its presence by imposing upon me its anamorphosis—by imposing upon me the taking into view of the point that it will have decided for me, but without me. Thus I must only measure what it gives me, when it only gives me its question that is still without a response. Nevertheless, from now on, it gives me something rather than nothing: it assures me, first, of a *here* that is irreducible in space (§ 5); next, of a present given in time (§ 6); and, finally, of the flesh in which my ipseity "takes" or sets (§ 7). But none of these givens belong to me or come from me. All come to me and alter me at the very instant in which they fit me to my unsubstitutable facticity. Henceforward, what can I legitimately think? Nothing but that the assurance I seek, because it surpasses every certainty, can only come forward from elsewhere, and never from me. Every response that I would give to myself would lead me astray.

Concerning Every Man for Himself, and His Self-Hatred

§ 8. Separation and Contradiction

Thus in the erotic reduction, nothing and no one assures me—the lover that I have become under the erotic reduction—except myself, who by definition cannot do so. By agreeing to hear the question "Does anyone love me?" it is as if I have opened beneath my feet an abyss that I can neither fill, cross, nor perhaps even sound—an abyss that I risk enlarging even more by developing the logic of the question "Does anyone out there love me?" For the question "Does anyone love me?" will in effect only be able to receive a response (if it ever could) by coming upon me from elsewhere than myself; it thus assigns me an irreversible dependency upon that which I can neither master, nor provoke, nor even envisage—an other than myself, eventually someone other for me (*alter ego*), in any case a foreign instance, coming from I know not where—in any case, not from me. So, while the search for certainty ("Of what am I certain?") may still hope to lead me back to myself, by certifying to me that at the least I am, even if I am still deceived, the request for an assurance ("Does anyone out there love me?") exiles me definitively outside of myself: even if it eventually winds up reassuring me against the threat of vanity ("What's the use?") by assuring me that someone loves me, it would assign me all the more to this "someone" (whoever he or she may be) that I will never be, and whose foreignness nevertheless will always remain more inward to me than my most inward part. The very one who could assure me must estrange me. In short, certainty can lead me back to myself, because I acquire it by subtraction, like a poor phenomenon, while assurance separates me from myself, because it opens within me the separation of an elsewhere. Whether it remains an empty request or, instead, fills me with its excess, it always marks me with a lack that is my own. By opening the very question of assurance, I become a lack to myself.

Of course, it remains true that I am and that I even am certainly, each time and for as long as I think; nevertheless, I find myself henceforth ineluctably under the rule of the erotic reduction, where I cannot avoid the question "What's the use?"; in order to resist that question, or in order only to understand it, I must immediately search for an assurance ("Does anyone love me?"). Now, this assurance can by definition only come upon me from an elsewhere that is definitively anterior, other, and foreign to me, an elsewhere that I lack and that defines me by this lack. There follows this principle: I am, therefore I am lacking. As much as the *ego,* insofar as it is searching for certainty, can dream of ending up in a tautology (I think, therefore I am, and I am insofar as I think what I think), just so, when the *ego* means to brave vanity (which disqualifies its existence, by intimating, "What's the use?"), it must admit an originary alterity, an origin that alters it—I am only assured of myself beginning from elsewhere. We must nevertheless hold firmly to this contradiction as the only remaining guiding thread.

This contradiction and this separation cannot be easily dodged by a sophism or by common sense. This contradiction results from a position of principle: when the issue is that of asking, "Does anyone out there love me?" I am neither the principle, nor at the origin, of myself. To prove it, let us see if we might nevertheless be able to deny this contradiction or this separation. After all, couldn't we revert to a simpler and more reasonable argument? Let us proceed as follows: the erotic reduction would not deprive me compulsorily of assurance and would not leave me defenseless in front of the question "What's the use?" provided that I myself respond to the question "Does anyone love me?" I could say, for example, that, even if no one else assures me (that he loves me), at least I, in the end, love myself—I love myself, and that is enough. In effect, no one is closer to one's self than the reduced "me," absolutely immanent to the self, with an immanence rendered more tangible by the awful solitude that is provoked by the erotic reduction. In this solitude, I discover myself reduced to my purest self, melted into a new metal, a kernel of egoity so dense that no nuclear reaction could ever fissure it, or separate me from myself. Why exclude the possibility that this strictly reduced me could, without any recourse to an outsider, suffice to love me and thereby to assure me of myself?

Are we not also dealing here with the ideal, whether implicit or claimed outright, of the wisdom of the philosophers: to end up at self-contentment, to satisfy the self with itself alone, to be sufficient to one's self? The means, which may vary, matter little (putting aside external passions in order to return toward the self, admiring the good use of one's own free will, adhering to universal necessity to the point of appropriating it to one's self, etc.), for in the end it is all about loving one's self. Or, short of loving one's self, the point is at least not to depend upon any other, so as to support one's self, to substitute advantageously the autarky of one's self for the assistance of an outsider, in short to have each one assure himself. The injunction of a god ("Know thyself!"), which sustains the ambition of philosophers, would largely suffice to balance the question "Does anyone out there love me?"—short of extinguishing it completely. Perhaps the whole enterprise of philosophy consists only in claiming that, from the epistemic reduction to the erotic reduction, the consequences remain good. The self goes along of its own accord—even to the point of going along as far as itself; the return to self would bring together the point of departure and the end of the course; the solipsism of consciousness would assure autonomy without transition, right up to the love of self.

On this point, the wisdom of the philosophers receives—for once—a confirmation from popular wisdom. Popular wisdom also claims to attain to this unique ideal: I have no greater duty than to take care of myself, by managing the satisfaction of my desires, the health of my flesh, the serenity of my psyche, in short by working out the conditions of life that allow me to survive the question "What's the use?" or indeed, that render that question ridiculous to me, vain in its own right. I must take care of myself ("Take care!"), because, we admit implicitly, no one else will do it for me, or be concerned about my self ("Who cares?").* Henceforth, this care of the self by the self becomes strictly a moral duty ("Charity begins at home"), failing which one will compromise every other duty toward anyone else; for, through my failing, I will have endured profits and losses ("My mistake!"; "Every man for himself"). The means available to such an ethic are not lacking; and when they are lacking—if I do not succeed in satisfying myself directly—there are still substitutes to be found. Thus social mimicry always puts others on stage (other selves than me), idols (appropriately named) who are happier than me and in whose glory I will be able indirectly to love myself; or at least be able to retain the possibility of loving myself, insofar as they claim to realize that possibility; it will be enough

---

*Phrases in parentheses in this sentence are in English in the original.—Trans.

for me tangentially to imitate their examples—and after all, why wouldn't I succeed in imitating them, by dint of lies I tell myself? In order to satisfy the question "Does anyone out there love me?" it would be enough to conform myself to the image of those who are loved by all, so that, fantastically, all will love me and, in the end, I too, by proxy, will end up loving myself. The anonymous socialization of my consciousness would assure, without transition, the autonomy of the love of self.

Armed with this consensus, why would I still need another to love me and to assure me that I am loved, since I love myself? Curiously, the more I am able at least to claim to find a meaning in the words "I love myself," the more it appears clearly absurd, indeed obscene, to temporalize them; instinctively I feel that I can neither say nor even comprehend formulations such as "I loved myself," or "I will love myself." Why this discomfort? Doubtless because the fragile evidence for "the love of self" remains safe only for as long as one keeps it in a nominal form, abstract and empty of personal content, so as to neutralize it. But it betrays its impossibility or its performative contradiction the moment one verbalizes it by assigning it a real actor: after all, who can say with meaning and conscience, "I love myself"? How could he verify the signification? In what would the act of accomplishing it consist? The difficulty grows when we undertake to temporalize this reflexivity into the past ("I loved myself") or the future ("I will love myself"): what did I do then that I am no longer doing in this moment, or what will I do that I am not yet doing now? In addition, if the issue is the relation of me to myself, a relation that is supposed to be one of immediate identity, how can it not remain permanent, how could I suspend it ("I loved myself"), or begin it ("I will love myself")? It may be that the formula has no signification at all. It is necessary to see in this language difficulty the index of what is in principle an impossibility: love of self can indeed be proclaimed, but it cannot be performed.

§ 9. The Impossibility of a Love of Self

Thus it is necessary to examine the fragile evidence that the love of self presupposes: I and I alone would be enough to love myself. How can an *I* become doubled, as the ambition to be assured *from elsewhere* demands, while at the same time remaining the same, as the intention to love *oneself* requires? If I must love myself, I have a choice: either we are concerned with only a single I, or the issue is two different I's. If we are concerned with only one I, how could it detach itself in order to assure this I from the outside, which must then become an other than itself? A single and compact I cannot become an other than itself, in order to give itself an assurance that responds to the question "Does anyone out there love me?" If the issue instead is an other than myself, how could this other I assure me that it is indeed me that it loves, since, by hypothesis, it will appear as foreign, as a non-I? Metaphysics knows something of this aporia, butting constantly against the distinction between the transcendental *I* that thinks, sees, and knows, but does not let itself be seen, or known, or even thought, precisely because it only ever knows, thinks, and sees the empirical *me,* a mute subject, of which it speaks without listening; as the transcendental *I* precedes the empirical *me* from the lofty heights of its representation, it can never identify itself with that *me;* for, if representation allows the *ego* to overhang that which it knows, representation exerts that overhanging viewpoint first upon the *ego,* its closest stranger. This split, hardly tolerable within the order of knowing, becomes absurd in the order of loving.

There are at least three reasons for this absurdity. First, because if I had to love myself like an other than myself, it would be necessary for me to precede myself. Those who have loved me originally (in principle, my parents) could only do so because they preceded me and they loved me before I was even in a state to receive their love; loved without yet being, I was thus preceded by the response to the question "Does anyone love me?" which I could not yet pose to myself. Now such a temporal anteriority flows from the very structure of this question, which always signifies, "Does anyone *out there* love me?" and implies aiming at an endpoint that is radically exterior to that which an actual love awaits, that is to say, an other. If by chance I had to exercise the function of loving myself, it would therefore be necessary that I assume the implausible claim of *preceding myself*: not only loving myself before myself, but loving myself with a truly originary love, which is to say, a love that is senior to me and to everything that I could produce.

Next, if a response to the question "Does anyone love me?" is to have the least chance of making me resist the suspicion "What's the use?" it would be necessary that it carry my complete conviction. Which implies, first of all, that I admit the fact that someone out there loves me; and next, and above all, that I admit that the decision (to love myself) not only matches up to but surpasses in power and conviction the vanity that strikes me with its deadly "What's the use?" This hypothetical love, of which I still do not know if it is, or what it is, would have to assure me nevertheless beyond every expectation, which is to say that it would have to envelope me in the mantle of an authority that holds no common measure with what I am and all that I may become. For the measure of this love requires loving without measure—without common measure with what I expect and imagine, failing which I will not believe in it. And, barring its excess, love remains lacking. Thus, without this preeminence over me and my expectation of the other who is supposed to love me, every love simply commensurable with vanity would only reinforce its dominion. This situation is well known: it happens that I might say, in front of someone who claims to love me, "Nobody loves me." How can I thus deny what she tells me? Because I in fact think: "What's the use of a love like yours?"; it isn't enough for me, to assure me that someone loves me and to convince me that my equal and my counterpart loves me, he who remains as poor in assurances as me, as subject to vanity as me, as deprived of love (for himself, for me, for whomever) as I am myself. If I had, strangely, to lay claim to loving myself, I would thus have to assure myself by myself of an authority who surpasses, by far, my own expectation and my own lack, so as not only to give me assurance, but above all to reassure that very assurance. To the question "Does anyone love me?" an answer that is only affirmative is not enough—only the excess that surprises and surpasses would suffice. Thus, to love myself, I would have to go beyond myself, in order to respect the measure of love, which has none. I would demand of myself *an excess of myself over myself.* But who can add one cubit to his stature?

Finally, and above all, what, if it were thinkable, would the gap within myself mean, as it is implied by the scheme according to which I would love myself? I can certainly divide myself and, without any contradiction, identify with myself, when the *ego* of which we are speaking puts itself into play within the order of the thought of understanding; I can at one moment think myself as an other, or indeed as an other object, and then pull myself back together in the following moment as identical to this very thought; I can have myself play the role of an empirical *me,* just as well as that of a transcendental *I.* In short, in thought, I can dig out a gap within myself, and fill it in just as easily. But, in front of the question "Does anyone out there love me?" the concern is not that I (as transcendental *I*) think of myself (as empirical *me*); the concern is loving myself. Loving requires an exteriority that is not provisional but effective, an exteriority that remains for long enough that one may cross it seriously. Loving requires distance and the crossing of distance. Loving requires more than a feigned distance, or one that is not truly dug out or truly crossed. In the drama of love, actions must be accomplished effectively over distance—distributing, going, coming, returning. That which I can bring about without contradiction within the order of thought—in turn identify myself with my thought through this very thought and then distinguish myself from it, engender myself in presence according to thought or place myself in parentheses, doubt my existence or demonstrate it to myself once again through thought—all of that becomes absurd within the order in which the question "Does anyone out there love me?" is heard. Here, the concern is loving, and thus what is at stake is a *distance* and an elsewhere that is even more real, serious, forbearing, and suffering than the negative of the dialectic—by far. Without the distance of this elsewhere, no one would ever love me. Thus I cannot love myself—except by leading myself astray into the insane illusion of imagining myself as my own elsewhere.

Thus, unable to precede myself, to exceed myself, or to cross the distance, I can neither think nor perform the formula "I love myself."

§ 10. The Illusion of Persevering in One's Being

One will nevertheless still object that this impossibility is merely formal. It does not stand up to a massive fact, erected in principle by metaphysics— every man for himself loves himself first, and infinitely.

I love my neighbor more than a stranger, my friend more than my enemy, my brother more than a distant relation, my wife more than my brother, and, finally, myself more than my wife. This gradation doesn't even have any sense or direction, because an absolute caesura immediately renders this series heterogeneous: I love myself with a love that is completely different from the loves that I eventually bear toward such and such others, because, rather than competing with them, this love of myself makes those loves possible. I do not risk loving others in spite of the love that I bear toward myself, but by virtue of it. As everyone knows, I can only give that which I already possess, or that which I have possessed and maintained. Only a moralism of scarcity could require that one deduct from oneself the love (and thus the being) that one can bear toward an other— since, on the contrary, I will never love anyone if I do not succeed first in loving myself, even if only a little bit. I love myself in my being in order to make possible not only myself, but all of that for which this me becomes the condition of possibility, or indeed the center: the network of exchanges, of conversations and conservations, of interests and affections,

which make of my life a definitive intersubjectivity, poor or rich, conflic-
tual or harmonious, but in every case opened by the love that I bear first to
myself. No ethics can do anything about this fact.

Let us admit that the formal impossibilities come up against this real
fact and that it is legitimate that I love myself infinitely. We will not be able
to consign this supposed fact—that I love myself infinitely—except as
a development of the circularity of the *ego cogito*: I hold to myself, and
through the self I appear to myself as infinitely near, to the point where the
self belongs to me, and I belong to it and I merge myself with it. From this
originary co-belonging there follows the adhesion of each to himself—
every man for himself. Love of this self—this every man for himself—
would assert itself as the first possible love, the love of the first possible,
and thus the only, self: love properly understood, love of the proper,
proper love of self; love begins with oneself, because it begins with the first
"each for himself"; one does not argue about original egoism, one carries
it out each day, at each moment—and every doctrine of love, even altru-
istic, begins with it. It could be that the demand to love oneself offers, beyond its formal impossibilities, a more radical meaning: at issue here would
be the reflection within consciousness of a more originary demand that is
no longer psychological but ontic—that of persevering in one's being. The
love of self would then become the simple index, incomprehensible perhaps if one remains at the level of logic, of an otherwise constraining demand, that of the being as a being.

Put otherwise, no being can be without unconditionally striving to
continue to be. Being implies for every being the effort to persevere in its
being (*conatus in suo esse perseverandi*). Being requires being, always and again,
in spite of all opposition. To be implies a demand to be without reserve,
without condition, without limit or end. It matters little whether I persevere in my being according to a more or less active mode (with an idea that
is adequate to my decision to be), or one that is more or less passive (with
an idea inadequate to that which comes upon me from being)—the essential consists only in my persisting in being and, by whatever manner in
which I am, that my *I* be. Thus what we were calling the love of self re-
flected only, within consciousness and its representation of desire, an im-
prescriptible transcendental demand; and our powerlessness to think it
without ending up in contradictions only proved that the psychological approach (love of self) remains just short of what it is required to think—being, for a being, is equivalent to presence and requires endurance in presence. In order to love oneself, it is necessary, more essentially, to persevere

in one's *own* being. The two boil down to the same—to the presence of each for himself.

Nevertheless, even thus transposed, this argument exposes itself to several objections, on perseverance and on being.

On perseverance, one must first ask if being requires for every being to persevere always and exclusively in the present, and thus to redouble presence in itself, or if it might not be a matter, in certain cases, of another temporalization, more complex and subtle, oriented toward the future. One must ask the question even more pointedly when the concern is not of a being's being in general, nor such and such a being of the world, nor above all a being according to objectivity, but being in the mode of the *I*. When what is at stake is this center of the world that at each time I am (I and no other), this being who does not belong to the world (because he opens the world) and this *I* for which no one else could ever substitute (for he would then open not my world in my place but, in his own place, an other world), we have to ask if presence, even radicalized in persistence, is enough to state the appropriate mode of being. Rather, wouldn't the *conatus in suo esse perseverandi* transpose, not without naïveté or violence, a very elementary mode of being, strictly fitting to intraworldly and physical beings—the principle of inertia, which declares that every body persists in its state (of rest or movement) for as long as another does not prevent it—into a nonworldly being, nonphysical and unsubstitutable for every other, into this *I* that each time I alone have to be, and of which no other, ever, can spare me the burden? Does it thus go without saying that the mode of being appropriate to this being who alone can say *I,* who alone admits no substitution, who alone makes it his duty to decide for himself, and who alone opens the world, be reduced without remainder to the trivial effort of persevering in presence? Let us admit even that the *ego* perseveres as much as you like—by this simple mode of being, what more will it be or what more will it know of itself as *ego*? Nothing. Because for an *ego,* being does not consist merely in prolonging its actuality, but first in remaining open to and by a possibility, not in persisting in acquired presence, but in projecting itself into the unforeseeable future. The dead man perseveres in his being—that is all that remains for him. Thus for me, the living person, being does not signify persevering, but inaugurating oneself into possibility.

Above all, what happens to being if the issue *here* is me within the erotic reduction, exposed thus to the question "Does anyone love me?" Henceforward, under the black sun of vanity (even if I claim to resist it through the love that I am supposed to be able to bear toward myself), what does perseverance in my being matter to me, what does being itself matter to me, since it is the entire question of being that finds itself henceforward placed in parentheses? How would I content myself with persevering in being when the question is no longer that of being, but of defending this being against the question "What's the use?" which destroys it? How could being, even persevering being, assure me, when the issue is that of assuring being itself against vanity, of assuring oneself against the vanity of being—in a word, of assuring myself that someone loves me? And besides, how could I make my decision to be and, above all, to have the unshaken strength to do so if being did not first remain for me lovable? For I can just as easily not esteem my being as lovable, I can always hate being, out of disgust or impotence; I can even deny myself the right and above all the duty to encumber the world of my fellows with my pathetic claim to persist in my pitiable being. Being—should a lover necessarily love it, and love it for itself, as fitting to him in the rank of lover? Nothing is less assured. A physical body, a being of the world, an object do not have to decide if they merit being, nor if they are able to do so—they persevere in elementary being, because they are excused from choosing it, willing it, or in short loving it. But I have to decide. Perhaps the atom, the rock, the sky, and the animal can, without anguish or scruple, persevere naturally in their being. I, however, cannot. In order to persevere in my being, I must first will to be, and, in order to do that, love to be. And I cannot do it for very long (except by neutralizing in myself that which distinguishes me from the atom, the rock, the sky, and the animal) if I do not quickly obtain a positive response to the question "Does anyone love me?" Now, not only does the *conatus essendi* not respond to the question "Does anyone love me?" but it does not even hear it, because it remains totally held within the natural attitude.

Under the rules of the erotic reduction, the question "To be or not to be?" loses its evidence and its primacy, such that the response brought by the *conatus in suo esse perseverandi* no longer has any pertinence. This question and this response disqualify one another, because they refuse even to hear the interrogation "Does anyone love me?"—because they draw back in front of the erotic reduction itself.

§ 11. Whether I Will It or Not

Let us nevertheless attempt a final experiment. Suppose against all logic that one could invoke here the *conatus in suo esse perseverandi* and even put it to work. It remains to test whether it can assure me, in whatever manner, against the vanity of being. Put otherwise, will the *conatus* make me bear up against the ordeal imposed by the question "Does anyone love me?" The answer to this question divides in two, according to whether I persevere in my being willingly or not (that is, necessarily), or because I will it (freely). In effect, the instance of my freedom enters without discussion, since what is at issue is *my* perseverance in *my* being as a being, the one and the other in the first person.

Take the first hypothesis: I do not persevere in being because I have decided to do so, but because it is a necessity, which determines the manner of being of the being that I am. In general and for every being of whatever type there may be, to be is equivalent to persevering; being amounts to presence, and thus to enduring and persisting in presence, without having even to decide or to will it. I make no exception to a principle that is just as valid for the atom, the rock, and the animal as it is for that which I am. It follows that I cannot fail to strive to be, or indeed exhaust myself in being, and at any cost. In metaphysical language: I strive to be in exerting myself by inadequate as well as adequate ideas, inactively and actively, in knowing or in not knowing what I do. In short, like a brute or like an understanding—in any case I will persevere, "je maintiendrai," I will cling to presence to the last possible moment. Or even beyond, because, by principle, I have neither to will it nor even to choose it. This hypothesis raises two radical objections.

First, if all being, and thus every manner of being, even the most difficult or abject, justifies my perseverance in being, or better, requires it, how far must I descend in being to satisfy unconditionally the principle of perseverance? To the point of unhappiness, to the point of indignity, to the point of animality, to the point of vegetative life, or to the point of what abjection? Does the being in which I will persevere on principle remain that of a being working in the world or of an intraworldly being, of a living being apt to die or of a phantom, neither dead nor alive? Will I truly not have to choose in front of this foretold degradation, or will I be able to suspend it in order to remain myself? Can the *conatus in suo esse perseverandi* force me to give myself over to inhumanity, in short to lose the reasons for being in order to remain in being? Suicide, in a word, could become for me not only a duty, but the only way to identify myself with what it is my duty to be; even if in most cases suicide only sanctions the rule of ressentiment in us, it sometimes—in rare cases—attests to the sovereign decision not to fall away from my manner of being. Better not to persevere in being than to be anything, and at any price. Next, supposing that I persevere in my being in a mode that does not make me fall away from myself, what does it matter if it conserves me or fulfills me without my having chosen it, without my having willed it, without me myself being there in any way? What does persevering in my being matter if I—I who decide and will what I become— am there for nothing, for no one, not even for me? To persevere in *my* being—but are we still talking about my being, are we still talking quite simply about me, if I have no role at all and I yield to the necessity of a principle decreed by metaphysics? In a word, is it still persevering in my being to persevere in a being that stubbornly persists without me? Without even evoking a response to the question "Does anyone love me?" is it still me at issue in this anonymous being, who perseveres, head down, in his mad, mute, and undifferentiated presence? Anybody and anything can persevere in being, without me and in my place: it does not touch me as such, it teaches me nothing when it is time to brave the erotic reduction. Sure, all beings can be contented, reassured, and comforted in that way; but for me, who ask myself, "Does anyone love me?" persevering even in *my* being remains for me a miserable vanity. What business do I have with this triviality—persevering in a being that does not love or that no one loves, which has neither to love nor to make itself loved, because it has no name and no individuality?

Now take the other hypothesis: I persevere in my being freely—because I am quite willing to do so. But can I will it? One could seriously doubt that the will has the least impact on being in general, even my own; because the will itself, whether it be an authentic faculty or a simple surface effect, supposes being and does not provoke it; at best it manages its modalities, its figures and its orientations; but producing and conserving being escapes its grasp, and thus also persevering in being. What would a proposition such as "to will to be" or "to will to persevere in one's being" mean? Doubtless nothing, nonsense. Yet it remains that, if I cannot will decidedly to persevere in my being, I can at least be quite willing to do so— I can agree to it, desire it. But what then does it mean to agree to persevere in one's being, if not *to love* being, and thus *to love* to continue to be? With the reappearance of this term, *to love,* do we not find ourselves back at the initial aporia: I can only love being (in order to persevere in it) if this resolution resists the question "What's the use?"—inevitable in the erotic reduction? I can only resist if I ask in response, "Does anyone out there love me?" and obtain a positive response that assures me. Thus, we are brought back ineluctably to the initial question: the *conatus in suo esse perseverandi* is no more an exception to the demand for an assurance from elsewhere than is the claim of every man to love himself. The ontic detour that the *conatus in suo esse perseverandi* claimed to assign to the autarkic circularity of the love of self changes nothing at base: the issue is still that of deciding whether or not we can, in order to resist vanity as established by the erotic reduction, get by without a love come from out there, which assures the lover. The *conatus* was only a decoy, and only won us a reprieve. We still have to brave the hardest question.

§ 12. Self-Hatred

We will thus give up on these two illusory points of departure, the love of self by oneself (§ 9) and perseverance in one's being (§§ 10–11). Not because they are ethically lacking (which, after all, remains undecided), but because they simply cannot be put to use. It is not their injustice that would make them hateful, but their impossibility, which renders them inapplicable. Nothing is more evident than love of self and perseverance in one's being, at least in the natural attitude; but as soon as we enter the erotic reduction, each appears as a logical contradiction, or more exactly, an erotic contradiction. To have done with these illusions, we will establish once and for all the exact opposite thesis—no one can love himself, and surely not with an unconditional self-love, because every man for himself finds, more original than the alleged self-love, self-hatred in himself.

Let us suppose that I claim, despite all evidence to the contrary, that I love myself infinitely. What, at base, would such an extravagance mean? Of what obscure worry is it the symptom? Precisely of its opposite. To insist on love of self betrays, in fact, my very clear consciousness of *not* possessing this serene love of myself; and more, of not being worthy of an infinite love. Why? Because I know, better than anyone else, that I am finite and that my eventual nominal value (we are not speaking of principle, or of essence, or of human nature, all words whose meaning I do not know here) overflows, streams, and oozes with finitude. Even if I were unaware of my finitude and my failure (supposing that I could hide them from myself for a long time), already the simple fact of insisting on an infinite love of myself by myself would prove to everyone that I am lacking such a love, since I experience the need for it and feel myself obliged to lay claim to it openly. For in the end, if in truth I loved myself infinitely, I would not even dream of laying claim to it or of proclaiming it; I would not even waste my time bragging of it; this enjoyment would seem at this point to go without saying, so that I would not even have to become aware of it—no more than today I have to become aware of my flesh or of my sexual difference, so much do they coincide exactly with my ipseity, the deployment of which they even precede. If I truly loved myself without effort or remorse, the simple consciousness of this reconciliation with myself would constitute me so intimately and so identically that it would immediately disappear from my eyes. I would love myself with a long and calm possession, without end, or lack, or even the least consciousness. If I loved myself infinitely, I would love myself without commentary, without argument, without state of mind—without knowing it. I would not even think of posing myself this strange question, "Does anyone out there love me?" If I truly loved myself, I would not even hear, resonating stubbornly in the back of my mind, the suspicion "What's the use?"; I would not even expose myself to the erotic reduction—because I would have already satisfied it without even knowing it or willing it. As a consequence, if I claim to love myself, I know and already admit to myself clearly that I have never arrived at such a love, but that I have the greatest need to do so. I proclaim my self-love precisely because I cannot accomplish it alone. I claim it loudly precisely in order to hide from myself that I have not attained it. In proclaiming that I love myself infinitely, I prove that I do not love myself infinitely, I attest to the gap between the love that I ask for and my incapacity to obtain it. Thus—this is the first stage—the simple *claim* of the love of every man for himself accomplishes ressentiment at its most terrible depths—self-hatred.

Substituting self-hatred for self-love could seem arbitrary, or even violent. After all, who has ever hated his own flesh? This worry is understandable, but cannot be taken seriously. The point here is not pessimism or optimism, which are silly categories, but to describe as exactly as possible what the erotic reduction makes appear in the center of the *ego,* once vanity forbids grounding every man for himself in thought that is equal to itself and exposes us to the question "Does anyone out there love me?" In such a situation of exposure (as if defenseless against a danger), it is necessary to recognize, by fair means or foul, that the *ego* cannot assure itself, because it cannot attribute to itself this elsewhere, alone from which an assurance may come. The hypothesis of self-hatred as the fundamental affective tonality of the *ego* within the erotic reduction imposes itself as a direct consequence of the impossibility, logical as much as actual, of the love of self. To which is added a factual confirmation: the greatest of philosophies claim to attain to the love of self, but do not arrive at it—at least not enough to stop some men, or indeed the majority, not only from experiencing self-hatred, but from exercising it upon themselves. I do not argue here by invoking statistics or news items, but by asking each one who reads these lines if he or she has not had to brave, if only once in his or her lifetime, the almost irresistible impulse to punish himself, with full if not serene justification, because he confirmed himself in his own eyes to be a failure, a disappointment, or, as we often say, pathetic. This is self-hatred as self-scorn—whence inescapably there follows self-punishment. Who could honestly say that he has never hated his own incompetence? If he denies it, I take him for a god or a madman; on second thought, not a madman—for a madman knows more than anyone the hatred of self, from which he proceeds—but a beast. This second hypothesis remains the most frequent—if only because he who claims to play a god plays the beastly fool. Self-hatred thus imposes itself as the ultimate affective tonality of the *ego* under the rules of the erotic reduction.

A second stage consists in *injustice*. Since the simple claim of a constant and serene love of self already insinuates a self-dissatisfaction, it is enough to demonstrate its contrary: such a love was not self-explanatory, and thus couldn't from the first be perfectly accomplished. Now it remains to conceive that which provokes and maintains this formal contradiction—nothing less than a real injustice. For, on the one hand, in order to love *myself* (or at least to claim to do so), I must acknowledge myself as a radically finite self: since I need someone to love me from out there, I must trace a limit—my own—beyond which this "out there" can appear in its exteriority, but on this side of which I occupy a territory that is finite, and therefore unquestionably mine; what is more, it goes without saying that, without this finitude, I would have neither consciousness, nor a need for the least assurance. But, on the other hand, in order to *love* myself, I must presuppose a love (from wherever it may come) that assures me, and thus which loves me infinitely, for otherwise it would remain conditional, and thus incapable of assuring me (§ 9). In claiming to love myself, I thus lay claim as much to a radical finitude (in demand of an assurance from out there) as to a positive infinity (accomplishing the assurance from out there). The formal contradiction thus deepens in inadequacy: the finite claims not to be able to be matched except by the infinite. For the *ego* wants to establish between two incommensurable terms not only an inadequacy, but an equation—the finitude of the self only feels itself adequately assured if an infinite love assures it; in short, the finite receives assurance from nothing less than the infinite. The finite, in order to resist vanity and its "What's the use?" requires an assurance, and thus an infinite love. This is a paradox, but not an absurdity, because the lover that I become reasons according to a strict logic—the logic of the erotic reduction. When the issue is responding to the question "Does anyone out there love me?" nothing is more logical than injustice: in effect, the finite requires the infinite as its due. The simple claim to loving oneself cannot be accomplished without injustice. But nothing is less unjust than this very injustice, for nothing is more justified than to require an infinite assurance, especially if one knows oneself to be finite. Who would be content, knowing how finite he is, with a finite love? Who would be satisfied, knowing how pathetic and worthless he is, with a worthless love? This is an injustice that is logical, rational, inevitable—in a word, a just injustice.

A third stage immediately emerges: *bad faith*. From this point forward, I know better than anyone that I am not worthy of the love that I nevertheless demand; I know perfectly the injustice in the claim to love myself even though I hate myself. I measure like no one else the abyss lying between that which I am and that which it would be necessary to become in order to merit someone's loving me from out there—*a fortiori,* in order to succeed at making me love myself. No one knows and suffers the contradiction that this injustice provokes more than I. Nevertheless, no one more than I experiences the necessity of surmounting it—since, if I did not succeed at loving myself, because someone out there loved me, it would only remain for me to succumb to the question "What's the use?" I can neither deny nor adapt myself to this gap between what I am—unlovable—and what I need to become—unhateable. Thus the only remaining alternative is to mask the gap. Bad faith thus becomes the only reasonable attitude, even as untenable as it must prove to be in the end. For the point at first is not at all to lie to an other—to simply hide from her that my worthlessness does not make me worthy of the rough outline of love that it claims; nor to dissemble from her my perfect consciousness of this demerit, since no one keeps fewer illusions about myself alive than me; in short, the point is not at all to lie to an other. The point is *to lie to myself,* so as to keep open the possibility of loving, either through myself or from elsewhere, the one for whom I have the most scorn: myself. For in the two cases, the one who would love me must both know and not know who I am. My right hand must not know anything of my left, the me that loves must be completely unaware of the me that is loved (and in fact hateful): love of each for himself, but with eyes closed, where the less I know, the more I can do. This schizophrenia becomes the only figure of the love of self that is still practicable—insofar as it is a desperate substitute for love from out there—

and thus the last effective posture of a still-working egoism. In order to love myself, I must, then, not recognize myself for what I nevertheless am in my own eyes—hateful. Self-knowledge not only does not go hand in hand with self-love, it prohibits it. At least this is how it goes as soon as one passes into the erotic reduction.

This inevitable inadequacy leads, in time, to the fourth stage: *the verdict*. I find myself in a situation that is psychologically and logically untenable. First, the contradiction of the claim to a love of myself, joined with scorn for myself, has led me to the posture of a deep-seated yet legitimate injustice. Adding itself to this first contradiction is the extraordinarily arduous effort, the pain of which condemns it, to lie to myself with the intention of accomplishing, despite my conscience, the love of every man for himself. From this point forward, the contradiction of the love of self and the effort to mask it enter in turn into conflict, because the first never stops knowing what the second wishes to hide (from itself). It follows that I have not only one but two good reasons to hate myself: first, the scorn that I bear toward myself, the inanity of my claim and my injustice—a positively negative reason—and, next, my inescapable powerlessness to hold on for long to the lie required to love myself despite my conscience—a reason that is negatively negative. At one moment or another, my defenses will give way, the pressure of the bitter flood will carry off the last barrier, in short, I will give up on loving myself and even on claiming to do so. And in fact, all those who gain access to the status of lover (and they alone), or put another way, every *ego* that succeeds in entering into the erotic reduction, experiences more than once in its life the hatred of self. We must not imagine that we are talking about an extreme situation. On the contrary, it is accomplished most often quite gently, in the almost soothing calm of a disaster announced by contradictions that have weighed heavily for too long, a clear and slow disaster, become perfectly intelligible through the evidence of the injustice, indeed, a serene disaster, wherein I feel, as a benefit, that justice is at last done. Soothing because, if I do not succeed in loving myself, if I can no longer even lie to myself enough to make myself believe in it, the fault lies no longer with me, who would have lacked strength, but with this other me, who is not worthy of being loved, neither from out there nor from his self. I thus render double justice to myself by giving up on loving myself: I do not love this me who does not deserve it, but I also justify myself in not loving him. What is more, I even give back the world its purity, which had been spoiled by my unjust claim to make myself infinitely loved, not in spite of, but by virtue of, my worthlessness. When at last I give up on muddying the order of things by accepting, logically, wisely, and justly, not only not to require that someone love me from out there, but in addition no longer to claim to be able to love myself by myself, I experience the harsh but full satisfaction of giving way not to strength, but to a piece of plain evidence: there were simply no grounds for loving, because nothing, including me above all, is worthy of loving. How about suicide to close the accounts? Or perhaps a simple settling of accounts, in which I take delight in having neither to love, nor to be loved. In hating myself, I do not at first put my life or, eventually, my death into question, but instead the possibility of my *ego* considering itself as a lover. In hating myself with goodwill, I attempt almost to annul the erotic reduction's hold over me. There is no point in loving, there is nothing to love, since even I have no success in making myself loved from elsewhere, or in loving myself. There remains my *ego* and its possible ontic certainty, which I am excused henceforth from loving, since I cannot do so. And so, my self-hatred no longer attests to any deluded love.

§ 13. The Passage to Vengeance

This balance in indifference—where I have nothing to love and nothing to hate—does not last. Self-hatred cannot be absorbed so easily in the indifference of the simple absence of love. Suspending the erotic reduction does not go without saying, precisely because it radically modifies the very concept of the *self*—in short, it is not enough for every man for himself to hate himself in order to exit the horizon of the infinite elsewhere of love. The hatred of self still refers back, at least as much as the impossible love of self, to the question "Does anyone out there love me?" and for an obvious reason: the *self* that one hates is hated precisely because one succeeds neither in making it loved from out there, nor in loving it oneself. The impossibility of love within hatred appears as more inward to hatred than hatred itself. The hatred of self does not last in the provisional serenity that we have known; soon it sets off a chain reaction with the other, or more exactly, with the hatred of the other. This chain reaction is linked by four other stages, which prolong the preceding sequence of self-hatred.

But how can I arrive—this is the fifth stage—at the hatred of the other, seeing that I have no need of the other in order not to love myself, and am, all by myself, sufficiently up to the task of hating myself? What is more, at this moment of the analysis, I still have no ordered access to the other, nor do I have any motive to hate him—at least, to hate him in return for the hatred that he eventually would bear toward me. But I find other, more powerful motives for hating the other besides hatred toward myself. Let us suppose that in the end I truly renounce both loving myself by myself and making myself loved from out there: for as long as I consider this choice within the field of the logic that has led me there, *I* can imagine myself able, through a mixture of stoicism and cynicism, to resign myself to it without hesitation. But now let us suppose that, crossing the domain of my logic without any consideration, some sort of other comes along, apparently without difficulty or even intention, making himself loved by all (or a few—that will suffice), to the point where he even succeeds in giving himself the illusion of being able to love himself by himself; in short, let us suppose the sudden appearance of what one calls a *happy idiot*—or at least what I apprehend as such: handsome, stupid, rich, and lucky, someone for whom everything turns out well, without any merit, difficulty, or failure, either. So we ask: what will become of my hatred for myself, supposedly calm and civilized, without violence or demands, discreet and private, when it encounters the first idiot to come along, provided that he is happy? Clearly, we must answer: my hatred for myself will not put up with the illusion and imposture of love that the happy idiot thinks he bears toward himself as a consequence of that which he imagines to come to him from elsewhere. Not only because my hatred knows the lie, but above all because it will not long put up with the fact that injustice, which it has, for its part, renounced, has shamelessly triumphed in the life of the happy idiot. Self-hatred, which has taken possession of me, demands justice: what I have destroyed in myself—the claim to love myself—has no right to triumph in anyone else. And there is an excellent reason for this: the other is neither worth more nor more worthy than me; he merits no more than do I a positive response to the question "Does anyone love me?" I will therefore ask: Why him and not me? Or: I am not worthy, but since he, who also is not worthy, claims to be so and believes he has obtained love (or even worse: has truly obtained it), I have the right to it *just as much as he,* even if, according to my own conviction, I have *in truth* no such right. I can certainly no longer uphold my claim to someone loving me, by saying that "I will it," but, by comparison with the happy idiot, I may still answer that "I am worth it." I cannot assume the *conatus* in the first person, but I can still attempt to assume it in the second person, for mimetic rivalry accords me indirectly what self-hatred directly prohibits. I am going to love myself anyway, at least by default, by transposing onto the other the weight of my hatred for myself which, thus shared, will henceforth become bearable—

at least for a time. The hatred of the nonhatred of self, the hatred of a love of every man for himself found in another who is by all appearances happy diverts the hatred of self by the self from me—at least for a time.

Thus—the sixth stage—for the first time the other has stepped onto the stage. But he enters wearing the unexpected mask of a thief, or, almost, that of a seducer, because he diverts onto himself and as if for his own benefit part or all of my hatred for myself. The other at last appears, but *as the one that I hate.* Or more exactly, as the one that I can, against all logic, prefer to hate rather than myself. Or again, as the one who bears in my stead the crushing weight of my own hatred for myself. The other always offers himself first as the one I love most to hate—seeing that he excuses me, at least in part, from keeping my hatred of myself for myself alone. Now, I am going to address this other that I do not love, whom in fact I hate, and whom I know only insofar as I hate him, in order to ask him to love me. And I am going to ask him this, all the while presuming, by analogy with my own case, first, that he does not love himself any more than I love myself, and second, that he guesses that I don't love myself either, for the same excellent reasons that make him hate himself to begin with. And yet, how, in hating himself and knowing that I hate myself, could he not hate me? Either he will conclude from my hatred as well as his own that I am worth nothing more than he, and will therefore logically hate me; or, if by chance he suspects me of not hating myself, but instead of claiming to love myself as any happy idiot would, he will hate me all the more, frankly and wholeheartedly. Thus I address to him, reasonably and absurdly at the same time, my request for a love come from elsewhere. Reasonably, indeed very reasonably: I have come, in effect, to the guiding thread of my longing: to have access, for the first time, to the other; though it is under the figure of the first one who can be hated, this other nevertheless offers the first possible face of the elsewhere, ceaselessly sought, but up to this point inaccessible. And yet absurdly, too: in effect, I only meet this other under the figure of the second one who can be hated after me, or of the first one who can be hated who is not simply me; and thus, according to the principle that hatred receive hatred in return, I request that someone love me from elsewhere from the one who precisely can only refuse me, and who, in a sense, must do so. Thus the contradictory request par excellence is accomplished: asking the one who can only hate me to love me—for the first time—from elsewhere.

A contradictory request, but not a senseless one. For the other appears to me in the figure of Janus—*the one that I hate and who ought to love me,* the one that I would like to love even when he hates me—because he fulfills, doubtless in spite of himself, a unique function: that of delivering me, at least in part, from the hatred of every man for himself, which crushes me. Clearly, I can only request this deliverance from the first anybody who comes along, this first other from out there, even if he hates me because he hates himself as well. It would already be a huge advance if he were to love me a little. If he were to show me some regard, even in the form of his hatred, it would always be more valuable than to remain alone, loving and hating myself at the same time. Whoever he may be, I entrust to this other come from out there the weight of the impossible performance of the improper and contradictory love of every man for himself. To him and him alone falls the dirty job of putting up with that which makes me loathe even myself—the work of loving myself despite my hatred for myself, or, what comes down to the very same thing, the sad responsibility to hate myself by virtue of the love that I should have borne myself. This other, whom I love and hate at the same time, indeed appears as a paradoxical phenomenon; but this paradox has its reason in me—because it looms up in fact out of nothing less than my original entry into the erotic reduction. The other, whom I love and hate at one go, reproduces, in the figure of a phenomenal paradox, the original contradiction that I inflict upon him—the contradiction of the hatred of myself by myself, by way of the result of my claim to love myself from elsewhere; he in fact only carries the weight of the impossible performance of my improper love of myself. But the other could not take upon himself so perfectly this contradiction that comes from the core of my self, if he did not reflect me exactly: he too practices the hatred of self, just as much as he demands of himself and of "out there" the unjust and impracticable love of himself. He welcomes so well within himself my contradiction because it simply reproduces his own, ready to be employed. The other looms up into visibility like a mirror that is too faithful, the simple hostage of my (loving) hatred of myself, the worker of the improper (hateful) love of myself, in short as my perfect idol, the invisible mirror of myself. And it is not the least accomplishment of the hatred of every man for himself to give rise to his own idol. As if he needed to mime the glory of a god.

Of course—the seventh stage—this first other, who appears to me precisely first in the figure of the one who hates me, can hardly do other than address a refusal to my request to love me. He must end up hating me. Let us admit, then, that, for all appearances, *he hates me.* This hatred is far from telling me nothing. On the contrary, it teaches me much by validating the preceding stages of the itinerary. First, the hatred that the other bears me confirms that I could not love myself, since the other cannot do it either; for the putting into play here of an other than myself shows that the issue is not simply an incapacity on my part, but instead a third-party impotence, repeatable for all and sundry. His hatred confirms that I should neither require that someone love me, nor claim to accomplish it myself. He, and with him everyone, may legitimately hate me, because my claim to make myself loved by them proves itself always in the end so exorbitant and contradictory that their exasperation simply does it fitting justice. My claim to love myself (and to assure myself as my own elsewhere) justifies without discussion their hatred for me.

Next, the hatred that this poor other bears me confirms that, more originary than my hating him is his hating himself, just as I hate myself. He does not hate me because of me, but because of himself. My potential failings do not factor in, only his failure to love himself or to make himself loved from out there. In fact and by right, the hatred that he bears me should make him worthy of my recognition—make me recognize him as a fellow galley slave on the same thwart; in the hatred that we bear one another reciprocally, we share first the parallel hatreds that we each exert upon ourselves alone; we attack ourselves well before, and more radically, than we attack others. Our parallel practices of the hatred of every man for himself bring us together much more originarily than the hatreds of every man for the others set us against one another, to the point that the latter become an epiphenomenon of the former, almost negligible with regard to the self-torture that torments both of us. I am almost unable to take offense at the other's hatred of me—why would he not hate me, since I am the first to hate him; and how would he have the means to love me, when he doesn't even have the means to love himself? A simple backfire, the return upon me of his hatred feeds first upon the even more consuming fire of his hatred of self.

Finally, there remains the by far most decisive attainment. Since the beginning the goal has been to answer the question "Does anyone love me?" and thus to attain an assurance that by definition is come from elsewhere; nevertheless, the first answer turned me toward the love of myself by myself, bent elsewhere back over me alone, and thus closed access to every truly foreign instance. Henceforward, the contradictory love of myself by myself ends up, through its vicissitudes, by opening an access to the other. In fact, it reaches him successively, as the one who should love me, as the one who can only hate me, and, finally, as the one who resembles me in so very far as he hates himself, just as I do myself. The other in the end makes possible the figure of elsewhere or "out there," access to which has been prohibited to this point, because he appears undeniably, though in the figure of the enemy, hated as well as hateful. And he appears thus as an actual elsewhere, at the request of the love of self by oneself, which both denies and requires him at the same time. To the persisting question of the possibility of breaking solipsism while still holding to the *ego,* we must answer affirmatively, and yet not positively: the other or elsewhere does not render him or itself actual by loving me, but by hating me. And I do not gain access to the other by claiming to reach him in his individuality, nor to know him there, nor, even less, to love him as myself, remaining within the natural attitude. On the contrary, I settle myself definitively within the erotic reduction in order to envisage the other precisely from the starting point of the pure and bare necessity of an elsewhere, demanded by the question "Does anyone love me?" From that moment, it becomes possible *a minima* to enter into contact with the other, or rather to allow him to enter into contact with me: for the point is no longer to lay hold of his fantasized interiority, nor even to feel him at the end of my gaze, but rather to feel myself touched by his gaze; or better, touched by his hatred, as by the point of his sword, which presses on me, almost to the point of piercing me. Henceforward, I no longer dream of elsewhere, I no longer argue about it—I experience it. And I do not experience it as love, but as that which my claim to make myself be loved provokes—as hatred. To whoever asks imprudently: "Does anyone out there love me?" an answer finally arrives, but says: "What comes to you from out there hates you."

Whence follows the final stage: I hate this elsewhere, finally actual in its hatred for me. As he has turned his hatred of self upon me, I turn upon him both my hatred of myself and his hatred for me. I hate the other, or more exactly, "other people," for the same excellent reasons for which they hate me: because their obtuse claim on someone to love them defies all justice; because their ridiculous attempt to love every man for himself proves itself impracticable; because their hatred of themselves not only frightens me, but ends up by disgusting me; because in the end they only have access to me through the hatred that I reserve for them and return. In them as in me, love of self is only good for hatred, received or given. We all have only one same assurance and one unique access to an elsewhere of some sort— the hatred that we bear one another. Nothing else unites us. From the claim of every man to the love of self by the self results the hatred of all for all and of every man for himself. Strangely, but necessarily, the *conatus,* in its apparent clarity, turns against itself.

§ 14. The Aporia of Assurance

This path ends in an aporia, one that is not discussed, but simply rehearsed. The erotic reduction imposes itself as I seek not so much a certainty, as an assurance. In the erotic reduction, I can hear the question "Does anyone out there love me?" and I must inquire after this "out there." It appears that the most direct way consists in assuring myself of such an out there by loving myself by myself. Now, not only can I not accomplish this claim, but it provokes the hatred of myself by myself, and then the hatred of the other, first for me, and then by me. Thus all love that begins as a love of every man for himself (impossible) ends up, by self-hatred (actual), in the hatred of the other (necessary). If I claim to love myself or to make myself loved, in the end I hate, and make myself hated. Thus the assurance from out there remains inaccessible. Vanity in the end bears it away. At this stage, the erotic reduction inevitably disqualifies my *ego,* even if it remains ontically certain—indeed, all the more, if it remains so.

This result leads me astray, it closes my path—which is what we call erecting an aporia. Here, the way and its aporia are one: the simple fact of undertaking the search for certainty and of pushing it to its end—assurance—and thus of posing the hypothesis of the love of every man for himself, is enough to lead me to the hatred of all for all and of every man for himself. The aporia follows necessarily from the point of departure. Could I eventually remove it? Doubtless, if I succeeded in changing the point of departure, or in breaking the chain of events.

Let us consider first the necessity of the chain of events. After all, doesn't winding up with the hatred of all for all and of every man for himself betray an exaggerated pessimism, one that is systematic and, in the end, unbelievable? Why not admit a legitimate love of self, which would counterbalance the drive toward death and self-destruction? And doesn't the hatred of self arise simply from pathology? Doesn't privileging it in this way constitute an obvious symptom? Couldn't sympathy, respect, and compassion unite the other and myself just as much? These objections are in no way foolish; nevertheless, it is necessary to put them aside, because they lose all pertinence once placed in the situation of the erotic reduction. No longer are we describing, as a psychologist or a sociologist, possible relations between humans, or certain feelings that I may bear toward myself, as in the natural attitude, with its allowances for undecided abstraction.

Rather, our concern is to consider with as much rigor as possible the status of certainty (couldn't one in fact disqualify it?); and next, to take note that it does not satisfy what the *ego* that I am requires, because it does not assure me when confronted with vanity (and who is unaware of vanity's power?); and finally, to enter into the question that opens onto vanity, and surpasses it—"Does anyone out there love me?" But, from this very moment, we enter into the erotic reduction and can no longer avoid braving, without delay, the demand to make ourselves loved. Now, this demand has its requirements and its consequences. Either the other loves me—but I still know nothing of this potential other, and, once again, I ask myself, by what right can I claim that he or she loves me, and not instead him- or herself, or any old other? Or I love myself—but can I do so without contradiction, and in this case, do I in all justice have the right? The two ways listed each lead to a barrier, and there is no third way. This is not about pessimism, but rather impossibilities under the rules of the erotic reduction. I cannot require that the other love me, any more than I can promise myself to love myself—as if I could offer an authentic elsewhere for myself, or as if I, in my incontestable finitude, could assure myself infinitely. But above all, who can seriously believe himself unscathed by all self-hatred, transparent, equal, benevolent toward himself, free of ressentiment and of the insolvent debt of a past that is out of reach? Here, nothing counts, except the phenomena that the erotic reduction allows to stand out and, eventually, to be described. If someone can show me how the other *must* love me, let him show it. If someone can show how I *am able* to love myself (from elsewhere, and infinitely), let him show it. And if, as I believe, no one could ever do these things, then all that remains is seriously to consider the aporiae at which we've ended.

Since we cannot break the chain of events, could we nevertheless change the point of departure? Why not hold to the criteria of certainty without demanding, in addition, an assurance from out there? Or, if one believes he must pass beyond the certainty of objects toward an assurance for the *ego,* why not base it, too, upon self-consciousness or upon some sort of performance of my own existence? In short, why impose a new requirement, or, if it is to be imposed, why have recourse to a new principle? But it is enough to formulate these reservations to see their inanity. We know, by experience as well as concept, that certainty only fits the object, and that the supposedly known "subject" exposes itself to so many disqual-

ifications that the qualification (the certainty) of its objects indeed no longer rests upon it. Now, there weighs upon this "subject" the weight of new
questions—vanity, nihilism, and boredom—that radically pass beyond the
old question, limited to certainty. Certainly the *ego* can win certainty of itself, and thus be, insofar as it thinks; but this circle is precisely only valuable for being and certainty; it can do nothing against vanity, which inflicts
the trial of a "What's the use?" even upon being and certainty. In order to
resist against vanity's assault, much more or something else, other than the
simple thought turned in upon itself, is therefore necessary—an assurance
is needed, which by definition can only come to me from out there; in
short, I must be able to respond to that question, "Does anyone out there
love me?" That which certifies the *ego*'s being no longer assures it under the
rules of the erotic reduction. To confuse these two questions by proposing
a single answer simply betrays a balking in front of the erotic reduction—
like a horse balks before an obstacle, out of fear. But whoever balks before
an obstacle usually falls.

Thus the aporia remains whole. It keeps us from going further than the
hatred of all for all and of every man for himself. We will therefore need to
brave vanity without any other weapons than this double threat.

Concerning the Lover,
and His Advance

§ 15. Reducing Reciprocity

A path closes up all the more tightly as we follow it step by step. The aporia results from the contradiction between the question and the conclusion: in beginning by asking if someone out there loves me ("Does anyone love me?"), I am inevitably led to the hatred of every man for himself, against the background of the hatred of all for all. Whoever wants to get himself loved gains hatred for himself, and then hatred for everyone other than himself, and, finally, self-enrollment in the hatred of all for all.

Can we avoid this conclusion? It is always possible to challenge the logic that leads to it and disclose a simple mistake in the order of reasoning. But this would augment the failure, because then only a fault in reasoning would be able to save my right to have myself loved, as if it would be necessary to forgo hating myself only by recognizing myself as irrational. That is a high price to pay to confirm the prejudice that love is only possible if one gives up thinking correctly. But what other way remains open? At least this one: it is necessary to forgo drawing out a concept of love beginning from the question "Does anyone out there love me?"—that is, to forgo gaining access to a concept by beginning from the demand that one love me—because neither I nor any other can, on this basis, assure myself of anything but their hatred. But then the aporia would not throw into question the general rationality of love, but only the pertinence of the question "Does anyone out there love me?" or at least the way in which we have understood that question up to this point. Put another way, in order truly to accomplish the erotic reduction, it would be necessary to gain access to a question that is much more original and radical. How do we get there?

Let us return to the question "Does anyone out there love me?" Why did we take it up at the outset as a way to gain access to the erotic reduction? There was an obvious motive: this question in effect isolates assurance in confrontation with vanity, by opposing it clearly to certitude in confrontation with doubt; to be is certainly no longer the issue, but rather to surmount the disqualification distilled by the suspicion "What's the use?": to assure oneself of love, and no longer to certify its existence. In this precise sense, the question "Does anyone out there love me?" indeed triggers the erotic reduction. And yet, the instance of love does not yet stand forth here except at a very closed angle. Not because it concerns me, the first *ego* waiting for an assurance from out there; for love and assurance could not intervene without a base of support that assigns them, and a stake that calls them forth; the fixing of the erotic reduction upon the *ego* remains absolutely indispensable. Rather, the difficulty arises from what the *ego* allows or does not allow us to glimpse of the erotic reduction. Indeed, with regard to the *ego,* love still only intervenes indirectly, as if negatively, following the search for an assurance against the threat of vanity. Love here plays only the hypothetical and nearly unattainable correlate to my lack of assurance when confronting the question "What's the use?" The erotic reduction still remains partial; as of yet, love only appears there by default. Assurance does depend upon the erotic reduction, but the erotic reduction does not completely achieve it, because the *ego* lacks assurance; and this *ego,* which itself lacks assurance, only apprehends love as a shortfall. The *ego* takes the risk of the erotic reduction under the threat of vanity, and thus in panicked fear of "missing out." Missing out on what? On assurance in love. The *ego* does not venture onto the field of love except in order to escape from the risk of losing itself, thus hoping for an assurance, a return of assurance, the chance to make up the shortfall. It achieves only a narrow and parsimonious pre-understanding of love: it doesn't have any, it needs some fast, and so it asks for it; the more ignorant it is of love's dignity, its power, and its rules, the more frenetically it demands it. The *ego* addresses love like a poor man who, with fear in his gut because he is penniless, never imagines he could be dealing with anyone but usurers, each more pitiless and rapacious than the one before; for him, assurance must be even more costly than certainty, with even more knowledge to sacrifice and more ascesis to endure than in hyperbolic doubt. Caught in this panic at its lack, what does the *ego* hope for when it takes its first step into the territory of love? What does the erotic reduction, in spite of the *ego,* open before it? At best, in the highest estimation of its fearful expectations, the *ego* hopes not to lose anything there—it hopes that love will give it assurance at a fair price. The *ego* is quite willing to pay to obtain assurance, but not if someone takes from it more than it will receive. The *ego,* from the outset, expects from love only a more or less honest exchange, a negotiated *reciprocity,* an acceptable compromise.

Of course, one could immediately respond that reciprocity has nothing to do with love and befits only the economy and calculation of exchange. And in fact the *ego,* still standing at the border of the erotic reduction, naïve and inexperienced in the things of love, is completely ignorant of love's paradoxical logic; it knows little about the lover within that it has not yet liberated; it only reads love as the expectation of and demand for an assurance at a reasonable price. How then does the *ego* calculate this price? Like a wretch, with mistrust and precaution: I want to receive my due—my assurance that someone loves me—and only then will I pay and will I love in return. In this way of looking at things, at first it had even seemed preferable to try to make less expensive deals: for example to produce assurance each for his own, without asking for it from elsewhere (§ 9), or, if it indeed was necessary to ask for it from elsewhere, to choose the most familiar neighbor, who resembles me the most and bothers me the least—he who hates himself like I hate myself, who hates me just like I hate him, my counterpart (§ 13). The *ego* had finally to give up on these expedients, but it remains in the same dispositions; the *ego* continues to calculate the smallest margins and holds itself to strict reciprocity; I will only love in return, after the fact, only if someone loves me first and only as much as someone first loves me. I will play the game of love, certainly, but I will only risk the least amount possible, and on condition that the other go first. Love thus is definitely put into operation for such an *ego,* but always out of panic, in a situation of lack and under the yoke of reciprocity— thus love does not really come into play, any more than the erotic reduction is truly accomplished. The obstacle that obstructs the opening of the amorous field—an erotic obstacle, not an epistemological or ontic one— consists in reciprocity itself; and reciprocity only acquires this power to set up an obstacle because one assumes, without proof or argument, that it alone offers the condition of possibility for what the *ego* understands by a "happy love." But could such a "happy love," closely controlled by reciprocity, remain happy? In any case, it could not remain a love, because it would fall directly under exchange and commerce. It is for a radical reason that love cannot confine itself to reciprocity nor base its decisions on a determination of fair price: the loving actors have nothing to exchange (no object), and thus cannot calculate a price (whether fair or not); in the realm of exchange, by contrast, the agents deal in objects, the permanent third party lying between them, about which they may make calculations, and the prices of which they may set. Thus it is necessary to reject reciprocity in love, not because it would seem improper, but because in love reciprocity becomes impossible—strictly speaking, without an object. Reciprocity sets the condition of possibility for exchange, but it also attests to the condition of love's impossibility.

This recourse to commerce thus indicates what was blocking the erotic reduction and was shrinking access to the order of love—I began not so much from assurance itself as from assurance as always already lacking, from my needy *ego,* struck with panic before a shortage and directly taking refuge behind reciprocity. We understand now why the initial question "Does anyone out there love me?" could not until this moment receive an answer, other than the hatred of every man for himself and of all for all: the love that it evoked in fact remained prisoner to the iron law of reciprocity—love, perhaps, but only if I am first of all assured, which is to say under the condition that someone love me first. In short, at this stage, to love means first to be loved. To be loved—to put it another way, to love still refers back to being, and thus merely confirms being in its metaphysical function as first instance and final horizon; once again being determines love, which has no other role than to assure being, as underpinning, against vanity. Love is of use to being, and serves being, but is not excepted from being.

§ 16. Pure Assurance

This diagnosis suggests a path that might open a way out of the aporia: radicalize the erotic reduction in order to reduce even as far as the demand of reciprocity. To the initial question "Does anyone out there love me?" which limits access to the horizon of love as much as it opens it, it is necessary to add another question, which picks up where the first left off—one that poses the question of love without, however, submitting it to the prior condition of reciprocity, and thus of justice; that is to say, one that does not presuppose that assurance happens first for me. How could we conceive that loving might not first be required to come from somewhere else toward me, but might instead unfold itself freely and without serving me? By admitting the possibility that this event issues from me in view of an other still undetermined—issues from me deep within an elsewhere that is more inward to me than me myself, preceded or validated by no as-surance at all. In short, the point is to ask, "Can I love first?" rather than, "Does anyone out there love me?"—which means, to behave like a lover who gives himself, rather than like one who is loved tit for tat.

Now such a possibility—this is the sovereign argument that restarts the entire inquiry—remains by definition always open, and no aporia will ever be able to block it. For the finding (or the simple suspicion) that some-one does not love me never prevents me in principle from being able to love first. That no one loves me (whether I know this for a fact or fantasize it is not important) never makes it impossible for me to love the very one who does not love me, at least each time and for as long as I decide to do so. She may not love me as much as she would like, or she may love me as little as she can, but that never prevents me from loving her, if I so decide. They can hate me as much as they want, but they will never force me to hate them, too, if I decide not to. The incomparable and unstoppable sov-ereignty of the act of loving draws all its power from the fact that reci-procity does not affect it any more than does the desire for a return on in-vestment. The lover has the unmatched privilege of losing nothing, even if he happens to find himself unloved, because a love scorned remains a love perfectly accomplished, just as a gift refused remains a perfectly given gift. What is more, the lover never has anything to lose; he could not even lose himself if he wanted to, because giving without a guarantee, far from de-stroying or impoverishing him, attests all the more clearly to his royal priv-ilege—the more he gives and the more he loses and disperses, the less he himself is lost, because abandon and waste define the singular, distinctive, and inalienable character of loving. Either love is distributed at a loss, or it is lost as love. The more I love at a loss, the more I simply love. The more I love at a loss, the less I lose sight of love, because love loves further than the eye can see. Accomplishing the act of loving not only allows for not fearing loss, but it consists only in this freedom to lose. The more I lose ut-terly, the more I know that I love, without contest. There is only one single proof of love—to give without return or chance of recovery, and thus to be able to lose and, eventually, to be lost in love. But love itself is never lost, because it is accomplished in loss. Loving surpasses being with an excess that has no measure, because it recognizes no contrary and no inverse. While being ceaselessly demarcates itself from nothingness, and is de-ployed only with it and struggles only against it, love never meets anything that remains foreign to it or that threatens it or limits it, because even the negative, nothingness, and nothing (what can be imagined that is more opposed?), far from canceling out love, offer it yet another privileged terrain, and allow it to accomplish itself all the more perfectly. Loving loses nothing from the fact of not being, because it gains nothing from the fact of being. Or better, to love consists sometimes in not being—in not being loved, or at least in accepting being able not to be loved. Nothing, neither being nor nothingness, can limit, hold back, or offend love, from the moment that loving implies, by principle, the risk of not being loved. To love without being loved—this defines *love without being*. The simple, formal definition of loving includes its victory over nothing, and thus over death. Love raises from the dead—we must understand this as an analytical proposition.

From this point forward, the old aporia explodes. Not only is reciprocity unable to take the question of love hostage (by bending the question "Does anyone out there love me?") and lead to the hatred of every man for himself (along with the hatred of all for all); but above all, loving only testifies to itself as such by suspending reciprocity and by exposing itself (giving itself over) to losing what it gives, to the point of its very own loss. Either loving has no meaning at all, or it signifies loving utterly, without return. The erotic reduction is radicalized and the question is formulated henceforth in this way: "Can I love first?"

Nevertheless, this radicalizing, fruitful though it has proven to be, gives rise retroactively to a serious difficulty. I was only able, in fact and by right, to glimpse the erotic reduction because there first emerged in me a demand for assurance, such that it disqualified the request for certitude. It was thus in the name and in the direction of assurance that I entered onto the field of love. Now the very logic that first made me pass from the interrogation "Does anyone out there love me?" to "Can I love first?" justifies the primacy of the latter over the former through the freedom to lose and to be lost; but doesn't loss or expenditure without return, as distinctive of love as these may appear to be, forbid me any assurance at all? Doesn't loving signify henceforward being the first one lost, and thus detaching myself from every assurance out there? For the lover that I become, the "out there" itself would no longer authorize any assurance, but would amount to an obligation given by me, to which I abandon myself. The conclusion is clear: as the erotic reduction is radicalized, the demand for assurance loses its legitimacy, and I should give up on it definitively.

In fact, this argument is not as good as it first appears, for two reasons. First, because it contradicts the logic of loss and abandonment, rather than illustrating it. Indeed, one reasons as if the act of loving, in giving itself utterly, was lost and abandoned in order to fall away, or even to disappear; but one can only draw such a conclusion by implicitly holding to the point of view of reciprocity and of commerce, where, in a situation of panicked shortage, the loss of what I give would amount immediately to my insolvency as lover and to my annihilation, for lack of the least bit of assurance. On the contrary, if one holds to the strict point of view of the lover, the fact of losing (or the risk of being lost) in no way entails one's disappearance for lack of assurance, but instead the accomplishment of love in its very definition—the more it loses and is lost, the more it attests to itself as love and nothing other than love. The more it loses (disperses, gives, and thus loves), the more it gains (because it still loves). In the erotic reduction, the lover who loses himself gains himself all the more as lover. In fact, the objection still describes the amorous loss from the starting point of the prejudice of reciprocity; it still confuses assurance with the autarkic possession of every man for himself.

Second, the objection fails to understand the essential paradox: the love of the lover always gains, because she has no need whatsoever to gain anything in order to gain (herself), so that she gains even and above all when she loses. Yes, one might respond, but in this game of whoever loses wins, I gain by loving first, without for all of that gaining the least assurance that someone out there loves me; thus one has to admit that love in its essence must give up on any assurance. And the confusion we were trying to clarify by radicalizing the erotic reduction has burst out all over again. Indeed, what is understood by assurance, when, as here, one thinks to deny it to the lover? Evidently assurance from out there, which guarantees the *ego* against vanity; but what is understood by such a guarantee? That vanity will no longer prevent me from loving myself enough so that I can will to be and persevere in my being; thus assurance, at this point, would remain ordered to my being, to the being in me and to me in my being; I thus still dream imperceptibly of escaping from the erotic reduction, which in fact I refuse and would like to flee. Inversely, when I pass on to the question "Can I love first?" what assurance can I legitimately hope for, as a lover? Evidently not the assurance to be able to continue or to persevere in my being despite the suspicion of vanity, but the sole assurance appropriate to the radicalized erotic reduction—not the assurance of being [*l'assurance d'être*], nor of being itself [*ni de l'être*], but *the assurance of loving*. By responding to the question "Can I love first?" with the loss of the gift to the point of the loss of self, the lover really does win an assurance—understood as the pure and simple assurance of the precise fact that she loves. When I love to the point of losing everything, I do gain an irrefragable assurance, one that is indestructible and unconditional, and yet solely the assurance that I love—which is enough. The lover finds an absolute assurance in love—not the assurance of being, nor of being loved, but that of loving. And she experiences it even in the absence of reciprocity. Let us suppose that a lover loves—but without return, because someone doesn't love her, or ceases to love her. Has she lost? What has she lost? She will have assuredly lost the assurance that someone loves her; but absolutely not the assurance of loving—provided at least that she persists in loving, without waiting for any love in return. She will keep this assurance as long and as often as she wants—that is, as long as she loves first and, above all, last. When a love rids itself of all reciprocity, who wins and who loses? Within the natural attitude, she who ceases to love wins—in effect, her gain consists in no longer loving; but, in point of fact, she has lost love. Within the erotic reduction, she who continues to love gains, because in this way she keeps love, or indeed, she finds it for the first time.

To the objection, then, one will respond that the point is not to say: "I love, therefore I am certain of my existence as a privileged being," but rather to say: "I love, therefore I have the assurance that I love first, like a lover." Primacy obviously changes status: it no longer indicates the privilege of the greatest surety, or of the greatest certainty, but the risk of greatest exposure. For I only have the assurance that I am loving, for as long as I am loving—that is to say that I assume the risk of loving first; I only have the initiative insofar as I can love, and can make a primary decision to love without return, and can make it so that love, through me, loves. I have the assurance first and foremost of making it so that love loves in me. *I have the assurance that I am making love.* And, as love assures against vanity, I discover myself to be assured by the love that I make, which makes itself in and through me, against the suspicion in the question "What's the use?" This assurance can certainly lead me off track, but like a paradox: it makes me change tracks and start back up on a different route from my first climb toward assurance. Instead of demanding an assurance oriented to my profit, and thus extracted from somewhere else by every means possible (including the hatred of each for himself until it produces the hatred of all for all), I radicalize the erotic reduction in order to receive the assurance in the very gesture of losing what I give, to the point of risking losing myself, without any return on my investment or on my property (my οὐσία, my fund or core, my good). I receive an assurance, but it no longer concerns being, having jumped over it; the assurance only directly concerns love, the love that I set in motion as a lover, not the love that I might lay claim to as the property of one who is loved. Assurance still comes to me, but no longer from an ontic elsewhere that would conserve me in my beingness; rather, it comes from an elsewhere that is more inward to me than myself: the elsewhere that comes upon me in the very gesture in which I give up what I have (my gift) and what I am, in order to assure myself only of what I truly make in this instant—love. I receive the assurance that I am making love and I receive it only from lovemaking itself and in view of itself alone. I receive from love what I give back to it—the making of it. I receive the assurance of my dignity as lover.

That will suffice for me as long and as often as I make love as a perfect lover. For love grows in loving, a fact that calls for two decisive remarks. First, I do not get beyond self-hatred (or the hatred of every man for himself, or the hatred of all for all) by a frenetic or imaginary excess of love for myself, as recommended by the weighty, authoritative opinions of psychology and psychoanalysis—had I only known, for example, that I have a ψυχή, or what is signified by this word, or even that the point is in fact to take care of it and to work on it! No, I pass beyond the hatred of every man for himself by overcoming the hatred in me of all for all, and vice versa. And as I cannot begin with my own case, which remains too close to me, too unknown, and too hostile, I begin by overcoming my hatred for others, who are better known, further away, and less dangerous for me than I myself am. In this first moment of the erotic reduction, even though radicalized, the issue cannot yet be the obtaining of self-love—loving myself, should it ever prove to be possible (and I have some good reasons to doubt it at this moment), would come as a conclusion, as the highest and most difficult of loves, for which I would need infinite help and the borrowed surety of grace, still inconceivable to me at this point (§ 41).

Second, in moving from the question "Does anyone out there love me?" to the question "Can I love first?" I do indeed receive an assurance—the assurance that I love decidedly, that I love as a decided lover. This assurance delivers me so much the more from the suspicion of vanity that not only does it free me from my tense attachment to a being that is preservable by means of perseverance, but above all it leads me back to myself, in my final ipseity. I attain it first of all because, in this way, my assurance no longer depends on an indeterminate elsewhere, at once uncertain (does she truly love me?) and anonymous (can I truly know her?); it is born from a decision that, doubtless, I never make with a full and free consciousness (am I free, am I conscious?), but which at the very least would not be made without my consent, since it is only accomplished if I and I alone make love. I eventually make it without willing it, without foreseeing it, indeed without making it completely, but in the end it is always necessary that I risk myself in making it and that it is I who goes forth, in person and in the flesh, without a substitute or a delegate. When the matter consists of me, this particular other, and my assurance, it is only I who can make love. At the very least, love is not made without me, the lover. The very fact that I make it without any condition of reciprocity, without return and at a loss, confirms powerfully that here, first and foremost, I am at issue, as well as my initiative, or at least my singular and irreplaceable consent. My acts as lover belong to me incontestably, without admixture or apportionment. It might even be that all my other acts, in particular those that come under understanding and representative thinking, may not only be just as well accomplished by anyone, but even must be capable of being accomplished by anyone else, in order to safeguard the universality that is constitutive of interobjective rationality (§ 7). In this case, I would have no true access at all to my final individuality, nor to my nonsubstitutable ipseity, except through the love that I make, because I can only make love at my expense. It may be that, at the end of my days, I will sum up myself in my acts as a lover.

The erotic reduction, henceforth radicalized, accomplishes—and it alone can do this—the reduction to the proper, for it leads me back to that which I can and must properly assume as my own (§ 37). Everything else still involves something other than me (the world), or others than me (the other, universal reason, shared understanding). I do not become myself when I simply think, doubt, or imagine, because others can think my thoughts, which in any case most often do not concern me but, instead, the object of my intentionalities; nor do I become myself when I will, desire, or hope, for I never know if I do so in the first person or only as the mask which hides (and is propped up by) drives, passions, and needs that play within me, yet without me. But I become myself definitively each time and for as long as I, as lover, can love first.

§ 17. The Principle of Insufficient Reason

By loving first, the lover that I become breaks with the demand for reciprocity: my loving no longer presupposes that someone love me first. Love coming down on me from elsewhere no longer constitutes the prerequisite condition for my own decision to love. The lover loves without delay, because he loves without awaiting or foreseeing someone loving him first, and without letting or making another come to him, one who would expose herself first and take the risk of the initial outlay; he loves at once, without waiting for anything in return—neither a real counter-love, nor even the possibility of conceiving a certain hope. Nevertheless, this posture might seem, if not unthinkable, at least implausible, and nearly unrealizable—a formal hypothesis, dreamed up without actual validity. It is therefore necessary to consider further how the lover comes to the point of not waiting, or of waiting for nothing, in order to love first.

One does not spot the lover right away: at the outset, she does not see herself, any more than she foresees herself. It is not enough for me to enter into the game of a group of others, nor into a social relation, so that I might glimpse the possibility of becoming or of seeing a lover. Let us suppose first that I inscribe myself within a network of functions determined by readiness-to-hand: all that remains is to put to work some ready-to-hand beings (tools, machines, processes in view of an end); I intervene among these ready-to-hand implements by putting them in motion and to work, by exchanging goods, by communicating information, in short according to the logic of economy. Clearly, reciprocity here determines the totality of these operations and, following the well-understood law of well-conducted business, I will do nothing for free, nor will I ever engage myself in anything without a guarantee. The principle according to which "business is business" forbids, in its exceptionless neutrality, not only my mixing, as they say, business with pleasure, or my doing business with friends, but even more radically my taking into consideration anything that might overflow and muddle the strict reciprocity of commerce. Whether I buy an airline ticket at a reduced price or negotiate a fabulous contract makes no difference: the ritual of exchange hides the partners from one another and masks them behind the transparent clarity of the agreement, the contract, or the settlement. I never deal with particular persons, but instead with substitutable interlocutors, which I eventually put into competition with one another and attempt always to reduce to their pure role as abstract agents of commerce, transparent participants in reciprocity. The less I see an other as a person irreducible to his function in the economy, and the less I venture to accord him a resistant individuality, and thus a privilege of independence or, indeed, of anteriority to me, the more correctly, effectively, and even honestly I will treat the piece of business that brings us together. Economy demands the anonymity of participants in exchange; they accomplish the exchange better above all when they do not try to know one another as such. In this situation, which is by far the most standard, the lover not only may not come forth, but must not.

Let us suppose nevertheless that the social network in which I inscribe myself does not allow itself to be completely reduced to readiness-to-hand or to economy: for instance, a random and provisional encounter, but in principle disinterested, where I go to "relax" (a party, a festival, a gallery opening, a sporting event, etc.). I can perfectly well join in, feel fully at ease, and indeed take pleasure, without ever engaging myself in person. It might even be that the euphoria of my encounters grows the less I engage myself; it may be that I exchange ever more tokens of friendship, of interest, and of seduction the more I never truly give them, distributing them instead according to a strict reciprocity, neither more nor less, as if we were dealing in an immaterial merchandise, invaluable and yet really and truly negotiated in a trade that is more subtle and more enriching than one involving things. I make myself everything for all, but never, above all, someone for someone else. Even if I risk engaging in a little seduction, or even push it a bit further, I am clearly still aiming at reciprocity; I simply practice deferred exchange rather than immediate exchange; I take a first step (or a second, or a third) only in a decided expectation of a return on my investment, all the more delightful because I will have to wait for it, all the more valued because it might return more than I invested. Besides, even if I allow my attention to focus on such or such, to the point of engaging in a more individuated conversation, which, if everything goes well, will produce a thoroughly particular interlocutor, this privilege still doesn't engage me in anything; even if imperceptibly a singles ad scenario—". . . for friendship, maybe more"—is put into gear, this other and I still retain mastery of the situation, we control, at least through vanity and under social pressure, what is considered to be "going too far." And if we do indeed go too far, even in the flesh, we still are able, following the profitability of reciprocal exchange, to break it off there and leave one another, without any fuss, litigation, or loss (why not stay friends?). Thus reciprocity governs all commerce, even the carnal sort.

When, then, does the lover appear? Precisely when, during the encounter, I suspend reciprocity, and no longer economize, engaging myself without any guarantee of assurance. The lover appears when one of the actors in the exchange no longer poses prior conditions, and loves without requiring to be loved, and thus, in the figure of the gift, abolishes economy. In trade and exchange, only reciprocity reigns—and legitimately so—because it allows us to distinguish good agreements from bad agreements, through the calculation of the reason that suffices in validating the one and invalidating the other. Reciprocity renders economy reasonable, by calculating as exactly as possible what one renders to the other for the service rendered and the payment made. The price fixes the reason of the exchange by guaranteeing its fair reciprocity. The price renders economy reasonable. If the lover decides, then, to love without any assurance in return, to love first, without requiring any security, he transgresses not only reciprocity, but also and above all he contradicts economy's sufficient reason. As a consequence, in loving without reciprocity, the lover loves without reason, nor is he able to give reason—counter to the principle of sufficient reason. He renounces reason and sufficiency. Just as, in the end, a war breaks out without reason, in a deflagration and a transgression of every good reason, the lover makes love break out. He declares his love as one declares war—without any reason. Which is to say that he does so sometimes without even taking the time or the care to make the declaration.

Nevertheless, such a denial of the reason to love, which characterizes the love of the lover, in no way constitutes a banal folly. The issue is not an inability of the lover to find reasons, or a lack of reasoning or of good sense, but rather a failure of reason itself to give reasons for the initiative to love. The lover does not scorn reason: quite simply, reason itself goes lacking as soon as love is at issue. Love lacks reason, because reason gives way before it, like ground gives way beneath our feet. Love lacks reason, like one lacks air the higher one climbs a mountain. Love does not reject reason, but reason refuses to go where the lover goes. Reason indeed refuses nothing to the lover—but, quite simply, when love is at issue reason can do nothing, it can do no more, it is worn out. When loving is at issue, reason is not sufficient: reason appears from this point forward as a principle of *insufficient reason.*

I can verify this insufficiency of reason in love with a few arguments. First, if I love first, without any assurance of return, reciprocity can no more give me reason to love than it can tell me that I am wrong or give me a reason not to love: I remain as free to love as I am free not to love. Second, because I love first, I can sometimes very well not yet know the one that I love; not only because, in a radical sense, I have no need of knowing her and, on the contrary, the anteriority of my initiative dispenses me from having to, but also because the project of knowing this other adequately, without and even before loving her (as an object), has no meaning. Third: if I love without reason or even at times without prior knowledge of the figure or of the facets of the other, I do not love because I know what I see, but inversely I see and I know in the measure that I, the first to love, love. The other appears to me for as much as I love her, for my anterior initiative does not decide solely my attitude toward her, but above all her phenomenality—because I am the first to put it on stage, by loving her.

The lover makes appear the one whom she loves, not the reverse. She makes him appear as lovable (or despicable) and thus as visible within the erotic reduction. The other is phenomenalized in the exact measure according to which the lover loves him or her and, as an Orpheus of phenomenality, tears him or her from indistinction and makes him or her emerge from the depths of the unseen. This allows us to rehabilitate a polemical argument, used as frequently by metaphysics as by popular morality, against Don Juan, but also against the lover as such. The lover would delude himself, it is said, by not seeing the one that he loves as she truly is, but instead, each time, only as his desire imagines her to be. He sees with the eyes of love, which is to say by blinding himself (the large woman is majestuous; the petite, delightful; the hysterical, passionate; the bitch, arousing; the silly, spontaneous; the argumentative, brilliant, etc.—and one can easily transpose these so that they apply to men, too). We reproach desire with deforming and reformulating, in order to desire better. The lover, in this case Don Juan, fools himself, and his confidant, Sganarelle, sees clearly: it is necessary to come back to earth, to look things in the face and not to take one's desire for reality; in short, it is necessary to exit the erotic reduction. But by what right does Sganarelle claim to see better than Don Juan what he himself would have neither noticed, nor seen, if the lover, Don Juan, had not first pointed it out to him? By what right does he dare, with a clear conscience, to reason as the lover, when he cannot, by definition, share either the vision or the initiative? Evidently, because he is completely ignorant of the phenomenological rule according to which the anticipation of loving first allows one to see at last such and such an other, for the anticipation to love first sees her as lovable and unique, while otherwise she disappears into commerce and reciprocity. It is said that Don Juan and Sganarelle see the same other, but with two different gazes—the former with the phantasms of desire, the latter with the neutrality of good sense. This is wrong, for in fact they see two different phenomena. The lover alone sees something else, a thing that no one other than he sees—that is, what is precisely no longer a thing, but, for the first time, just such an other, unique, individualized, henceforth torn from economy, detached from objectness, unveiled by the initiative of loving, arisen like a phenomenon to that point unseen. The lover, who sees insofar as he loves, discovers a phenomenon that is seen insofar as it is loved (and as much as it is loved). In contrast, Sganarelle sees nothing of this other and only reasons against Don Juan because he reestablishes reason, of which the lover has just taken leave. It is precisely by reestablishing the economy that Sganarelle compares objectively the qualities and the faults of what the lover loves with other possible loves; he calculates anew the good and bad reasons, the gains and losses; and reason only reappears in order to justify or disqualify a possible reciprocity, a retributive justice. But this restoration has a price: one cannot claim to measure what the lover loves outside of what is for sale except by evoking phantoms alongside this new phenomenon henceforth arisen, crystallized and irrefragable; one cannot measure the lover's beloved except by comparing him or her to the phantoms of other possibilities, to another "he" or another "she"—that the lover could have loved, and should have loved, with better reasons; without seeing what is right in front of his eyes—that these phantoms have no rank among true phenomena, that the initiative of the lover has eliminated these very possibilities, and that they have all simply disappeared in front of the evidence of the new phenomenon, henceforth seen and revealed. Reason cannot reason except by comparing, but, from the moment of the lover's declaration, the former possibles collapse when faced with the unique facticity that has come forth, and they fade away, like shadows swallowed up by the light. Of course, one could always see things in other ways than does the lover, with more reason, for instance; but this is precisely the point: the lover has gone beyond the field of validity of comparisons, of calculations, and of commerce; he can no longer see otherwise, nor see anything other than what he sees—and what he sees decidedly no longer has the status of a thing, but of a beloved. The lover's domestic servant can do nothing more for the lover, because he regresses to the hither side of the radicalized erotic reduction that the lover fulfills, or rather, which fulfills him as lover.

Nevertheless, let us once again admit the question, why does the lover commit himself first, without any assurance, to love this one and not that one? If we have understood that, for the lover, no comparison can give a reasonable explanation (because the one that he has seen no longer counts among any other possible), there remains only one acceptable response: the other, become unique, herself occupies, by virtue of her role as focal point, the function of the reason that the lover has for loving her. The lover loves the beloved because the beloved is the one and only, and because the lover makes him- or herself the lover—because it was him, because it was me. The lover has no reason to love the one that he loves other than, precisely, the one that he loves, insofar as he, the lover, makes this one visible by loving him or her first. From the lover's point of view (and his alone), love becomes its own sufficient reason. The lover thus makes love by producing the reason according to which he has good reason to go without every other reason. The insufficiency of reason to give love reason thus marks not only the principle of insufficient reason, but erects above all the lover as reason in himself. The *causa sui* that the love of self claimed in vain (§ 9) transposes itself into a *ratio sui,* but a *ratio sui* that is accomplished, this time, according to the radicalized erotic reduction—no longer by asking, "Does anyone out there love me?" but by exposing oneself to respond in person to the question "Can I love first?" The circle is decentered from the *ego* toward a certain other.

§ 18. The Advance

I have just followed the same path as Don Juan. For Don Juan knows, perhaps better than anyone else, how to provoke the erotic reduction and impose it upon those who, without him, would have had neither the idea nor the courage to enter into it (not only Sganarelle, but also Anna, Elvira, and Zerlina); he, the first, takes the initiative to love, without any other reason than to accomplish the erotic reduction itself. What is more, his desire does not so much provoke the erotic reduction as result from it; those to whom he declares his love, like those against whom he declares war (often the same people), appear in their increasingly extreme singularity uniquely because the erotic reduction designates them as loved, whether well or badly, but in any case lovable, in a situation to meet the lover. Nevertheless, I will not be able to follow this path any further, because Don Juan does not maintain what he so clearly inaugurates. He takes the initiative by exposing himself continually to the question "Can I love first?" thus continuously provoking the radicalized erotic reduction; but he becomes entangled in reproducing it exactly, almost mechanically, like a forest fire that starts up again with each new outbreak of fire, or rather like a fire in a fireplace that does not catch, and thus needs to be constantly stirred up. Where does this persistent and pitiable repetition come from? Doubtless from the fact that Don Juan practices the reduction solely in the mode of seduction.

Before distinguishing themselves from one another, reduction and seduction (both erotic) come together to put into operation the same advance, the same anticipation—I love first, without any other reason than this one whom I risk loving, without awaiting her response, without presuming reciprocity, without even knowing her. Reduction and seduction each proceed by anticipation—out of balance at first, carried along by their proper impetus into a fall, which remains a race for as long as it catches up with itself by virtue of its prolongation. But their divergence begins precisely with the mode of this advance. In seduction, the advance remains provisional and ends by canceling itself out, because once the other is seduced (led to give consent), I no longer love in advance or to the point of loss, but rather with a return, in full reciprocity: I will simply have made an advance on love, for which I will be reimbursed with interest. Just as the other will inevitably wind up returning to me the love I initially credited to her, my possession will catch up with it and will assimilate it to my *ego,* which will once again become the center of the circle. From that point, seduction betrays the erotic reduction, not because it seduces, but because it seduces neither enough nor long enough; because it ends up reestablishing reciprocity according to the natural attitude; and because it mimics the lover's love in order finally to invert it. This is confirmed by seduction's final moment: not only does Don Juan reestablish reciprocity in the final instance ("elle m'aimera, je le veux"), but he overturns it in his favor ("elle m'aimera et moi, non"), so that someone out there loves him without his any longer loving first, or even at all. Seduction wants to make itself loved without, in the end, loving—I only go about the advance with the firm resolution of losing it as soon as possible; I only lose myself in the advance so that someone comes to me and I thus find myself again; or rather so that I find her without her ever finding me again. The advance disappears, like a lure I dangle, assuring me a free gain. In seduction I take pleasure, but the pleasure is solitary.

In contrast, the reduction starts off in an advance that is definitive and without return, an advance that will never cancel itself out, and never catch up with itself; I start off out of balance and I only avoid the fall by lengthening my stride, by going faster, in other words by adding to my lack of balance. The more I do to avoid falling, the more I advance without any hope of return. For even if I reach the other, this does not give me possession, precisely because I only touch her and open an access to her by the impact that I provoke, and therefore according to the measure of the impetus that I take and that I must maintain; the other does not stop me like a wall or an inert and delimited lump, but offers herself to me like a path that opens, always continuing in proportion to my entry forward; the advance thus requires a permanent fresh start, wherein I remain in the race and alive only by repeating my imbalance; each accomplishment asks for and becomes a new beginning. In conformity to the definition of the phenomenological reduction in general, the erotic reduction (radicalized under the form "Can I be the first to love?") is only definitively accomplished in never ceasing to repeat itself. The *ego* will never again become the center; until the end, it must decenter itself in view of a center that is always to come, an other back to whom I lead myself.

Nonetheless, does this still formal opposition between seduction and reduction truly matter, deep down, for the lover? What does the difference between a provisional advance and a definitive advance change in the question "Can I love first?" It touches upon the essential. For with a provisional advance, the other herself remains provisional: a new advance will have to be started, by scaring up any old other, making new advances upon Zerlina, after the declarations made to Elvira, Anna, and the rest of the catalog. By contrast, in a definitive advance a single, unique other suffices in principle superabundantly, ceaselessly arousing a new start. And yet, even this uniqueness of the other does not tell the essential difference, because already the uniqueness is a result of the difference. For the other only becomes unique for me on the condition that she is confirmed to be infinite—that she is able, by herself, not only to support, but to provoke an ever repeatable start of the initial advance, of my initiative to love first. But is there not a patent contradiction at issue here—how can the other, come from this world, and thus definitively finite, open the distance to an infinite re-starting of the advance, to an ever repeatable advance of the lover? Put vulgarly, how would the other in the end not overdo it [*saturer*], and the lover not become tired? A vulgar response: Don Juan grows tired, and I grow tired of Elvira or of Zerlina, because we quickly size them up. Put the other way round, we size them up so quickly because, after a certain moment, we do not re-start our advance. The other thus appears to me as finite, because my advance toward her has slowed, been extinguished and disappeared, not the inverse. It is the end of the advance that makes the other finite, rather than any finitude of the other justifying the end of the advance. The other becomes finite for me because she enters little by little (as my advance diminishes) into my field of vision, is immobilized there, and ends up by facing me, massively, frontally, objectively, instead of remaining the vanishing point that I aimed at in advance, without truly seeing it or ever comprehending it. Henceforward seen full frame, like an object, the other is immobilized in a place in the world and I can take her measure—in short, size her up. What we call possession of the other simply exploits her previous objectification; but this objectivity already implies her finitude, and thus the end of the advance. My powerlessness to re-start leaves the other to become a thing, my object, the finite that I size up, and from which I eventually turn away. Don Juan does not love too much— on the contrary, he loves too little, too short of the mark, without impetus; he loses his advance. Don Juan loves too little, not because he desires too much, but because he does not desire enough, or desire long enough, or desire persistently enough. He claims to hold his liquor, but he does not hold his love; he does not hold out in his desire, he does not hold out the entire distance. In a word, he does not hold to the erotic reduction. For I, the lover, only hold to the erotic reduction as long as I maintain the advance and re-start it. I find pleasure in the other because my advance and her imperceptible delay allow me to avoid the possession of an end.

Thus the advance provoked by the lover, provided that he at least respond to the question, "Can I love first?" definitively characterizes the radicalized erotic reduction—to the point that the reduction is only accomplished so long as the advance is repeated. This advance unfolds and is illustrated by several remarkable postures.

The lover *bears everything*. Indeed, by definition, the other owes no reciprocity whatsoever to the lover; or better, the other only appears as the beloved and only arises as an erotic phenomenon within the situation of the erotic reduction, and thus only at the initiative of the lover, who risks himself first; only in this way does the other escape from the fragile and provisional visibility of the object, which I can size up and, when I'm done, turn away from. Whence comes this paradoxical, yet inevitable, consequence: at the outset, when the declaration of love bursts out, the lover decides everything, and the other nothing—precisely because before the erotic reduction no other could yet be in play, and only objects offered themselves to sight, and thus to possession. The lover thus renders the beloved possible, because he enters first into the erotic reduction. Let us describe the process by which the lover raises an object to the rank of the beloved. The lover presupposes that which he aims at; but, at first sight, what he sees (or guesses at) still only offers an object to the gaze; now, since it is a matter of loving according to an advance and an endless re-starting, everything but an object is necessary; and facing me, in appearance, there stands only an object. Whoever admits that only an object is to be found must abdicate the role of lover and, like Don Juan, pass on to another object. The lover, however, does not abdicate: he presupposes that before him, despite the appearances of an object, an other rises up, that is, not only an actual beloved (beloved by me), but also a potential lover. The lover is going to love this assumed other as if he or she already wanted to, knew how to, and could make him- or herself be loved, and, in his or her turn, love like a lover. Of course, the lover does not ask for reciprocity or anticipate it, but simply postulates that this other does not have the rank of an object. He attests to this in presupposing—without any guarantee, or certainty, or condition—that he or she too can take the posture of the lover, enter into the erotic reduction, and, in short, love. The lover decides that the other is worthy of the title of other (beloved, not object). Thus he also makes love in the sense that he supposes that the other will end up by making it as well. The lover does not only make love, he has love made (§ 33).

Next: the lover *believes everything,* endures everything and lasts without limit or help, with the sovereign power of he who loves before knowing himself loved, or worrying about it. The lover makes the difference—he alone differs. He differs from all those who want to love on condition of reciprocity, those metaphysical or natural-attitude *ego*s that are obsessed by their equality to themselves, to the point of wanting to enlarge it into a new equality—between what they imagine of themselves, and what they require receipt of from elsewhere. The lover also differs from all the visible objects, and thus from subsistent and ready-to-hand beings, because he loves by advancing himself into a distance, where they must not appear, so that their commerce will not muddle the erotic reduction. Nothing supports the lover, thus it is necessary that he bear everything, in particular that his presupposition—that the other will end up by entering into the erotic reduction—not come, or not come yet; and the very addition of "not yet" amounts to believing everything. The lover believes everything, endures everything and, more precisely, puts up with remaining alone in the situation of the erotic reduction. He alone has as his own the erotic reduction—he remains the idiot of the erotic reduction. But nevertheless the lover assumes this idiotic solitude as a sovereign privilege, acting on a motive that we have already sketched. In the banal, nearly universal case wherein one of the two is no longer in love, or indeed was never in love, who should be designated the least unhappy of the two? It is necessary to make a distinction; in the natural attitude, the least unhappy seems to be the one who loved the least, or who stopped loving earlier—because he has lost less, and suffered less when love disappeared; by contrast, in the erotic reduction, the least unhappy appears as the one who loved the most, because he does not stop loving, even when the other has disappeared, so that he alone maintains love afloat. He has not lost everything, because he still loves. Indeed, he has lost nothing, because he still remains a lover. In the erotic reduction, if one truly wants to win, it is necessary to love and to persist in this advance, without condition—thus the last to love wins the stake. What stake? To love, of course. The winner is—the last lover, the one who loves to the end. For the lover loves to love. That does not turn him away from loving a beloved, but instead allows him to love the beloved, even if the beloved does not love him, or simply loves no one, or indeed even takes exception to her status as other to be loved. The lover loves to love for the love of love. Henceforth, just as he bears everything, the lover can believe everything and hope for everything. To believe and to hope here signify to love without knowing or possessing. Unknowing (which believes) and poverty (which hopes) nevertheless do not indicate any scarcity or shortage, but rather the properly infinite excess of the lover, as he loves without the condition of reciprocity.

Finally: the lover loves, or at least can sometimes love, *without seeing*. Indeed, a lover cannot know what she loves in the way that she would know an object, and in fact she has no need; if she knew it in such a manner, she would be able to constitute it and size it up once and for all; neither does she know it as a subsistent being, whose presence and persistence in identity she could verify at any moment; nor does she know it as a being ready-at-hand, of which she could, at the opportune moment, make a use that is adapted to her needs, her desires, and her projects. She in fact needs to know neither objects nor beings at all, because in order to love, it is necessary for her to practice the erotic reduction of objects and of beings of the world in general, so as to open the distance in which their commerce vanishes and the abandon without return may begin. Properly speaking, she does not know that which she loves, because what one loves does not appear before one loves it. It is up to the lover to make visible what is at issue—the other as beloved, appearing as erotically reduced. Knowledge does not make love possible, because knowledge flows from love. The lover makes visible what she loves and, without this love, nothing would appear to her. Thus, strictly speaking, the lover does not know what she loves—except insofar as she loves it. There follows an incomparable privilege: since she phenomenalizes what she loves in so very far as she loves it, the lover can even (or especially) love what one does not see (if one does not love it)—and, to begin with, the absentee. The absentee in space, certainly: a known living person who for the moment is far away (it matters little here whether voluntarily or involuntarily), or even one who is definitively departed (due to a quarrel). But also the absentee in time, a living being still unknown and potential (the one "who already waits for me," me alone, in the indistinct crowd) and who will identify me; and what is more, a living being only to come, and known by proxy (the hoped-for child, or indeed the child that is feared); and above all the living being dead and gone, whether a known deceased (to whom I may want to remain faithful), or an unknown dead man (who haunts my search for identity). In loving the absentee, the lover in no way succumbs to delirium but instead limits herself to accomplishing exactly the radicalized erotic reduction, which, as we have seen, depends upon nothing belonging to being, or indeed which provokes the nothing itself. At one stroke the lover is freed from the emblematic limit of metaphysics, the difference between being and not being—for she loves just as much what is not as what is; indeed, she loves all the more freely by loving that which is not yet, that which no longer is, or even that which does not have to be in order to appear. She also washes herself of a suspicion weighing upon phenomenology—that of privileging visibility within phenomenality; for the lover loves what she does not see more than what she sees; or rather, she only sees because she loves that which, at first, she could not see. The lover loves in order to see—as one pays to view.

Because the lover possesses nothing, and must do so, it remains for him *to hope*. Hope indicates here a privileged mode of access to that which can unfold within the phenomenality opened by the erotic reduction, precisely because one can only hope for that which one does not possess, and for as long as one does not possess it. In the strict sense hope does not and cannot have an object, because objects call for possession; the more that possession grows, the less it hopes; hope and possession cross one another, inversely proportional. This is suggested by the old expression, "to have hopes"—that is to say, not yet to have the possession of an inheritance, but to find oneself in the position of waiting for it, more or less certain. And the lover has hopes; in fact he has nothing but hopes, which offer the particularity of never converting themselves into so many possessions, not because they go disappointed, but because what he hopes for does not belong to the order of that which one possesses, nor to that which possession governs. He in effect never hopes in objects, but precisely in what surpasses objectness, or even beingness: the lover, in the very moment of the most headlong advance, which frees him from reciprocity and from economy, still hopes by full rights in assurance, the assurance that someone loves him and defends him from vanity, and thus also from the hatred of each for himself. But this assurance would sink instantly into its contrary if he waited for it like the possession of an object that is certain. For this very possession would contradict itself—possessing the beloved, come from somewhere else like an object, would ineluctably end up in jealousy (§ 33); it would not even be effective—because the beloved must, in order to assure me against vanity, unfold infinitely, while every object remains finite. Love, coming from out there and going to infinity, can only come upon me if I renounce possessing it and hold myself strictly to the radicalized erotic reduction. Love thus only becomes thinkable according to the mode of the hoped for, of that which can only come upon me as the radically unseen and unwarranted. As such—as that which I can neither possess, nor provoke, nor merit, it will remain the unconditioned, and thus that which, on this condition, can give itself infinitely. Hope thus hopes for everything, except that which it could possess. It hopes for everything and, to begin with, the unhoped for. It assists possibility.

The lover bears everything, believes everything, even what he does not see, and hopes for everything. And, now that the erotic reduction is accomplished, he alone remains. Nothing can triumph over him, because his very weakness makes his strength. Whence comes his advance.

§ 19. Freedom as Intuition

The lover's advance is nevertheless exposed to an objection that becomes all the stronger as it is multiplied. For the request for assurance, which from the beginning determines the lover in the situation of the erotic reduction, could in the end fail, in several ways. First, because it clearly remains doubtful that someone out there loves me, whether I ask for it naturally, or I pass into the radicalized erotic reduction ("Can I love first?"); the hope to which I have just had recourse confirms me in the assurance that I have none right now, and that all certainty has likewise failed me. And there's more: not only do I have no assurance whatsoever that anyone loves me, but I also have no assurance whatsoever that I love, that I truly love; for, by virtue of the advance, I do not really know whom I love, nor why I love her, nor in fact what loving means; that which makes it possible for me to love—the pure initiative, without sufficient reason—also makes this love of mine enigmatic; whether I love truly without reason (gratuitously, for nothing), or there are in fact reasons within me that I am unaware of that are determining me (reasons that come from the unconscious, from my flesh, or from society), in both of these cases, nothing assures me that it is still I and I alone who takes the initiative to love, because I do not know what "I" and even what "to love" might mean. The danger that most threatens my ambition as a lover doubtless does not consist in my not knowing whether someone loves me or not, but rather in my imagining myself able to love or able to know what loving means. How do I avoid this objection, which weighs all the more heavily because it depends directly upon the erotic reduction, in which loving is summed up by the initiative of loving in advance and without reason? And this objection could threaten even the accomplishment of the erotic reduction—for in the end an assurance received from out there does not go without saying, and the simple fact of demanding it implies neither that one will obtain it, nor that one may legitimately lay claim to it. In short, by taking the initiative to love in the role of lover, in advance and without reason, I would quite simply lack judgment and prudence.

Nevertheless, it could be that this objection only draws its strength from a misunderstanding of the erotic reduction; it boils down once again to the assertion that, in order to love, it is necessary to know whom one is loving, why one loves, and if one is loved in return; all of which are perfectly legitimate demands, but solely in the natural attitude, where nothing is done without sufficient reason, or reciprocity, or knowledge of the other as an object. These reasonable precautions lose all validity as soon as the border separating the natural attitude from the erotic reduction is crossed. And yet, this answer does not prevent the objection from returning under a slightly different form: if the lover only becomes possible beginning with the radicalized erotic reduction, the lover presupposes it; he cannot provoke it, since he results from it. There is a circle here, and it thus becomes more arbitrary to pass on to the erotic reduction, than to pass it by.

Unable to dissolve the objection, I can take support from it. I will thus concede without discussion that I do not have the least assurance that someone out there loves me, nor that I am the first to love. But this lack of assurance does not forbid passing on to the reduction, since the reduction only becomes possible when the very question of assurance, and thus of the lack of assurance, is acknowledged; the lack of assurance does not disqualify the lover from taking an advance; on the contrary, the lack of assurance makes it possible for the lover to advance by opening distance for him. If this is admitted, what results? That I am no longer assured of anything? That in the radicalized erotic reduction my lover's advance leaves me naked and empty? Absolutely not. For, even if I possess no assurance whatsoever that I love first, I at least have the assurance of having decided to do so. Just as love given remains perfectly given even if the gift is refused, since the scorn that the gift suffers in no way interferes with the abandon that the gift accomplishes, so too does the lover who decides to love first acquire the certainty of having decided, even if his advance does not love perfectly without reason, since this imperfection in no way affects the *decision* to advance without reason. Doubtless it is not enough that I decide to love first for me to accomplish without remainder such a love in advance; but it is indeed enough that I decide to love first for me to accomplish without remainder the *decision* of such a love in advance—in short, for me to receive the assurance of acceding to the status of lover. To decide to love in advance is enough to give me the assurance of the lover— the only assurance that I can aim for and hope for—because the decision to love in advance, if it does not decide my actual love, decides at least that I have decided to love in advance. To qualify as a lover, I do not have to perform love's perfect advance: by definition no one can promise that, since it depends on no cause whatsoever, not even my will; but in order to be qualified as a lover, I have only to decide to perform love's advance, a decision that depends only on me, even though it always plays out at the limits of my abilities. To decide to love does not assure loving, but it does assure deciding to love. And the lover attests himself lover precisely through this decision—the first and the purest, without a cause, without return, a pure projection into the erotic reduction, without any other reason than itself. Assurance comes to the lover when he decides simply to love, first, without the assurance of reciprocity. Assurance comes to him when he decides definitively not to wait for it. Or rather, the assurance that comes to him—to love as a lover—no longer coincides with those assurances that he renounces—that someone love him in return, or even the assurance of loving first, perfectly.

In displacing the qualification of the lover from the performance of the advance to its pure decision, one does not lower the requirement imposed upon the lover by the erotic reduction from actuality to simple formal possibility. First of all because to claim to love first and effectively is, let us repeat, meaningless: at the instant of his initiative, the lover does not know if he acts of his own accord or under an influence, nor under what influences; nor does he know any better what he is truly undertaking, or how far he will succeed. And we cannot ask more from the lover, incomparably more than what his conscious power can cover.

Above all, by leading the advance (to love first) from an actual performance back to the possibility of a decision, the reduction does not collapse, but instead is radicalized. For to decide to love first, in advance, amounts unquestionably to the lover's deciding for and determining his self. In effect, when I ask: "Where am I and who am I?" I am searching for the place where my ipseity plays out and is phenomenalized—which is to say, the place where I make my own decision. But I do not identify myself when I decide for myself alone through an anticipatory resolution, which only anticipates me alone; in this case, I remain the prisoner of the narcissistic mirror of myself, in which I become phantasmagorically at once both spectacle and spectator, actor and judge. On the contrary, I identify myself when I no longer anticipate myself alone, but instead others, the other than myself; for she, who does not coincide with me and who attracts me within the distance that I no longer master, can describe and inscribe me as such—other than myself, henceforward situated under the protection of the other. In making my decision *to love the other in advance* I appear to myself for the first time as I make my decision—exposed to the other for the possibility precisely upon which I decide. Paradoxically, I do not appear when I make my decision by and for myself, but only when I make my decision for the other, because she can confirm for me who I am: in deciding for her, it is through her that I appear. In my decision for the other, my decision to love in advance an other than myself, my most proper phenomenality is decided. I do not come to a decision about myself alone, but rather through the gaze of the other; not through an anticipatory resolution without witnesses or grounds, but through love in advance, in the distance wherein I expose myself to the other (§ 37). The decision to love thus remains valid, even if I do not actually accomplish love in advance, provided nevertheless that I resolve to do so—formally, that I make the decision to decide. Making love in advance perhaps does not depend upon me, but *loving to love* (*amare amare*) does. Nothing can separate me from the freedom of playing the lover.

In this way, we can posit that to love is fully equivalent to loving, and qualifies me already as a lover. We can also note that the distinction between loving the other in fact and only loving to love him or her (or loving to love) here remains imprecise; for I only experience immediately my love for loving, without ever being able to certify to myself that I love the other gratuitously, truly, or sufficiently, and without ever being able to measure it; in order to reach certainty it would be necessary not only for me to love according to the other's measure, which means without measure, but above all for a third party to make him- or herself the arbiter or, what amounts to the same impossibility, for the loved other to assure me; but who among those who share my finitude could claim to decree such a judgment? The transition between the love of love and the love of the other remains tangential and gradual for us, entangled as we are in the flux of our finite and factual affair. No lover claims seriously or easily to love the other purely, beyond his or her conviction of having loved to love in view of this other: he would like to love, but he never succeeds in proving it, to himself or others. In what, then, do we recognize the radical lover? In the fact that he almost never dares to declare, "I love you!" precisely because he knows what it will cost. Whoever is assured that he actually and correctly loves either does not know what he is saying or is lying (to himself); he would already be doing much if he loved to love without mental restrictions or bad faith. Between loving to love and actually loving the other, we cannot mark a clean difference—we are dealing with a border zone, crossed by comings and goings without any stops, and above all without any stable resting place. Each advances as far as he or she can and as far as he or she wills (as far as he or she can will; as far as he or she wills to be able), hoping to love the other a little, thanks to the love of love.

To love loving comes down to me; in this decision, I come to and come round to appearing to myself as such. Whence arises this liberating paradox: it is enough for me to make *as if* I loved to decide to love and thus to acquire a full status of lover. *As if* betrays no regression, no pulling back, no compromise, but instead unveils the privileged space of the initiative reserved for the lover—that which only depends upon him. It depends only upon him to love in advance (with or without the means to accomplish it, it matters little) and thereby to raise himself to the dignity of the lover. In deciding that I love in advance and without reciprocity, without knowing what the other thinks of it, or even if the least other knows anything about it, I have the sovereign freedom to make myself a lover—to make myself amorous. I become amorous simply because I want to, without any constraint, according to my sole, naked desire. Thus the strength of love in advance emerges: I can reasonably love even if I do not know that I am loved (or indeed even if I know that I am not loved), because in deciding to love first, I actually experience that I love. This assurance alone is enough for me. When I "fall in love," I know, at my risk and peril, what I feel and what is affecting me—to wit, that I devolve to the other, whether or not she returns my love, whether or not she knows it, indeed whether or not she accepts it. My being in love with her does not depend on her, but rather on me, alone. And that is enough.

Enough for what? Enough for an intuition to fill me, or indeed to submerge me. There is a paradox here, which could be surprising if, in the end, it did not impose itself: the state of "being in love"—those words define all of its danger, even its injustice—does not depend upon its addressee or recipient; it depends only upon its giver, me alone. It defines me and wells up from me only. In fact, it is only up to me to become loving. The lover experiences it quite lucidly: I do not become loving by chance, at just any moment in my everyday life (happy are those who are the exceptions!), nor by deciding coldly to do it; I know that sometimes there are periods that emerge in which I clearly decide not to become loving deliberately, but eventually to allow myself to become so. For if there are times when I allow myself to be absorbed by the management of objects in the world (the erotic reduction thus remaining impossible), and certain times when I must consent to the work of mourning for a love that has ended (the erotic reduction thus remaining engaged in its negativity), other times open in which I have nothing better to do than to allow myself to love loving, whether because vanity pushes me to ask (myself), "Does anyone out there love me?" or because the erotic reduction radically questions, "Can I love first?" Desire is not yet at issue—it can only come later. At issue is the very condition of desire, which first requires this consent, and the possibility that it opens. More radically: when, in the blur of the first encounter, without any information or the least assurance of reciprocity, I make my decision to go and see, or even to "go for it," this decision depends only on me. In front of a gaze that is not cruel or already misted over, I can very well hold myself back and stay put; I can also allow ambiguity to hover by "just looking"; or I can decidedly attempt to provoke the sparkle that I am hoping for, or that I dread. And, in each of these occurrences, I can make a decision out of simple curiosity, out of a slight sadism, out of playfulness, out of interest, or out of passion. To push my advance or to hold it back, to deploy it generously or to pretend to follow: it all depends on me. No one falls in love involuntarily or by chance, even if only because—all involuntary emotion admitted—he must ratify it after the fact, in order to know when and to what he is surrendering. I know very well when I become loving—at the precise moment in which I ask myself, and reassure myself by claiming that I am not in love ("I am not in love, I have nothing to worry about, I can stop at any moment"), in short at the moment in which it is already too late. Whether I am beginning to become amorous, or I already love loving, or I imagine myself loving, in each case I am willing it and, in this acquiescence, am deciding for it. The affection that I experience at the beginning of my amorous state imposes itself upon me in fact as an auto-affection. And this auto-affection will not leave me for some time, because it comes with my consent, and cannot touch me without it. The amorous state touches me the most deeply (affection for self), because in the end it falls to me alone to consent to it, and thus to decide for it (affection through the self, auto-affection).

When I consent to becoming amorous, and agree that I become loving of my own accord, what is decided is not summed up in a simple subjective emotion that would be individual and prereflexive. Rather, what is decided will invade me with an affective tonality that is powerful, deep, and durable, and which, little by little or quite brutally, will contaminate the totality of my inner life: not only my emotional but also my intellectual life, not only my conscious but also my unconscious life. Or better: more inward than my most inward part, this tonality will overdetermine all of my apparent decisions, all of my public argumentations and all of my private debates; it will ruin the most limpid logic and the interests that are the least questionable; it will eventually drive me to the most extreme social and relational choices, will push me toward the most risky outbursts and the most suspect compromises. What will be at issue in this tonality, for months, for years, perhaps forever, is a horizon encompassing all of my decisions and all of my thoughts. What status can I attribute to it? It does not have to do with an emotion, or a passion, or even less with a delirium, but first of all with what phenomenology calls a lived experience of consciousness [*un vécu de conscience, Erlebnissen*]. But this lived experience, while it is indeed provoked within me by me (insofar as it depends only upon me to love loving), is not limited to my subjectivity; it indissolubly involves the other as its intentional reference, always aimed at, even and above all if I do not yet actually reach, him or her. Insofar as it is aiming at such and such a specific other, who obsesses me even when remaining virtual, this lived experience proves itself to be radically intentional—intentional of this other. Thus the affective tonality that exposes me as amorous, or rather that qualifies me as a lover, gives me an intuition that is polarized toward an other than myself, the one that I already imagine loving, without yet knowing what I am saying. By intuition I here mean that which could fill the signification aimed at by intentionality, so that by eventually becoming adequate to the signification, the intuition allows a strict phenomenon to appear. Nevertheless, it does not exactly work this way; to become loving by my consent, and thus by my decision, amounts to receiving an intuition that is still so vast and so vague that it could fill an indeterminate number of significations, and thus render visible an indeterminate number of diverse phenomena. Effectively, this vague availability is easily verified (by following banal experience and popular wisdom) in the worrisome propensity of the same amorous affective tonality to give rise to passions, intuitions, and thus phenomena of the other that are very different, or even contradictory, and which pass, brutally and apparently without rhyme or reason, into one another; in love, I can fix myself arbitrarily upon one or another other, or swing arbitrarily between them, with about-face reversals as violent as they are sudden; even supposing that I focus myself for a considerable lapse of time upon the same other, I can certainly imagine adoring her, devoting myself to her, or enjoying her, but, if the circumstances disappoint me, I can just as well suddenly come to suspect her, betray her, or indeed even hate her. With the same affective tonality, which functions like an intentional intuition of a potential other, I can will to constitute phenomena that are as precise and visible as they are different and contradictory, which is to say phenomena that in the end are fluctuating, provisional, and nearly phantasmal.

Where does this instability come from? Evidently not from a failure of intuition, since intuition remains ever ready to fill any signification; indeed, my decision to love loving is enough to render intuition available to validate, without reserve or condition, any of the significations that I will, or that the current affair proposes. The danger comes precisely from the abundance, autonomy, and limitless fluidity of my intuition—endlessly restarted by my decision to love loving. The instability of amorous phenomena thus never comes from a poverty of intuition, but instead from the opposite: from my incapacity to assign to it a precise signification that is individualized and stable. Always available and already there, intuition shows itself to be superabundant in front of a signification that is first and foremost lacking (What other?) and most of the time provisional (Will I love a long time before veering into jealousy or hatred?). In short, the affective tonality of loving to love proves itself to be an intuition that is at once intentional toward the other and without an assignable other—an intentional intuition, but without an intentional object; a fulfilling intuition, but without a concept to fill. The intuition that furnishes me with the affective tonality of loving to love arises in excess, but is dispersed without form. It remains a vague intuition, which renders my love of loving vagabond—morally flighty, but above all phenomenally incapable of staging the least identifiable other. A blind intuition, which never sees any other. Saturated with itself, it gives loving to love, without showing anything.

Thus, intuition—in the affective tonality of the amorous state—comes to a decision following the resolution taken by the lover, and, since this resolution always plays out in advance, it gives itself before the other appears as such (supposing that he or she will ever appear). The intuition shows itself as always already given to the lover by himself, provide that he had radicalized the erotic reduction by asking himself, "Can I love first?" As he progresses in the performance of this reduction, the intuition thus provoked by his decision will grow, to become, at the limit, a saturating intuition. And all the more saturating in that, in a first and long moment, it wanders, vague and virginal in an assured, or only assigned, signification. The affective tonality of finding myself in fact in love—of attaining the status of lover—does not yet lead onto any signification: the other does not intervene here. The intuition of loving becomes blinding, because it only depends upon the lover who, once more, makes love first. But, this time, his priority closes the horizon for him.

§ 20. Signification as Face

As lover, I attempt to rise to the other as a phenomenon, which the radicalized erotic reduction would set forth through the question "Can I love first?" But the ordinary definition of the phenomenon cannot, in this very specific case, remain unchanged. I cannot simply maintain the claim that the phenomenon shows itself when one of my intentional significations finds itself validated by an intuition, which comes to fill it adequately.

This is the case for two reasons. First, because, in the radicalized erotic reduction, I alone make the decision to love in advance and, as I love to love, I provoke through myself and by myself alone the intuition (in this case, the amorous affective tonality): this auto-affection actively produces, in immanence itself, intentional lived experiences, which can validate nothing other than myself: my amorous lived experiences only confirm my status as lover, and that I make love; they do not render the other that I love visible or accessible to me (supposing that I really do love *one*). Thus the difficulty here no longer consists in confirming a signification (always available to my spontaneous intentionality, yet still in itself empty) by intuition (eventually lacking, yet forcing itself upon me). Rather, the difficulty lies inversely in fixing a precise signification to the superabundant and vague intuition, which the decision to love in advance provokes; the point is no longer to validate a signification by an intuition, but rather an immanent and available intuition by a foreign and autonomous signification.

Whence comes the second reason: this signification should validate my intuition (my decision to love loving) as the other; the sought-for signification must, in fixing my intuition, make the other manifest to me as a full-fledged phenomenon. To allow this to happen, it will not be enough that the signification attempt to represent the other to me, since the signification would degrade the other to the dishonorable rank of an object, which I could constitute at will and modify at my leisure. It will be necessary that this signification make me experience the radical alterity of the other—none other than just such an other—while the vague intuition, which I produce spontaneously by my decision, keeps me from the other and allows me to love (in fact, to love loving) without a fixed point. Signification, here lacking, must above all not represent the other to me, but must prepare me to receive alterity. Since it is precisely the case that I do not experience this alterity in the advance toward loving to love, I will have to experience it in signification's coming upon me. How can a signification ever make me experience the alterity of the other, or more exactly, the alterity of just such an unsubstitutable other? The signification in question will only arrive if it comes upon me from this alterity itself, if it no longer arises as that against which my intentionality would end up knocking, but rather as that which affects me from out there, beginning from itself. By virtue of a signification provoked no longer by my intentionality but instead by a counter-intentionality—exteriority's irrefutable shock, contradicting my aim, my forecast, and my expectation. In order for the other to manifest him- or herself to me as a whole phenomenon, I must not wait for the contribution of an intuition, but rather the unpredictable arrival of a signification, coming to contradict my intention *with its own*. In order to see the other, I must not attempt to make him or her appear like a phenomenon oriented according to my centrality; on the contrary, I must wait for a new signification to thwart my own significations and impose upon me, for the first time, an alterity that transcends even my advance toward loving to love. For every common-law phenomenon, my forecasted significations await the confirmation of intuitions yet to come. For the other, under the rule of the erotic reduction, my superabundant but vague intuition must continue to await the unforeseeable advent of a signification, which holds it fixed.

Thus the signification of the other, unlike the intuition of loving to love, will not belong to me; it will come from an exterior elsewhere by an advent, the experience of which alone will bring the proof of alterity. How could such a signification ever affect me, to the point of shaking me deeply enough, so as to assign my lover's *ego* to just such an other and none other? I have, in fact, known for a long time how such a signification could affect me—ever since I learned to envisage the face of the other. The face—of the other: there is a tautology here, for only the other imposes upon me a face, and no face opens upon any other ordeal than that of alterity. What does a face show? Strictly speaking, it gives nothing to be seen, at least if one were hoping to see intuitively a new visible, more fascinating or attractive than the others. In effect, the face shows nothing more than does any other surface in the world and, as a source of intuitions, it does not benefit from any privilege over the other parts of the human body. They too offer a surface that is sensible and accessible to all of my senses; I can likewise see its contours, touch its surface, smell its odor, suck the skin, even listen to its being bruised, just like any other thing in the world. What is so special about the face? Nothing, intuitively speaking. Even less than nothing, if we consider that the eyes—in all appearances the most notable characteristic of the face—offer to our seeing only the emptiness of the pupils, and thus nothing at all. The face furnishes me with no new intuition. But does it oppose me with its spoken word? Not always, or necessarily: its silence often is enough to immobilize me. And yet, the face stops my gaze and my attention like nothing else. It detains me, precisely because it opposes me with the origin of the gaze that the other lays upon the world and, eventually, upon me.

This hypothesis remains: the other's face holds me with the gaze that it lays upon me, by the counter-intentionality that its eyes exert, by a nonspectacle and a nonintuition, and thus perhaps by a signification. But what signification? For I could still lend it one of my own significations—the ones that I impose upon objects and upon beings in the world; and also those that my lover's intuition, which loves to love in advance, deploys endlessly in its wandering: desire, expectation, suffering, happiness, jealousy, hatred, etc. Nevertheless, it is not these significations, my own, that are at issue, because, produced as they are by my spontaneous decision, they impose upon me nothing from out there, but instead impose themselves upon the other; with these significations, I would cover up the other and hide him, or worse, destroy him. In a word, if I follow the significations that I impose upon him, I can ignore him, use him, possess him—even kill him. Kill him? This is the decisive signification—because I must not even conceive of it, because it turns against me, and because it imposes upon me a prohibition, and thus an alterity. To kill him—I cannot impose *that* upon him, without it turning against me, and his face imposing itself upon me, like something that I could neither produce nor refute. Empirically, I can in fact kill this face; indeed I could kill nothing other than such a face, because it alone calls for murder and makes murder possible, just as murder renders the face that much more visible. But why? Because everywhere out there, it is not yet murder that is at issue: for the animal, for example, the issue is only one of passing from life into death. Why, then, is it an issue of murder here and only here? Because the face alone signifies to me, in speech or in silence, "Thou shalt not kill."

By what right and by what authority does the face impose on me such a signification? This question neither admits nor asks for a response, because the only thing that matters is *the fact* that the face signifies to me precisely this signification. It is all about a fact, as constraining as a fact of reason, even more formal than a simple right. For a right only has value if, in actuality, it is ratified by force. But the signification "Thou shalt not kill" survives the violation of the right within it—I can kill, but then I become a murderer, and will remain one forever. The consciousness of and remorse for this murder could very well fade—but not the irrevocable fact that I am a murderer, a fact that will mark me forever, everywhere upon the surface of the earth and for the rest of my time. All the perfumes of excuses, of good reasons, and of ideologies can do nothing; nothing could ever kill within me the fact of the murder that I have committed. The face thus imposes upon me a signification, which is opposed to the empire of my *ego,* which up to this point has met no resistance—I must not submit myself to the face, and there where it arises I must not go. Strictly speaking, we ought not to speak of the other's face, since the alterity of the other only imposes itself upon me there where a face opposes itself to me; neither should we, following logically, speak of the face in general, nor of the other in general, but only of *just such* an other, designated by *just such* a face—it being understood that I never envisage a universal or common face, but always *just such* a face, which opposes to me *just such* an alterity, in telling me not to kill him—not to come to where he stands.

The face opposes itself to me; it thus imposes upon me a signification, one that consists only in the ordeal of its exteriority, of its resistance, and of its transcendence in relation to me. But, if I admit this result—and how could I not admit it?—shouldn't I necessarily give up on the horizon of love? For I attempt to phenomenalize the other, but as a lover; I try to fix my intuition upon a signification come about from the other by way of counter-intentionality, but the intuition here is an amorous one, one of loving to love; I attempt, of course, to accede to the exteriority of the other, but following the advance taken in the radicalized erotic reduction. However, doesn't the signification that rises out of the injunction "Thou shalt not kill" come strictly under the ethical, and not the erotic? How could an ethical signification fix the resolutely erotic intuition of the lover—the vague intuition of loving to love? And more serious: does not the ethical give access to the signification of the other through the universality of the commandment, thereby excluding the individuation that is precisely required by the lover? These two disputes—the ethical or the erotic, universality or individuation—have not ceased to occupy the lover, who only conquers himself by trying to settle them.

§ 21. Signification as Oath

At this point where the lover now stands, let us consider for a moment the first dispute. We note right away that however powerful and legitimate the strictly ethical understanding of the injunction "Thou shalt not kill" remains, it nevertheless does not exhaust the injunction's signification. For to understand "Thou shalt not kill" solely as an injunction (and formal ethics must understand it in this way) implies referring it back to the one—I in this case—who must respond to and answer for it; thus, by an unforeseen reversal, "Thou shalt not kill" would determine me rather than the other, whose most proper signification it nevertheless delivers. Before understanding this signification within the ethical horizon, then, shouldn't one allow it to open out as the pure exteriority of the other, and ask not what the obligation means for me, whom it clearly obligates, but first of all what it means with regard to the other, who obligates me in it? In effect, how does this signification reach me, if not as the pure advent of an exteriority, by a counter-intentionality that keeps me all the more at a distance as it touches my heart? The injunction "Thou shalt not kill" signifies—signifies for me—that there, where it arises, I cannot go, except by killing this exteriority. It signifies the pure exteriority that as lover I searched for in taking the advance of loving (to love) first; as pure exteriority, the injunction thus does not contradict the radicalized erotic reduction, but fixes its amorous intuition that up to this point has remained vague. In hearing "Thou shalt not kill," I can and must, by virtue of being a lover, hear "Do not touch me"—do not advance here, where I arise, for you would tread ground that, in order for me to appear, must remain intact; the site where I am must remain untouchable, unassimilable, closed to you in order that my exteriority remain open to you—the exteriority that alone will fix your intuition and make visible to you a full-fledged phenomenon. The phenomenon, which unites your immanent intuition to my definitively distant signification, is born of your retreat in front of my advance. The erotic phenomenon that you want to see will only appear to you if you fix upon this intact signification the excess of your intuition to love loving. You will only receive this phenomenon by not taking hold of it, by not killing it, and thus first of all by not touching it.

I find myself in a radically new situation. And yet it is not a question of a psychological novelty (after all, encountering the other, if possible, would doubtless imply such a duality within distance), but rather of a phenomenological novelty. In the end the erotic reduction amounts to the posing of a single question (encompassing "Does anyone out there love me?" as well as "Can I love first?")—that of knowing if just such an other can by all rights show him- or herself to me, that is to say *beginning from him- or herself.* I perceive henceforward the answer: the phenomenon of the other, following the guiding thread of the erotic reduction, distinguishes itself from all else in that its two aspects—intuition and signification—do not belong equally to my own egological sphere. It does seem to work the same way in all the other phenomena, where intuition (categorial, of essence, or empirical) comes to me from the exterior, to fill (in part or adequately) a signification that is found to be already given. But here, the question is not one of simple exteriority, which in the end never puts into question the lordship of my *ego,* the sole constituent in the final instance. Here, an exteriority that is otherwise originary reaches me, distinguishing itself by absolutely new characteristics.

First, exteriority is no longer accomplished with intuition, since the lover gives rise to exteriority unconditionally by his or her decision to love loving; for the amorous affective tonality, which I thus produce, remains vague, without a point of fixation; it implies and releases in me an alterity, but leaves it still undetermined—an alterity that is purely negative, an exteriority that is unlimited, yet potential, and always anonymous.

Second, exteriority, on the contrary, issues, here and here alone, from signification, which only a given other, singular and definite, can impose upon me by opposing the distance in which I must attempt neither a touch nor a siege.

Third, the exteriority of this signification, even confirmed by an adequate intuition, allows me the evidence of no object whatsoever: here transcendence no longer results from objectivity, because it does not belong to the world, nor is it offered to the least constitution; certainly it gives itself, but according to a mode that is not worldly and not objective; it gives itself beginning from itself, following a counter-intentionality.

Fourth, exteriority marks its initiative by speaking; the arising of speech, when it wants and as it wants, to whomever it wants, puts forth an authority that has no common measure with the language it puts to work, its content, its meaning, and its rules; language can become an object again, but not speech insofar as it is the speech spoken by the other, who can take it back.

In all of these characteristics, signification shows that it imposes itself upon me as having come from the other *by giving itself as capable of not giving itself.* I only receive it because it very much wants to give itself and because it arises from the ground of an elsewhere (that which I await ever since the question "Does anyone out there love me?") that I cannot even dream of producing, or provoking, or even invoking. Signification does not come upon me here in a way that is like that of all the other phenomena, from the ground of the unseen and thus from the world and from its original opening; signification, when it consents to put itself into play, issues from another world—or better, not even from a world, but from an other more exterior to me than any world, because the other, too, defines a world (or indeed, henceforward he or she is the first to do so). In the erotic phenomenon, it is not solely a question of an inversion of the relationship between intuition and signification, but rather the gift of an unconstitutable signification, unforeseeable and absolutely exterior to my lover's intuition (loving to love in advance), by an *ego* that catches me because I did not foresee it, cannot expect it, and will never comprehend it. The amorous phenomenon is not constituted beginning from the pole of the *ego* that I am; it arises of itself by crossing within itself the lover (I, who renounce the status of the autarkic *ego* and bring my intuition) and the other (she who imposes her signification by opposing her distance). The erotic phenomenon appears not just in common to her and to me, and without a unique egoic pole, but it also appears only in this crossing. *A crossed phenomenon.*

In order for such a crossed phenomenon to be accomplished, the signification that has come through counter-intentionality must not fall short of my intuition. How does this signification give itself? Surely not by an intuition in which I ought to see something real—which the other, by definition, can never be. On the contrary, the signification of the other gives itself without ever becoming an available thing, but, rather, insofar as it consents to abandon itself, insofar as it gives itself as being able not to give itself. It gives itself while saying that it gives itself, *as if* it were giving itself and *as capable of not giving itself.* The other can only give her signification of

herself by signifying to me, in speech or in silence, "Here I am, your signification." In order to signify to me this signification, a moment is nevertheless not enough, for it must fix over time my lover's vague erotic intuition. It is thus necessary that the other signify to me, "Here I am, your
signification" not only in time, but for a period of time that fixes me—thus
a time without delay, or restriction, or assignable limit. The signification
only imposes itself upon me if it gives itself without foreseeing taking itself
back, and thus gives itself in self-abandonment without condition, or return, or prescription. "Here I am!" only gives a signification to my erotic
intuition by daring to claim to give itself without holding back, without return—forever. The other thus must not only say to me, "Here I am!" in
the moment, but she must also promise it for every moment still to come.
She must not tell me the signification, she must promise it to me. The
signification, which alone allows my intuition to make the phenomenon of
the other appear to me, arises like an *oath*—or it is forever lacking.

For only this oath allows the full erotic phenomenon at last to be put
on stage: henceforward intuition, which is put forth in the immanence of
the lover who is in the situation of the radicalized reduction, is docked with
the signification that the face of the other assigns to it. In this way a fully
achieved phenomenon is constituted, one that nevertheless offers two exceptional characteristics in comparison with the majority of other phenomena. To begin with, this new type of transcendence does not confer
upon the phenomenon its fulfilling intuition, but rather its signification.
Next, what transcends the immanence of my *ego* here no longer refers back
to a region of the world, but still to an *ego,* that of a supposed other; this
phenomenon without equivalent no longer plays between an *ego* and the
world, but between two *egos* outside of the world. Should we still even
speak of *a* phenomenon? What does it manifest, if I not only do not master the signification (the noematic face), but two *egos* frame it and confer
upon it two distinct intuitions, so to speak (two competing noeses)? Formally, a single response seems possible: neither of the two *egos* can see the
other in the strict sense of receiving its intuition as that of a phenomenon
of the world, in order to fill the signification that it would have first fixed—
as if the other would intuitively confirm the intentional aim that I would
have already taken at her beforehand and, eventually, without her; each *ego*
must here attempt to fix its erotic intuition, immanent and deployed in advance, upon a signification received from the other. The common erotic
phenomenon will thus not consist of a new visible or a common spectacle:
since two intuitions of opposed and irreducible origin enter into play, there

will appear to each of these two *ego*s a different phenomenon, filled with a different intuition and presenting another visible (precisely, the visible *ego,* which inverts the seeing *ego*).

The common phenomenon, instead, will consist in the unique signification, to which two intuitions come to moor themselves—because each *ego* assures the other, by oath, with a unique signification, "Here I am!" Of course, the other does not appear to me as an immediately visible spectacle (she would thus regress to the rank of an object); rather, she appears to me insofar as she lends herself to the function of a signification, which fixes and finally secures my erotic intuition. And reciprocally, I only appear to an eventual other by lending myself to the function of signification, which will assign what has up to that point been a vague erotic intuition to a fixed phenomenal site. The two *ego*s are accomplished as lovers, and mutually allow their respective phenomena to appear, not of course according to an imaginary and fusional logic—by exchanging or sharing a common intuition—which would abolish the distance between them, but by assuring one another reciprocally of a signification come from elsewhere—by lending themselves to the play of a crossed exchange of significations—thus firmly consecrating the distance within them.

Must we still speak of a common phenomenon, or, rather, of two distinct phenomena? Neither: we speak of a *crossed phenomenon,* with a double entry—two intuitions fixed by a single signification. One signification, and not two; for each of the two *ego*s lends itself to the same operation and gives itself as one and the same signification, "Here I am!" In effect, no *ego* claims to describe itself empirically like a *me* endowed with such and such properties, but means to reduce itself to the pure assertion "Here I am!" Each of the *ego*s assures the other of the same and unique signification—that which my immanent erotic intuition requires and to which I lend myself by assuring in an oath, "Here I am!" The two *ego*s do not join together in a common, directly visible intuition, but rather in a common signification that is indirectly put into phenomenality by two irreducible intuitions. A single phenomenon, because a single signification; yet a phenomenon that nonetheless has a double entry, because manifested according to two intuitions.

The lover thus does see the unique phenomenon, which he loves and which loves him, by the grace of this oath.

Concerning the Flesh, and Its Arousal

§ 22. Individuality

I the lover see a unique phenomenon that I love and which loves me, because I share its unique signification with the other, so that each of us fulfills the equal and common "Here I am!" of an intuition, which remains proper and unsubstitutable to each of us—the very act of the oath, which we each perform in the first person. I promise exactly what the other promises me, and our two oaths superimpose upon one another perfectly, becoming one. Indeed, they are able to corroborate and merge with one another exactly, without becoming blurred or confused with one another, because their unique signification remains purely formal: it consists only of the position or rather of the exposition of the *ego,* which places itself at the disposition of the other—a sort of passage from the nominative to the vocative in the first person, wherein I let myself be summoned by the other, who appears from that point as the dative, to which I assign myself. In pronouncing the words "Here I am!" I pass from the status of the nominative *ego* to the status of he who lets himself be called and summoned in the vocative ("Me? I am here, *hic*"); or rather, I expose myself henceforward to your point of view, different from my own, and my place is defined in relation to yours ("I am there, *illic*"). But above all I recognize the privilege of the other, envisaged now as the pole of my exposure and my point of reference; I thus acknowledge her as the one to relate myself to—the attributee of my oath, originarily in the dative. Originarily indicates that I am no longer first as an *ego,* who would take the other into account after that fact, but that I rise up directly as a lover out of balance before the one who advances, a primeval "Here I am!"—while the other no longer appears as the object aimed at by my intentionality, but imposes herself as the primeval (dative) addressee of my exposure. She and I are born, or even reborn (the erotic reduction abolishes a world and creates a love affair) as lover and beloved—and vice versa, for she too endures the same conversion.

But there is a difficulty. It doesn't lie in the sharing of the amorous phenomenon, for the fact that two intuitions corroborate a single signification attests precisely to the privilege of such a phenomenon: the rendering visible of the communion of a duality. Instead, the difficulty lies in their common signification, which remains completely indeterminate; indeed, it even must remain so, because it only becomes common insofar as it is formal, or in fact empty: "Here I am!" as such signifies nothing and even has no meaning, for as long as no actor performs it; beginning only with this act will a real "me" fix in a real "here" a statement heretofore without hearth or home. "Here I am!" states nothing in itself, but has value as a simple deictic, applicable to everyone and implying nothing; it depends upon the performance of a possible lover and, even in this case, it remains a simple expression that is only occasionally signative. Without the occasion of an actual lover, "Here I am!" expresses no signification. Consequently, the sharing of it between the lover and the beloved (me and the other) becomes problematic: we only agree so perfectly with one another on this signification because it remains not only occasional, but essentially empty, abstracted from all formulable content. In saying "Here I am!" to another, I tell her nothing, even if I eventually ensure her of something— of my person. And any other lover could just as well perform the same expression—ensuring another of one's person—without expressing any other signification than I do. The abstraction of the pure "Here I am!" matches with its universality and falls back into the aporia of every categorical imperative—"Act in such a way that the maxim of your will could at the same time always serve as the principle of a universal law": anyone can and must perform it for every action, precisely because it says nothing, to anyone. Thus, my lover's oath only coincides exactly with the oath of another because it signifies nothing in itself and thus applies to each and everyone.

The strength of this objection lies in the supposed abstract and empty character of the expression "Here I am !" a simple deictic that would only have a borrowed or occasional signification when an *ego* performs it, supposing that a universal and transcendental *ego* performs anything at all. But then again, if the oath-giving lover were not confused with the transcendental and universal *ego,* this very objection would fall apart completely. Now, not only is the lover not to be confused with the *ego* (neither empirical nor transcendental), but he or she openly opposes him- or herself to the *ego:* "Here I am!" puts the lover rather than any such *ego* into play, insofar as the lover is radically individualized and unsubstitutable. Without here taking up again all of the previous analyses, it will be enough, in order to reestablish a full-fledged signification in the words "Here I am!" to establish the radical individuation of the one—that is, the lover—who says them.

First, the lover is individualized by *desire,* or rather by the desire that is *his* and no one else's. Indeed, unless it merely obeys natural and physiological necessities (in which case we would be speaking of a simple need), desire cannot be universalized so that it applies to me and to anybody else; nothing belongs to me more than that which I desire, for *that* is what I lack; that which I lack defines me more intimately than everything that I possess, for what I possess remains exterior to me and what I lack inhabits me; such that I can exchange what I possess, but not the lack that possesses my heart. And, more than anything, the lover only desires the one that he has decided to desire, or rather who decided him, the lover, to desire; for desire, doubtless because it rests upon the lack of the desired, declares itself all the more powerfully when it bursts out without argument, indeed without reason; it is born in the lover just this side of explanations and of justifications, because it rises up out of lack itself, through a work of the negative and according to the indispensable absence of what it desires. Born of the pure lack of the other, the lover's desire affects him without his truly knowing why, nor through whom—and that is what individualizes him deep down. I become myself and recognize myself in my singularity when I discover and finally admit the one that I desire; that one alone shows me my most secret center—that which I lacked and still lack, that of which the clear absence focused for a long time my obscure presence to myself. My desire speaks me to myself by showing me what arouses me. This moment, in which desire fixes me in myself by settling my gaze upon that particular other, is recognized without fault—it is the moment in which, discovering a face, a voice, or a silhouette, I confess *in petto* that "this time, this one's for me"; in the sense in which I could say such a thing to myself when finally a race seems winnable, or just before playing a dirty trick (throwing a punch, taking a shot); at this moment, I realize that I am going to become, or I am becoming—no, that I have already become the lover of this other; at this instant this other becomes for me a personal affair and appears to me different from all the others, reserved for me and me for her; the other destines me for her and individualizes me through her; she assigns me to myself by assigning me to her. I recognize this instant by an already mentioned indication (§ 19): it is the instant in which I tell myself that I am *not yet* in love, that I am still the master of my desire, that I am going because I want to, and other such lies that I do not truly believe. At this instant, in which it is precisely too late, in which it has already happened, in which I am made by the other and by my desire—I am no longer the same, and thus I am, at last, myself, individualized beyond the point of return.

Next, the lover is individualized by *eternity* or, at least, by the desire for eternity. Let us consider a fact of experience. At the moment of attempting to utter an almost inexpressible (§ 19) "I love you," either squarely and with eyes wide open, or with arms embracing the other and eyes at the point of closing under the force of desire, the lover just as much as the beloved will have to have, even if only for an instant and after a cumbersome series of "other times," the conviction or at least the appearance, or indeed the voluntary illusion of the conviction, that, this time, it will be for good, that this time this will be for good and forever. At the moment of loving, the lover can only believe what he or she says and does under a certain aspect of eternity. Or, more exactly, under an instantaneous eternity, without the promise that it will last, but nevertheless an eternity of intention. The lover just as much as the beloved needs the possible conviction that he or she loves this time forever, irreversibly, once and for all. For the lover, making love implies irreversibility by definition (just as in metaphysics the essence of God implies his existence).

This is confirmed *a contrario*: to say "I love you for a moment, provisionally" means "I don't love you at all" and accomplishes only a performative contradiction. Making love for a time is the same as not making love, or as not playing the lover. Of course I can very well say "I love you" while clearly doubting to be able (and doubting to want to be able) to love forever, indeed with the quasi-certainty of failing before long; but I can never say it without maintaining at least a tiny possibility (which is simply to say a possibility) that this time I will love forever, once and for all. Without this possibility, as slight as one might want, not only could I not psychologically imagine myself making love, and even less actually do it, but, by right, I will condemn myself to lying. And this lie will not only deceive the other (who perhaps has no illusions and does not ask for so much); above all it deprives each of us from making love. We will do a lot of sweet-talking and, if all goes well (or badly), copulate, but we will not, for all of that, make love. For neither of us will accomplish the erotic reduction, nor reach the condition of the lover. The very question of love will disappear. On the contrary, if a possibility of eternity, as attenuated as you like, remains, even the eventual disappearance of "I love you" will not abolish what was once accomplished—we have made love as lovers. And it will remain forever that this was actually one time an erotic reduction, validated by an oath. Regret, nostalgia, and the goodwill of memory draw their legitimacy and their dignity from the fact that I was truly able to say (perhaps without accomplishing it, but truly nevertheless), "I love you once and for all." The promise of eternity protects even the lovers who could not hold to it, and assures them once and for all the rank of lovers.

Thus the oath is accomplished in every way, in its success as much as in its failure. What was said will never be able not to have been said. Whence there follows the individuation of the lover. First because he or she asked for it by claiming to run the risk of loving once and for all; by attempting, if only for an instant, to make love once and for all, I have already accomplished this temporal unicity, I have separated the time that does not pass from the time that passes, I have, in time, erected the irremediable; what once was said once and for all cannot be undone or denied. In time, I have marked, if only for a time, an eternal moment, which belongs only to me, which came about only through and for me, and, thus, which individualizes me once and for all. Once and for all—to have said it is sufficient to wound me with a wound that marks me forever and delivers me to myself.

The lover is individualized, finally, by *passivity*. This passivity in fact sums up all the impact that the other exerts upon me, the lover; an impact from which I receive not only what the other gives me, but also myself, who receives it. As lover, I allow myself to be struck by the seal of that which comes upon me, to the point that, in receiving it as the mark of the other, I also receive myself. I do not individualize myself by self-affirmation or -reflection, but by proxy—by the care that the other takes with me in affecting me and allowing me to be born of this very affect. As lover, I thus individualize myself under the power of a triple passivity, the three impacts of which add to and deepen one another. The first passivity is clear: the oath (the signification of the amorous phenomenon) makes me depend upon the other. In effect, only her response, "Here I am!" validates my own "Here I am!"; for my advance to utter it first and without assurance would remain a vague, undecided impulse mired in my own sphere, if the other did not ratify it as her signification, too, and thus as our common signification. The signification of my amorous phenomenon only truly befalls me if I receive it; otherwise it would still derive from me—in advance, yes, but from me alone. Thus I appear to myself as lover only if my very advance is received from the most intimate exteriority.

This first shock overlays a second, older passivity: the advance itself. For precisely because the advance would not yet open to me the phenomenon of the other, whose signification was still lacking, it would at least open the floodgates of intuition: I loved, already, with an intuition still without reference, yet poured out nevertheless. Sustained by the decision to love as if I could, that is to say by the naked assurance of loving to love, this intuition decidedly exposed me to what I did not know, even while knowing certainly that it did not belong to me. My erotic intuition—loving to love, loving *as if*—could very well have no fixed intentionality, nonetheless it deployed an actual intentionality, albeit a blind one. To love without knowing whom I love: this remains a loving and a knowing that I love. This knowledge without anything known or seen already advanced toward the other under the influence of her absence. This advance sets in motion an intuition all the more radically passive, in that, while it is mine and autonomous, it unfolds in me without me—I decide to be in love and, already too late, find myself amorous without knowing or mastering anything more. I am caught in my own game—with a detachment that is all the more alienating in that I do not even know who, or what signification, or what face overtakes me, or above all if an oath will ever unveil the actuality of an other. The intuition affects me with a disarming alterity, which comes to me still without any other.

This more obscure passivity imposes another, final passivity: the taking of a risk. The advance made me pass from the question "Does anyone love me?" to the question "Can I love first?"; no one can make this reversal for me, I cannot make my decision about it through an intervening person, and I cannot confer upon someone else the power to accomplish it for me; otherwise he or she would be the lover, not me. The advance is made in the first person, or it is not made; it thus reveals me to myself because it makes me risk myself. This risk consists in ridding myself of the activity of an *ego,* which would pose itself through its self-identity, its self-representation, its demand to love itself or to make itself loved for itself, so as to play the lover without guarantee of return: to love without knowing oneself loved, to make oneself recognized without oneself knowing anything. The advance makes me advance into open terrain without reciprocity; and definitively, for, just as the intuition will remain mine and solitary (to love loving, to decide to love *as if*), so my oath will remain mine, and thus solitary; doubtless an other's oath could validate my own; certainly these oaths will cross, will add to one another and, at best, will coincide, but they will not balance or compensate one another, and will not reimburse our advances. The oaths only have the ambition to prolong for as long as possible our forward-tending disequilibrium. The most assured love remains the most risky, with a risk assured just as it was taken—with a common accord. This shared passivity individualizes us like two castaways, holding on to the same piece of debris, treading water.

From this moment forward, I know who loves in me—the one to whom it happens in the first person and once and for all. I will love, and eventually I will be loved, in the measure that I recognize this passivity from its origins and in the measure that, far from resisting it, I accompany it with the least of my movements.

§ 23. My Flesh, and the Other's

Passivity makes me, insofar as it makes me become a lover. But how does it come about, if we are speaking of passivity in the customary sense—the absence or the inverse of activity? For my passivity as lover evidently has nothing in common with the inertia of the nonreactive mineral that feels nothing; nor even with the passivity of the animate, which only reacts to programmed arousals, because it poorly feels. At issue here must be a completely other, new sort of passivity, which, passing beyond organic, physiological, and even perceptive necessities, invests all that I am, insofar as I am the only one able to love (and thus also to hate).

Such a passivity clearly comes under the phenomenon of the flesh (§ 7). For only the flesh, or rather *my* flesh—I do not have flesh, I am my flesh and it coincides absolutely with me—assigns me to myself and delivers me as such in my radically received individuality. It comes about (more precisely, I come about through the guiding thread of my flesh) by virtue of its two privileges, which could seem at first to contradict one another, and of which, nevertheless, it will be necessary to establish the coherence. As flesh, I take on a body in the world; I become sufficiently exposed so that the things of the world have an advantage over me, such that they make me feel, experience, and even suffer their dominance and their presence. Not that I take a place among the things of the world, taking my position there as just one more thing, wedged in among others and simply part of the crowd; I do not insert myself among the army of things, I expose myself, since I face them; I do not become so much a thing of the world as I allow the things of the world the right to affect me and to reduce me to my passivity. But which passivity? Certainly not that of things—which in any case have no access to passivity: how could inert things affect me and act upon me? How could things without flesh give rise to flesh in me, which they absolutely lack?

Henceforward, everything is overturned: we must admit as a principle that things, as bodies, cannot affect me, since, even in movement and in the play of forces, they remain entirely inert and insensible. Fire burns and heats nothing—if not me, who alone feels it; water envelopes and cools nothing, if not me, who alone feels it; earth upholds and buries nothing, if not me, who alone experiences it; air awakens and lifts nothing other than me, who alone gives myself up to it. In fact, the things of the world quite simply do not affect me such as they are, nor do they make me feel anything about them in themselves—for the simple and radical reason that they do not feel themselves or experience anything as their action. Their supposed activity only makes itself felt if (and only if) their forces and movements, instead of playing with other things equally inert and insensible, bear upon a body that is particular, unique, and without common measure with them—my own. For my body, which it is quite necessary to call physical because it is nakedly exposed to the things of nature, enjoys above all the exceptional privilege of feeling them, while they never feel anything at all, especially themselves. These things, active as they may be, remain inert—in the sense that an inert body is not transformed, does not metabolize, does not explode. Only my body, because (or while) it is exposed physically to things, does not remain inert like them, but feels them. It feels them because this body, and it alone among all bodies, has the status of flesh. As flesh, it feels what is not it and, on this condition alone, the force, the impetus, in short the presence of what can affect it. The things of the world can very well act upon one another, but they cannot touch themselves, or destroy themselves, or engender themselves, or affect themselves, because none of them feels any other. Only flesh feels that which differs from it. It alone touches, approaches and moves away from something other, suffers from or enjoys it, is affected by and responds to it, because it alone feels. The claimed action of things upon me would never appear without this privilege of allowing myself to be affected, and thus never without my sensibility, without my flesh. In short, things do not act upon me, for their very action results first from my passivity, which renders them originarily possible. My passivity provokes their activity, not the inverse.

My flesh thus offers the only physical body that has the privilege of feeling another thing (body) than itself.

How do we conceive of this unheard-of privilege? Against what the natural attitude, with its good sense, suggests, I would feel nothing other (than myself) if I could not first feel myself, with an undertow more original than the wave that seems to result, but which, in fact, announces the undertow and, at once, allows itself to be sucked in by it: auto-affection alone makes possible hetero-affection. I only feel the things of the world because, first, I experience myself, within myself. The sense of touch illustrates this turnaround in an exemplary way, because my hand, which alone can touch another thing (and not merely enter into contact with it), only touches it precisely because it feels that it touches it; and it only feels that it touches it by feeling itself touch it, that is, by feeling itself at the same time as it feels what it feels. At once, my hand feels, with a single movement of thought, the thing and itself feeling that thing; and, if it opposes one of its fingers to the others, it winds up feeling its flesh feeling its own flesh feeling. There is no flesh in the world (indeed, the world is defined by its radical lack of flesh), but there is no world without flesh that feels it— a single flesh, my own. My flesh surrounds, covers, protects and opens the world—not the reverse. The more my flesh feels, and thus feels itself, the more the world is opened. The interiority of the flesh conditions the exteriority of the world, rather than opposing it, because auto-affection alone makes possible hetero-affection, which grows to its measure. Thus does my passivity lay itself out, to the rhythm of an activity that is more secret and original than all the movements and impetuses of inert bodies. Thus is my individuation accomplished, to the measure of what my flesh feels, which tells the story of the world according to the prism and the historicity of its own self-affection. I feel the world depending on whether I feel myself, and it blooms following from my individualization of myself in the memory of my affections. Thus I gain access to my incommensurable, peerless passivity.

Nevertheless, is this reconsidered passivity enough to define the lover in me? No, because it still only plays with inert things, or with my flesh itself. The lover, in contrast, is properly born through and for the other, in front of whom I promise, "Here I am!" and who promptly replies in kind. Thus it is necessary now to describe how my flesh can feel the flesh of the other, and above all how I feel myself. The difficulty no longer bears upon the sensation of alterity: we already know, through the experience of my flesh in the world, that hetero-affection goes hand in hand with auto-affection and that, far from running counter to one another, they grow in concert. The true difficulty resides in the access of my flesh no longer to other inert and insensible things of the world, but to another flesh, wherein the other feels, because he feels himself there. How will I ever be able to feel not just something rendered sensible through my flesh, but the feeling of this other flesh, which is in no way a thing but instead a self experiencing itself? In principle, I at least know this: I will never be able to feel this feeling itself directly *in* my own flesh; for, if I felt it through a fusion of some sort, I would immediately reduce this feeling to the rank of a simple sense datum among others, and thus of a thing of the world, and I would miss the flesh as such; or, if by an absurd hypothesis (a communication of properties), I felt this rare feeling, in which the other feels himself, I would identify myself absolutely with him and his flesh would intermingle with mine, and thus he would disappear as other. These two impasses set aside, what may I hope to feel of another flesh? What path do I follow to feel the flesh in which the other feels himself or herself? In fact, perhaps I have not yet measured all that my flesh is capable of; for, up to this moment, I have only thought and experienced my originary feeling and feeling of feeling in the horizon of perception, in which it is fitting to experience the things of the world. But, as soon as it is a matter of feeling, and feeling in my flesh not just things, but another flesh, there is no longer any thing to perceive, and the flesh can expose itself without translation, immediately to a flesh. And the flesh that exposes itself to another flesh, without a thing, without a being, without anything as intermediary, shows itself naked—the nude-to-nude encounter of one flesh with another. This modification of the flesh, which passes from its perceptive function to its nude phenomenality, eroticizes my flesh and thus radicalizes the erotic reduction.

How does the flesh strip itself naked? The question is first posed, clearly, in front of the flesh of the other—I can only desire a phenomenon that I can see, and I can only see another flesh, a flesh other than my own (which I in fact can never see). But the difficulty emerges right away: in seeing another flesh, I once again see something, for instance a physical body, a being, often already an object. The simple fact of denuding it—of removing the last piece of clothing, like the last screen—changes nothing; on the contrary, the final surface (the skin) can immediately become once again the surface of an object, which annuls all phenomenality of the flesh. Thus medical nudity, far from manifesting me as flesh, re-transforms me into an object of examination, measurable under every angle, diagnosable like a physical machine, a chemical metabolism, an economic consumer, etc.; stripped before the draft board or for a clinical examination, not only do I not appear as flesh, but I appear more than ever as an object. And surgery in no way strips me naked, either, but instead uncovers new visible layers, which, moreover, become less and less visible as one plunges deeper into the physical body. That the remaining object sometimes elicits my desire changes nothing; on the contrary, the evident object of desire (for nothing hollows itself out more, in order to expose itself with less reserve) goes back up entirely to the surface of the visible, where the things of the world are piled; it thus renounces definitively the most secret depths of the feeling of self. Therefore, in order to remain the object of desire, the object strives maliciously not to strip itself too much, or too quickly—for the stripping nude destroys what is desirable in it, because the stripping nude transforms it into a simple object; in fact, the object can very well possess itself, consume itself, allow itself to be destroyed, but it cannot (at least not for very long) make itself be desired—the object does not hold the distance of desire. Desire can only kill the other, who would have the weakness or the imprudence to allow him- or herself to be made an object. The other thus delays his or her placement in the rank of objects: he or she remains covered in order to delay his or her death. But in the end, when the object appears, the flesh sinks into the darkness.

If the denuding of the flesh is not equivalent to the uncovering of the object, but is rather opposed to it, then eroticization does not proceed from denuding, even if it sometimes allows it; whence comes the paradox that eroticization (provoking the desire of the other) consists most often in showing that one does not show—for the flesh distinguishes itself from the body precisely in that it cannot and must not appear on an equal footing with objects, on the same stage as the things of the world. It is only phenomenalized by escaping from view, by refraining from appearing. Nevertheless, it is not a matter of playing with the gaze, or of exciting attention by frustrating it, in order to show more by showing less—the little game of seduction, which would be more suitable to the truth of philosophy. (We should not be scandalized by the relationship, for in the end prudish truth, which says yes and no, which uncovers itself and covers up again, shares with the sexual parade the fact that both play upon the world's raw stage, in the open, without any retreat, on the forestage without any wings.) It is a matter of accepting a determinant phenomenological principle: by definition, no flesh can appear as a body; or, more radically, if one understands this appearing in the simple sense of offering itself naked to the gaze, it is only fitting for a body and never for a flesh, precisely because that which gives the flesh its privilege—the capacity to feel and feel itself feeling—cannot appear directly under any light. And this impossibility of all flesh to make itself seen is all the more useful for a flesh that does not belong to me, for the flesh of the other, this other flesh only ever supposed, and never experienced, by me. The aporia of the access to the other is thus redoubled by a second aporia, at least as formidable—the invisibility of all flesh.

But, if the other's flesh (like all flesh) cannot fall under the gaze, because it must not be seen, how will it be phenomenalized? Must we resign ourselves to exclude it from play, as metaphysics does? And yet the other's flesh is truly phenomenalized, but under a unique mode that must be admitted: it is phenomenalized without, however, making itself seen, by allowing itself simply and radically to be felt. By allowing itself to be felt in such a way, of course, that I feel that I am feeling it (by the definition of my flesh), but also that I feel that it feels me (by the definition of the other); and what, then, does this flesh of the other feel, if not that I feel it and even that I feel it feel me? And, at the end of this interlacing, what do our two fleshes feel, if not each the feeling of the feeling of the other? The confusion of feelings, which I am no longer able to untangle when (like now) I want to tell them, does not put me in check—because I am only attempting to phenomenalize the confusion of two fleshes and of their respective feelings, which are abolished in one another without any consideration. Nevertheless, how can I distinguish between the feeling of a thing of the world and the feeling of a flesh? Let's describe them. Normally, when my flesh (my hand, but also every other member) feels a body, it experiences itself as an avatar of my body of flesh exposed to bodies of the world (which are bereft of flesh); my flesh identifies them as simple physical bodies precisely in that they resist it by virtue of their spatiality, and thus their impenetrability (hardness or elasticity make no difference, because in the end compression resists just as well, indeed better). Bodies thus declare themselves by resisting my flesh; they affect my flesh by refusing to allow it access to the space that they occupy and the extension wherein their forces are deployed. Each body appears as a physical body bereft of flesh, because it refuses access to it—it resists, defends itself, repels. I experience bodies (and not a flesh), because bodies expel me from their space and I experience myself as flesh (and not as a physical body) because I cannot resist against this resistance; I beat a retreat, withdraw, and hunker down within myself, in short I undergo, suffer, and experience myself precisely as *my* flesh faced with bodies.

From this point forward, everything becomes clearer and I know how to distinguish *another* flesh from a body. For if there is ever an other flesh, and thus an other's flesh, it must by definition behave the opposite of physical bodies, which is to say, like my own flesh behaves as opposed to them—by not resisting, by withdrawing, by allowing itself to be stripped of its impenetrability, by suffering being penetrated. There where I feel that something *puts up no resistance to me,* and that, far from turning me back into myself and thus reducing me, this something withdraws, effaces itself and makes room for me, in short that this something opens itself, I know that I am dealing with flesh—or better, with a flesh other than my own, the flesh of an other. On the contrary, I remain in the world—and I recognize the fact according to this criteria—for as long as someone resists against me and I must defend a free space to occupy (a dwelling) among other spaces that are already occupied, unavailable, and thus impenetrable. Everywhere in the world, I touch walls, limits, and borders; not only am I not *in relation to* the world as an openness, but I am *in* the world as though in the midst of enclosures, of private properties, of reserves that are off-limits; I do not open the world from the outset, but always find myself there penned in, assigned, or even forbidden to stay. The world does not receive me in a wide-open way—it always begins by stopping me. My flesh thus causes me to experience that I do not comprehend the world, but, rather, that I am comprehended there: I am, according to being, precisely insofar as comprehended. Being probably only consists in this comprehension, which limits me, a horizon in the strict sense, a horizon by definition finite. Being finitizes me according to its essential finitude. It holds me and restrains me. In order to get myself out and away, it is necessary that my flesh enter into commerce with another flesh, in and through which I will stretch myself out for the first time (in any case, am I not born into and of flesh, where I stretched myself *before* entering into the least world?). I can only free myself and become myself by touching another flesh, as one touches land at a port, because only another flesh can make room for me, welcome me, and not turn me away or resist me—that is, comply with my flesh and reveal it to me by providing it a place. And where would the other flesh make a place for mine, if not *within itself*? Since the world makes no room, another flesh must do it for me—by squeezing in for me, by allowing me to come in, by letting itself be penetrated. I feel, all at once, both my flesh and the other flesh, by feeling that it cannot resist against me, that it wants not to resist me, that it takes me in its place without comprehending me there, that it puts me in its place—places me in its place—by letting me invade it, without defending itself. By entering into the flesh of the other, I exit the world and I become flesh in her flesh, flesh *of* her flesh.

The other gives me to myself for the first time, because she takes the initiative to give me my own flesh for the first time. She awakens me, because she eroticizes me. Whence follow the definitions of pleasure and pain, which are valid for *every* encounter of one flesh by another (§ 35). By pleasure, we understand my reception by the other's flesh, such that it gives me my own flesh; this pleasure augments as I receive further my flesh from the flesh of the other and as my flesh is augmented by this nonresistance; reciprocally, passivity grows according to the augmentation; or, what amounts to the same thing, passivity grows in proportion as the augmentation fills it. In fact, passivity and augmentation define for the same reason, and simultaneously, the two fleshes. Contrary to the naïve evidence of metaphysics, the augmentation of a flesh is not made through its activity to the detriment of the other's activity, but through their double passivity. For the growth of one is made as the passivity of the other provokes it; and the passivity of the one is deepened as the augmentation of the other allows. Augmentation does not come actively from itself, but passively from the nonresistance of another passivity, more powerful than every activity. In effect, passivity only grows because it very much wants, with all its flesh, not to resist and thus to face another flesh, which it embraces with its own growth. Inversely, by pain, we understand the resistance of the other's flesh to my own (or even the resistance of mine to hers), such that it contests or refuses my own flesh; this pain augments as my flesh diminishes, until my flesh withdraws into a corporeity that is spatially defined or closed-up, and which no longer gives access to anything or anyone. For pain deprives me of my flesh, just as pleasure gives it to me, since my flesh when it is suffering not only retracts, but must learn to resist against what resists it; and so it becomes hardened; contaminated by the resistance of the other body, what was once flesh makes itself into a body, a heart of stone, a tough body, adapted for bodily combat with the world. My flesh vanishes when its unique condition of possibility, the flesh of the other, disappears. And the other's flesh fades away when my own is blurred.

One thus conceives of the insufficiency of the all-too-common theme of the caress, superficial in every sense. The eroticization that gives rise to the flesh does not result from a touch that is simply less possessive, groping, or predatory than another. It is not sufficient to limit the contiguity of two physical bodies to a contact, as tenuous as one might like, in order to make two fleshes arise; we would still remain in the world, as if upon an improbable frontier zone, between that which belongs to the world and that which no longer belongs to it. Even if only one flesh touches a body (though no body ever touches another body), still one flesh never touches another flesh, because the one immediately draws back and fades away before the other, not even resisting enough to allow for an impact—except that of feeling itself feel the other feel, on this side of space. If one absolutely must speak of a caress, it would be necessary to free it of all contact, so as to banish from it all worldly spatiality, and thus think it beginning from what renders it possible—the indistinction between my flesh's feeling and its feeling itself feeling, for my flesh feels not only reciprocal feeling, but also the other flesh's feeling of itself. As this feeling no longer belongs at all to the world, and even makes me leave it, my own flesh no longer touches anything, because the flesh of the other does not constitute something; my own flesh does not experience this other flesh as the contiguous resistance of a thing, but discovers it as that which, on the contrary, does not resist it, and, thus, it discovers that it can stretch out there and grow. The caress, then, would never touch and would never come into contact with anything (like one comes into contact with an enemy), because the flesh of the other only allows itself to be felt as the imperceptible retreat of that which does not want to resist—of that which only delivers itself through the deliverance that it accords to the growth of my own flesh. Its growth or, what amounts to the same thing (what is equivalent to and, above all, what responds to it), its passivity deepened under the growth of the other flesh. It is no longer a question of the sense of touch, or of any other sense—because I see by feeling, just like I feel with a look, or by hearing, or even by taste—but instead of a radicalized incarnation.

Thus, the still abstract decision to make *as if* I loved first and to receive the signification of the other in the common "Here I am!" of the oath is accomplished in the unique eroticization of each flesh by the other. The flesh that henceforward has been thoroughly eroticized, beyond what it can and even what it cannot do, accomplishes the lover in one who is gifted—one who receives himself from what he receives, and who gives what he does not have.

§ 24. Eroticization as Far as the Face

From that point forward, the other gives me what she does not have—my very flesh. And I give her what I do not have—her very flesh. My very own flesh (it makes me become myself, which I was unaware of before then) comes upon me and augments in the measure in which the flesh of the other provokes it. Each discovers him- or herself the depository of what is most intimate of the other. This inadequacy, where I only know as mine what comes upon me from out there, definitively disqualifies every naïve (metaphysical) critique of the inadequacy of my idea of the other; for, far from alienating me, only this erotic inadequacy allows me to accede to myself, and passivity is no longer opposed to activity, in my flesh or in the other's flesh: the flesh only lives to intermingle the two. Except if we interpret our flesh as two impenetrable bodies and our thought as two contiguous representations, it seems evident that I do not become myself by activating myself to possess more extension, and thus more body around myself, but by becoming my flesh, by eroticizing myself through the flesh of the other, and thus *not* by possessing myself, but by letting myself be (dis)possessed. One can only possess a body (one's own, or another contiguous body, it doesn't matter), and possession closes access to the flesh. No flesh is possessed, above all with an adequate idea; first of all, because no flesh can ever be seen; and next, because flesh is experienced precisely as an inadequacy, the happy inadequacy of growth.

Thus the other appears with the rank of an authentic phenomenon, but according to the phenomenality of his or her flesh—not directly (like a thing or an object), but indirectly, and yet all the more immediately, as the one who phenomenalizes me as my flesh. The difficulty of the phenomenon of the other thus lies not in its supposed distancing, poverty, or transcendence; it lies on the contrary in its absolute immanence: the other appears in the very measure in which she gives me my own flesh, which opens out like the screen upon which hers is projected; her own phenomenalization is played out in her taking flesh; reciprocally, my taking flesh renders manifest her emplacement in glory. Each of us becomes the phenomenon of the other, by each becoming flesh through one another. This reciprocity does not go beyond the oath; it depends upon it, and completes it. It depends upon it because, without the oath, neither the other nor I could rationally assume the crossing of our two fleshes, each appearing not in itself, but in the other and uniquely in the other. It completes it because without this shared eroticization, the common oath would remain an abstract linguistic performance, which would not phenomenalize itself anywhere and would not individualize me any more than anyone else (§ 23). And eroticization, no more than the oath, cannot be understood as a fact: it has to do neither with a thing, nor with a visible spectacle. Strictly speaking, there is never anything erotic to see—what is seen immediately becomes once again a ridiculous or obscene object; in order for the stage to remain erotic, it is not necessary to see it, but to be aroused by it, that is to say, whether we like it or not, to be implicated in it, to abandon ourselves there and thus to allow ourselves to become flesh. It has nothing to do with a fact, either, because one can never objectivize the eroticization of flesh; for, following the rigor of the terms, eroticization only offers indices of itself, which one must believe or not; one may always cheat by pretending to feel what one does not experience, or even (less easily) that one does not experience what one nevertheless very much feels. It has nothing to do with a fact, but rather with a process toward an accomplishment, or with a disposition for an act, comparable in this way to the phenomenological reduction, which the erotic reduction redoubles and annuls.

At least three negative characteristics follow. First, every static opposition between activity and passivity becomes outmoded: I activate myself even insofar as I admit that I am affected, I allow myself to be affected the more that I give in to my desire; the other affects me even insofar as she lets me experience her passivity. Even if one may say that passivity activates itself and that activity lets itself go, by right these two terms lose all pertinence as soon as one knows that flesh experiences itself by feeling that nothing resists it, and that it is aroused less by the abandon felt than by its own unrestrained impetus. As surprising as it may appear, in the situation of eroticization no one possesses anyone, or finds him- or herself possessed, for no flesh as flesh dominates or finds itself dominated, leads or follows.

Second, the process of eroticization admits neither interruption nor limit, since it aims at everything being made flesh in me as in the other, so that nothing of us any longer obeys the phenomenality of bodies or of the world. Pleasure consists (but, we have seen, it hardly consists) only in experiencing my taking flesh. Thus one cannot privilege any particular sense as the better operative of eroticization: all the senses participate in one way or another, and their fusion alone allows the conception of what philosophy calls common sense; if it were necessary to distinguish one, we would rather stigmatize the impropriety of sight, almost inevitably prone to objectivization. Consequently, neither could one privilege certain organs: there are no erotic organs, only sexual organs. First of all, this is because these organs belong to the physical body, not the flesh; next, these organs merely implement sexuality, which only very partially covers eroticization; and last, these are organs of reproduction, which, as such, do not as yet (§ 39) have to do with the phenomenon of the other. That these organs play a privileged role in the process of eroticization can hardly be disputed, but also proves nothing; of themselves they do not provoke eroticization, which often perfectly outlives their failing, or even their use (§ 35); conversely, their implementation depends most of the time upon eroticization. One may ask whether my entire body is sexed, but one cannot doubt that my entire flesh can, and thus must, be eroticized. Third, contrary to what commerce repeats constantly, auto-eroticization has no meaning, nor the least actuality, any more than does an auto-arousal: always, if only through fantasy and imagination, it is necessary that another give me my own flesh that, nevertheless, she does not have, and which I, who become that flesh, nevertheless cannot give to myself. I affect myself without exception, in my own flesh, through the other: it is only a question of distinguishing degrees, according to whether I imagine her in her real presence or not, by knowing her or not, her recognizing me or not, etc. But in every case, the absent one remains ever present, with an irreducible and indispensable alterity, even when the alterity remains simply fantasized.

Thus it is a process without end or assignable limit. The flesh never stops submerging the body. If nothing of me must remain outside of the flesh, my flesh must take into its account all that the world and the mirror had attributed to me as a body belonging to me; I must take flesh integrally in order to retake possession of myself. The first stage of eroticization accomplishes it, transcribing this body, where space claims to contain me and where the world can still afflict me, into a flesh, which lets me become myself without resistance; in short, the first stage substitutes for the body that I have (as an assigned or secondary residence, almost in spite of myself) my flesh, where I feel enjoyment (and suffer) in person; it augments me in the advance, as the erotic reduction's lover. But this first stage results, as we have already seen, from a second, by right more originary, stage: my eroticization (my taking flesh) comes to me from the other, who alone can give me this very flesh; thus it is also necessary to succeed in transcribing in my own flesh that of the other, who gives me it immediately and manifests herself there indirectly. From this point forward, my eroticization discovers itself in charge of the flesh of the other, to whom it offers its only possible phenomenon. And, since it is necessary that I make the other be seen in my flesh, who appears nowhere else, I must, in allowing myself to be eroticized, eroticize her, too, thoroughly. The other too, without exception or remainder. This mutual erotic process admits neither limits nor conditions—because it alone assures us our phenomenality as lovers, which implies that the other becomes for me flesh without restriction or exception, just as I become it for her, too. My flesh does not experience a part but rather the totality of the other, and vice versa. Nothing of her or of me must remain on the side. Ideally, eroticization should recapitulate everything in a wave, which submerges and raises all flesh univocally. Eroticization without remainder is accomplished everywhere in the same way (§ 42).

Whence there follows the astonishing rightness of the usage, though at first glance profane and ugly, of the word *baiser*.* Trivially, one thereby understands the taking possession of another body (abduction, coition); but, in order to signify this coupling (often the zero degree of eroticization), one takes up a term, indissolubly both substantive and verb, that concerns first of all the act of the mouth, slightly open in order to touch another flesh—in order to give to the other his or her flesh. In so doing, the trivial acceptation of the word in fact perfectly verifies the phenomenological situation, where my flesh is not limited to my mouth, and neither is the flesh of the other limited to her mouth, but instead, by touching one another mouth to mouth, our two mouths set off a wave that traverses our two bodies, so as to transcribe them wholly into two fleshes, without remainder; the mouth begins the process, because, already open, without distinction between exterior and interior, it offers itself from the outset as flesh; it incarnates first the lack of distinction between touching and touching oneself, feeling and feeling (oneself) feeling. But, if nothing resists it (and, precisely, the flesh that it begins to give to the other is defined by its nonresistance), that is, since nothing resists it, the kiss [*baiser*] of my mouth upon her mouth (where each mouth gives flesh to the other without distinction) inaugurates the infinite taking of flesh. All that remains for the whole of the other and of me to take flesh is to extend the kiss beyond the kissing and kissed mouth. The eroticization of everything is involved, including what seemed, under the medical or speculative gaze, the least susceptible of becoming mine, of becoming my flesh—the sexual organs. For, by right, they should remain completely foreign to eroticization: they belong to the body, not the flesh; they work for the species, without me, or even against me; they do not even have an independent reality, but borrow the canal of other functions, those that are the most animal; and above all,

---

*Every student of French learns, usually very early on, to be careful when using the verb *baiser* or the noun *le baiser* because, depending upon the context, they can mean either "to kiss"/"a kiss" or "to fuck"/"a fuck"—and in contemporary usage, more often the latter than the former. This double meaning in one word is obviously untranslatable; we shall use the verb "to embrace" and the noun "embrace" as closest approximations in contexts where the other meanings do not fit.—Trans.

they remain, in the "cold" state, hardly arousing. But emplacement in flesh includes them; it ends up by submerging them, as if by an erotic kenosis; far from the sexual organs provoking the process of embracing [*le procès de baiser*], we should be astonished that the embrace could go so far as to include them and to emplace even them in flesh. Coition also embraces, kisses with a kiss of its mouth—penetration receives (or at least sometimes can receive) flesh, and gives it. The univocality of the word *baiser* does not rest upon a forced metonymy: it uncovers an actual metamorphosis. In retrospect, this univocality justifies the use (introduced in § 16) of "to make love" to name the lover's advance (§ 18), which radicalized the question "Does anyone out there love me?" through the question "Can I be the first to love?": the erotic reduction was already at issue, henceforward assigned to the taking of flesh as the manifestation of the other in her only possible phenomenon—my own flesh, become such through eroticization. Like other formulas, "to make love" and "baiser" witness, without truly knowing it, to the phenomenological requirement of an erotic univocality of the taking of flesh, which, without exception, is the condition for its accomplishment. The whole of us can be exalted in the flesh, so that each flesh makes itself the phenomenon of the other flesh, and thus of the other.

Nevertheless, this result gives rise to a new difficulty. If my own flesh, eroticized by the other who gives it to me, manifests the unique phenomenon of the other, does the other still show (herself) (as) a face in this flesh that is mine? And a more serious difficulty: does the face keep its phenomenological privilege as infinite noema beyond all my noeses? To the first question we must respond that, once eroticized, the other shows (herself) even more evidently (as) a face, because she receives from me her flesh in glory, or rather, she receives from me a glory that illumines first the face in her flesh: never has she smiled as much as now, when she climaxes—in her flesh, which appears at its fullest. But this itself leads to the true question: the face—we admit this definitive attainment—draws its privilege from its putting on stage for me the injunction "Thou shalt not kill!"; it manifests this commandment by decreeing it silently but imperatively, as an ethical demand, which establishes the other in an absolute transcendence; foreign to the world, other than me, having rights over me by the intentionality that he or she imposes upon me, the other appears directly as an iconic face (without any façade to see), who envisages me at a distance. From that point forward, if, as we have just described it, the erotic wave invades not only the other's flesh, but even as far as his or her face, does not the other disappear as such as this glory submerges him or her—

disappear, that is, as the ethical phenomenon of "Thou shalt not kill!"? Doesn't the wave of eroticization, drowning the face, also pass beyond the other?

We must recognize that the privilege of the face, supposing that it remains, no longer depends *here* on a distance, nor on an ethical height. Here, the face of the other, if she still wants or is able to speak to me, certainly no longer says to me, "Thou shalt not kill!"; not only because the other has no doubts about this point; and not only because she says to me, in sighs or in words, "Here I am, come!" (§ 28); but above all because she and I have left the universal, even the ethical universal, in order to strive toward particularity—mine and hers, because it is a question of me and of you, and surely not of a universally obligating neighbor. In the situation of mutual eroticization, where each gives to the other the flesh that he or she does not have, each only aims at being individualized in individualizing the other, thus exactly piercing and transgressing the universal. Or at least, each attempts to do so. In fact, it matters little whether one situates the eroticized face (hers, mine) beyond or on this side of the ethical visage, provided that one recognize that *here* the universal has no rights, nor the final word. Which confirms the impossibility here of substitution: I can neither substitute another other for this one, nor above all myself for her; my flesh will never be able, either, to substitute itself for hers, nor vice versa, because it experiences itself in experiencing it—and because this is what it is all about. And with the universal, the ethical also loses its privilege: the point is not to give up on my priority in order to recognize it in the other, nor to render my duties to him or her; the point here is to keep my advance upon her, so as to surrender arms to her by delivering to her her flesh, which I do not have, and by receiving my own from her, who gives it to me without having it; we have only to give ourselves up, each to the other, and give ourselves reciprocally the status of gifted—the one who receives him- or herself (his or her flesh) from what he or she receives (the other's flesh).

Yet for all of that, if the universal ethic becomes blurred, the other's transcendence, far from fading away, stands out like never before. In effect, what does the face of the other say to me (in whatever way she speaks to me), when the wave of eroticization submerges her? She tells me that the taking of flesh recapitulates now all her former body, that nothing more in her resists her flesh, and thus also that she absolutely no longer resists me; at this instant, her face witnesses to the accomplishment without remainder of her flesh and, in this sense, all her flesh rejoins her face in the same glory. Or if one prefers, far from her face sinking into the flesh, all her flesh becomes a face, like a "glorified body" is summed up in a single glory, the very glory of its face. Look at the flesh of a young mother, holding her newborn in her arms, flesh rising up as far as her face, where, indiscriminately incarnated, there is vanishing suffering, pleasure diffused, and joy returned upon itself. Look at the Risen Christ (and not always only the cadaver of the Crucified) on the Isenheim altarpiece, whose face, except for the eyes, whitens and almost disappears in the glory that submerges his flesh—thenceforward definitively living, irresistible for having known *not* to resist anything, even the worst death. The eroticized face also recapitulates all its flesh; in its gaze, I see—if I see anything at all—the irrepressible wave of its flesh surging up in it, giving it to itself for the first time. Thus I see there its flesh, insofar as it is felt and feels itself feel, thus insofar as it is definitively individualized, gifted to itself, in short insofar as it is definitively *inaccessible* to my own flesh. I see there the accomplished transcendence of the other, through which she differs forever and always from me—her flesh in glory. If she still looks at me, she makes me comprehend that she receives, in this very instant, the ability to distinguish herself from me, precisely because she vibrates under the impact of her flesh, which I give her because I do not experience it, and can thus abandon it to her. And inversely, she sees in my gaze that I am finally becoming my flesh, at an irremediable distance from hers. We commune, but within the distance of our two fleshes. They cross, through the same erotic reduction, in a unique amorous phenomenon—each appearing in the other without ever intermingling.

The crossing of our flesh in our suspended gazes renders our common soul finally apparent—at least to us, the lovers.

§ 25. To Enjoy*

We, the lovers, cross our respective and respected flesh. And we do this without confusion or mixing, since the two fleshes remain all the more irreducible as they rise up from their respective feelings, and as they give to one another what they do not have. Without separation or division nevertheless, since they experience the same erotic accomplishment, and each sees in the glorious face of the other the same feeling, feeling itself feeling. The two gazes, henceforward flesh, become through the same gesture im-

---

**Jouir and the noun *jouissance* will be translated, according to context, by "to enjoy," "to climax," "enjoyment," "climax," and "climactic enjoyment."—Trans.

manent and transcendent to one another. By discovering herself more inward to me than myself, the other stands higher than ever. The indirect
union (between two irreducible fleshes) remains immediate (of a unique
crossing, wherein each flesh receives itself from the other).

Thus I can legitimately conclude that I enjoy the other, instead of simply using her. For, strictly speaking, I can only use a thing, and in my interest, while here I adhere to the other for herself, insofar as her flesh no
longer belongs to the world of things. I adhere for she herself, because I
cling to the other, so as to give her her flesh; her flesh, indeed, because I do
not have it; and I do not possess it, because in fact I myself would have no
flesh if she had not given it to me. I adhere firmly to her flesh for her—so
that she might receive it. Thus I enjoy her. Put another way, I do not enjoy
my pleasure, but hers; and if, by chance (which does not go without saying), I also climax, this pleasure gushes forth only from hers, as its undertow; if I climaxed without her climax, I would simply not enjoy, but instead
would limit myself to using her anew. Of themselves, a discharge and a
spasm do not allow enjoyment, even if by chance they accompany pleasure.
Infinitely more than pleasure, even multiplied and violent, is necessary for
enjoyment. The crossing of flesh is necessary. In this way many badly
posed questions fade away: Does "union" abolish the "incommunicability
of consciousnesses"? Does self-love contradict love of the other? Does climax render one "selfish" or disinterested? etc. (§ 42). Henceforth I can forget all of these artificial oppositions, which return in fact to a number of
arbitrary hypotheses that I had to construct in the first meditations, precisely where it was necessary to accede to the erotic reduction. These an-
tinomies now attest that the question of love had not yet been correctly
taken up, or described; it was only correctly taken up from the moment we
recognized the phenomenological necessity of a radical reduction to the
given—of the erotic reduction of the *ego* to the lover, to the advance, and
finally to the flesh in glory.

For all intents and purposes, the erotic reduction has just been accomplished; it has attained the lover in his or her final immanence. It has
suspended intentionality, objectifying as much as ontological, and even supposedly drive-motivated intentionality (which still belongs to the world), in
order to discover the pure field of eroticized flesh feeling itself in another
flesh. But, now that nothing remains—not the least thing—what remains
for me? More precisely: where can I stand? I stand there where I receive
myself as flesh—in the flesh of the other, who dispenses to my flesh alone
more than a world, and better than a world. I dwell in this flesh, I take

root and become a lover. Nothing resists me any longer there, and nothing fails me. The assurance that I sought for, when I was lost and asking, "Does anyone out there love me?" I henceforward attain in the flesh that one gives to me and that gives me to myself. It thus becomes possible and even necessary to take up again the description, still negatively marked, of the world under the sun of vanity (§§ 5–6), this time positively, according to the accomplished erotic reduction and beginning from the crossing of flesh.

Where do we find ourselves? In what space is the phenomenon of love accomplished? And to begin with, is it still a matter of a space? Doubtless, no: I no longer consider myself here as a physical body that would be situated among other physical bodies, in the interior of the same compossibility (§ 5). Now, without this arrangement of a physical body, assumed mine, with other physical bodies, no homogeneous space (real or formal) can any longer be defined; one must be able, in effect, to be situated between other physical bodies in order to use coordinates of location (x- and y-axes, longitude and latitude, GPS or Galileo, etc.); the three dimensions of natural space (height, width, depth) remain valid only for what belongs to nature, and thus to the world, like an object or simply a being, situated among others, comparable within a homogeneous order. But, through the erotic reduction, I experience myself henceforward as pure flesh; this signifies that I no longer experience myself by the resistances of objects that, around me, restrain me in an allocated space and orient me forcibly in universal space. As flesh, I feel only myself, and thus I orient myself beginning from myself, without any other reference than my flesh itself. Or rather, on the contrary, I orient myself in relation to myself only in a neutral space (the two—neutral and space—go together perfectly); for I do not possess my flesh, but receive it from the other, who gives me to myself in the same time in which she gives it to me; as lover (that is to say, one who is gifted to another gifted one), I receive myself from the flesh of the other; I am thus situated according to the focal point when I receive myself; as received flesh, I only take my bearings from the flesh of the other. When the lover makes love (in all senses of the expression, since in fact it has only one sense), he finds himself (literally: he ceases to lose himself, he finds himself again) facing the eroticized gaze of the other in his very flesh. My lover's space, or rather that which is substituted for space in the reduction, namely the erotic environment, retains dimensions and, thus, coordinates; I still take my bearings: below, above, in front, behind, to the right, to the left; but for all of that I do not take my bearings according to an objective space, an intelligible extension, or a worldly opening, in short in the neuter; hence-forward below, above, in front and behind, to the right, or to the left are no longer defined except by reference to the flesh of the other. I situate my-self in this flesh (I penetrate it and it penetrates me), thus starting from it; I know where I am, whether I am in front of or behind it, to the right or the left of it, below or above it. This flesh alone decides my situation, be-cause it defines my unique — erotic — environment. And as the flesh of the other ceases to move about in relation to the ghost of objective space, which already disappears for us (we no longer see it or feel it), and as the flesh remains a point of immobile erotic reference, my situation in the erotic environment only depends on my relative situation in relation to this flesh of reference; I do not find myself above or below the physical world, nor to the north or south of the geographic world, nor at the entrance or the bottom of the world of real estate, I find myself again above or below this flesh, far from or near it, in or outside of it. It takes the place of place, of coordinates and of cardinal points, or rather it dispenses with these for me. Which is confirmed by the univocality of *baiser,* established earlier — it is not a matter of such or such part of the physical body, because it is no longer a matter of space, but of the erotic environment; as it is defined only in relation to the other's flesh, all that has to do with it becomes not a part of the flesh (which does not have any parts), but this flesh itself; I treat this flesh in its entirety in the same manner — I can and must embrace it [*la baiser*]. I situate myself exactly *here,* there where my embrace goes.

When do we find ourselves? In what time is the phenomenon of love accomplished? And to begin with, is it still a matter of time? Doubtless no, because I am no longer in the world's time, where what happens does not last, but rather I am in the erotic reduction's time, where, let us recall, the future is redefined as the time of expectation of an elsewhere where noth-ing passes (happens), the present as the time where the elsewhere happens or passes and makes the present of its passing, and finally the past as the time where the elsewhere has passed beyond the moment of its present (§ 6). Let us take up again these three dispositions of temporality thus re-duced. The *future* of the erotic reduction consists in the expectation of an elsewhere, where nothing happens or passes. And in effect, in the crossing of flesh, I await the flesh of the other to give me my own flesh; my flesh comes upon me all the more that the flesh that gives it to me receives itself from my flesh, since each flesh feels itself feeling in the measure that the other flesh lifts every resistance to the increase of the first — and recipro-cally. Expectation, however, awaits nothing (no object, no being) other than

its own accomplishment, since eroticization unfolds in the pure immanence of a process that is without external limits or transcendent bounds.
Expectation, awaiting only its increase, thus can last for as long as the mutual lifting of resistances liberates the respective flesh of each one; and by
right the nonresistance of one flesh to the other does not have to cease after an objective and calculable delay; it can increase, and thus last as long as
each flesh is able not to resist the other, and the other does not cease advancing in this nonresistance—and reciprocally. Now, as each flesh assumes these two functions, it would be necessary to say that the expectation can last as long as each flesh is able *at the same time* not to resist the other
and to advance in order to increase all the more; this advance and this withdrawal only contradict one another if we come back to the natural attitude
(here, metaphysical), where scarcity is opposed to abundance; but in the
radical erotic reduction, where desire identifies scarcity and abundance,
not only is the advance and the withdrawal of each flesh receiving itself
from the other not a contradiction, but they reinforce each other, clamor
for one another, and arouse one another. Each flesh receives the other
(withdraws itself without resisting) all the more that it receives itself (advances without resistance). The advance and the withdrawal of a flesh
await the advance and the withdrawal of the other for as long as they are
able to feel themselves feeling. That is to say, for as long as nothing comes
to pass—for as long as the process lasts by increasing, is hardened by
growing, or in short remains a process. This increase should never be accomplished, if finitude did not determine my flesh; what one names, without precision or pertinence, "mounting desire" corresponds, more than
any event in the world, to the classical definitions of change—an act without term, without end, in short the accomplishment of an act insofar as it
remains without accomplishment. In order for our two fleshes to be eroticized to the core, it would be necessary that they not cease to exchange
their advances and withdrawals, and not cease to maintain them and mutually to arouse one another to them. Thus the future of the phenomenon
of love is deployed—without an end. In itself, the process of eroticization
of the flesh as far as the face foresees no endpoint. According to the erotic
future, one question appears meaningless—the one that asks: "When will
this be enough?"; for the correct measure in love must pass beyond every
measure: unless there is too much, it is still not enough. In the erotic future, "Here I am!" says, "Come!"

  As for the *present* of the erotic reduction, it is understood as the time in
which elsewhere comes to pass and makes the present of its passage. But

how could a passage which, in passing, necessarily disappears, nevertheless happen, and accomplish itself enough to leave behind it a gift, that is, give a present? How could that which passes not sink into the past, not only give itself in the present, but give this present as a present—a durable present, a dense given that lasts, when all will disappear? How can the present be freed from the metaphysical aporia, wherein the present by essence imposes its concentration in the instant without duration, which (like the point without extension) only exists on the condition of disappearing without delay? And during this atom of existence, should it not also harden in subsistent presence, a dead mineral rather than flesh? In order to respond, it is necessary to go back to the process of the eroticization of crossed flesh: as we saw, the accomplishment lasts only as long as it remains unaccomplished; desire lasts for as long as it does not cease to increase and, thus, for as long as it is not achieved in the present; it lasts in and thanks to the fear of finishing, of giving way to its plenitude. It only lasts if it happens or comes to pass, and thus passes beyond itself, surpasses itself, without ceasing not to cease. It must always be going and coming, withdrawing and advancing faster in order that the unaccomplishment still be accomplished. The flesh that is crossed only lives by the contradiction of being only for as long as it is not yet. If the accomplishment were accomplished, it would disappear as a process; in order for it to remain alive, it thus must delay arriving. Lovers enjoy and last, when they know not to feel themselves feeling to the bottom yet, for the bottom would stop them, like a shoal where one runs aground. But they also know that they will not be able to avoid running aground in the end, or making one another reciprocally run aground. For finitude, still unintelligible at this point (§ 27), is going to exert itself, it is going to preempt the emplacement in flesh: there will be an end to this race from one flesh to the other, this race to the sea, always begun over again. The erotic conversation, which consists of never concluding, is going to have to conclude ineluctably (which signifies not success, but running aground). One can name this contradiction the orgasm. Suddenly, the movement of my desire advances no further, it merely coasts: it can go on no longer, it slackens, it lets go. Just like a sprinter who, having given all he can to catch up to and pass his intimate adversary, his beloved rival, feels that he can go on no longer, admits that he is worn out and, suddenly, bursts—thus the lover unravels, unwinds, follows with his gaze the other flesh that passes him, disappointed with himself, yet secretly delighted that the other progresses with a longer advance. The other flesh is in ecstasy further than he—in ecstasy because it has resisted *less* than has my flesh, the victor because it was strong enough to become even *weaker* than I. The other knows how to remain more faithful to her taking flesh, and thus more abandoned to my flesh, than I do to hers. The other thus passes me—but not in the sense that she disappears. For what the other makes present to me, what the other gives me as a present, in short that which the other makes present to me consists in the accomplishment of her flesh that is more accomplished than my own, of her flesh which lasts longer than my own, because it does not yet stop not resisting me. This very passage, which passes beyond me, makes itself present—it happens or comes to pass before and upon me, swallows me (in order that I experience it) and saves me (in order that I testify to it) at the same time. Our difficulty in saying, and thus in conceiving, this passage given to the present (this passage of the present to the present) is due to our still speaking the language of metaphysics, which opposes presence and absence, possibility and actuality, while in the erotic reduction here led to its endpoint, these differences, ontic or ontological, become indifferent. What we cannot say, we can at least see and feel, like the amorous phenomenon, the phenomenon of the other within me. And another question becomes absurd in the erotic present, the one that would ask: "For how long?" In the erotic present, "Here I am!" says, "I am coming!"

In the erotic reduction, the *past* is understood as the time in which elsewhere has passed beyond the moment of its present. At first glance, the situation of this past seems less paradoxical than the situations of the erotic future and of the erotic present: the process no longer surpasses itself, it passes away and sinks into the past; the crossing of flesh has struck its shoal. But the real question crops up here, which asks whether this running aground is equivalent to a complete failure. At this stage, a systematic answer to this question remains impossible; it will only come once suspension (§ 26) and automatic finitude (§ 27) are clarified. Nevertheless, let's sketch a response. The achievement of the process, where each flesh receives itself from the other, in so very far as no flesh has what it gives, but gives it nevertheless insofar as it does not resist, remains ambivalent: eroticization is achieved because its very accomplishment contradicts it, insofar as it was a matter of a process unachievable as such. This contradiction may nevertheless be understood in two opposing ways, according to whether or not one distinguishes two modes of the erotic past: running aground and failure. According to one way of understanding the contradiction, the finitude of eroticization (which we take note of without yet being able to conceive it) has simply exerted its right of preemption and accomplished the unaccomplishable; but the interruption of the rising of the currents does not give nothing at all; it makes the present of a profit-taking, finite but already surpassing every expectation—the enjoyment of each flesh by the other. The past signifies, then, that by ceasing to surpass itself, the process of eroticization has nevertheless made access to itself pass into the account of each flesh; each of the lovers draws near, if not to the other one, at least to his or her own flesh and becomes all the better him- or herself. And finitude, which has interrupted a process, not only does not in principle oppose the repetition of such a process in the future, but, by awakening the consciousness of *running aground,* suggests it to our two fleshes, or even asks it of them. The process will be reborn of itself, not infinite but *staccato,* by separated impetuses, by fragmented efforts, by unaccomplishments that will yet end up being accomplished; but it will repeat itself, always the same in its imaginable differences. The erotic past is thus defined as a latency of possibility and a necessity to repeat the crossing of flesh. Time will last as long as lovers take up this repetition, that is to say, as long as they validate in their respective flesh the oath that made them appear to one another. According to the second way of understanding the contradiction, the running aground is confirmed as a *failure,* because finitude no longer stigmatizes the necessity of a repetition, but its impossibility—the end of the game. We will not enter here into the psychological analysis of the motives for this abandon, for the abandon here has a strict phenomenological status: it designates the powerlessness of one who is gifted (the lover, a flesh) to continue to receive himself from what he receives; and when the gifted exposes himself to another one who is gifted (the crossing of flesh), the abandon comes down to the denial of eroticization, and thus to scorning the phenomenon of love. The past, then, opens upon no repetition whatsoever, but rather forbids it by proclaiming eroticization over and done with. Over and done with—not suspended for lack of desire (or more exactly, for lack of the strength not to resist in one's flesh the other flesh), but for lack of the desire for desire. Eroticization is born of desire, which grows from scarcity, as if from its own mode of abundance; one declares eroticization over and done with when scarcity no longer marks the superabundance of lack, when the lack itself is lacking. I lack the other, but for all of that, nothing becomes depopulated. Not only does the flesh no longer eroticize itself, but it retracts; then the face of the other becomes blurred, the *ego* is reestablished and, in the end, the erotic reduction is dissolved. A past of repetition or a past over and done with, running aground or failure.

In both cases, at least, one question becomes absurd for the erotic past: "How many times?" In the erotic past, "Here I am!" says, "Again!"

§ 26. Suspension

The erotic phenomenon of the other, such as I have just described it, has the property of endlessly ceasing (without accomplishment and at every try), while it ought never to do so. For that very reason, when it ceases, it ceases more cleanly than any other phenomenon, more necessarily, and in any case more brutally. Everything passes, of course, in the long run—movements between beings of the world, subsistent objects, my emotions, and even my most lasting passions. Everything certainly passes, but time is necessary, a labor of erosion and forgetting, which keeps mourning busy, and everything does not disappear all at once. Here the process not only never attains its accomplishment (for it admits none), but it stops without any gradual slowing, by disappearing in the instant. The flesh tries hard to extend this instant that it has not ceased waiting for; but it will only be a matter of a retention, or even of an already imagined memory, and never of a prolongation. Orgasm is not a summit, from which one would descend in stages; it resembles a cliff that opens onto a void, where one falls all at once.

All at once, then, nothing remains. Failing to grasp why, let us attempt to identify what disappears. Strangely, nothing real, no *thing*, is lacking: we find one another still there where we were, in the same place, in the same state; in reality nothing has changed; the world appears nicely in order, like before. If then something has disappeared—for in fact there was a suspension, a stoppage—we must conclude that this thing was not a thing, or at least had nothing about it that one might describe as a real thing. How could this be? In this way: what appeared arose in the radicalized erotic reduction, during which I received my flesh from that of the other and gave to her her own; by crossing one another, our flesh crossed without merging; from the point at which everything stops, in an accomplishment that is unaccomplished precisely because it is finished, my flesh ceases to be eroticized, and thus it ceases to give flesh to the other who, no longer being eroticized, no longer gives me my own flesh. In this way, the suspension of eroticization also and first suspends the reduction that it radicalized. The flesh disappears in us as flesh, and, forced outside of the reduction, we reappear as simple physical bodies, nothing more. The flesh, at the instant in which it is glorified and, become almost immaterial, explodes in a pure flash of light, becomes suddenly a body—nothing but a body, just as massively worldly as the others that border it, and as the world that encloses it. One could very well say, then, that nothing real has disappeared, since all that has disappeared is flesh—which precisely does not depend upon reality, nor belong to the world of things. One could even say the inverse: by disappearing, the flesh causes to reappear something that the reduction had put into parentheses—the physical body, ourselves, no longer as lovers, but as beings of the world. Excluded from the reduction, we return into the world, into the ranks of things, into the terrestrial atmosphere.

Henceforward, we recognize that we are naked—not because we have committed the erotic reduction, but, on the contrary, because we have ceased to perform it. The nudity that covers us indicates that we see ourselves, again and perhaps for the first time, as physical bodies lost in the world; the world takes hold of us once again, by making us wear its uniform, garments of skins. Unless we clothed ourselves precisely in order to mask the bodies that we become in spite of ourselves; for we could never clothe our flesh, which is in any case invisible and henceforward missing; thus we cover our bodies in order to hide from ourselves and from others the disappearance of our flesh, in order to mask the shame of belonging once again to the order of bodies according to the natural attitude. The body usurps the flesh in us, like a residue from its disappearance, the ashes from a fire. One thus can rightly speak of a death of eroticized flesh—not because it is eroticized, but because it ceases to be eroticized and dies as flesh. Nevertheless it is necessary to make a distinction: the flesh of the other and my own do not disappear in the same way.

For me, by putting a stop to eroticization, I do not lose my flesh (how could I, since it gives me to myself?); I lose in my flesh the access to another flesh, and the grace of experiencing in that flesh the nonresistance of what feels (itself) feeling; but I retain the exercise of the privilege of feeling myself as soon as I feel a resistance from an object in the world. In my case, the end of eroticization (the suspension of the erotic emplacement-in-parentheses) only deprives my flesh of the other flesh, and not of its own feeling of the world; I can even remain in the situation of the lover, no longer endowed with flesh by the flesh of the other, but nevertheless perfectly in the radicalized reduction, engaged under oath and assured by it. Even without eroticization in act, I keep a flesh, even a lover's flesh (§ 35). The gap between flesh and eroticized flesh repeats the gap between the flesh and the body, and these two gaps trace a third; these gaps consecrate the independence of my flesh as such, neither body nor eroticized flesh; quite simply, in this posture, I feel (myself) feeling, without, however, knowing from where I receive this flesh, which comes to me from out there; my flesh enjoys and suffers, without seeing what gift allows it to do so.

By contrast, for the flesh of the other, I cannot postulate this intermediary status of a flesh that is neither corporalized nor eroticized. For I only acceded to the other's flesh in its eroticization by my own, and in the eroticization of my flesh by the other's; thus I could only feel that, by not resisting me, the other had the rank of flesh, and therefore she felt me just as I did her, according to the mode of feeling (oneself) feeling; as soon as eroticization ceases, I therefore lose the sole phenomenologically serious criteria for distinguishing such and such a physical body as another flesh—all that remains for me are probable arguments (analogy, empathy, the coherence of behaviors, language, etc.); even if they are enough in the current conditions to presume the phenomenon of the other, they never manifest the other to me straight on. Above all, in extreme conditions, they do not allow resistance to the denials of flesh to the other; we have seen that racism, and thus also the global killing that it logically implies, thoroughly exploits the weakness of these probable arguments; racism only takes hold because it excludes the eroticization of the other and thus can deny him as such. Without eroticization, the flesh of the other becomes problematic, in fact inaccessible. The other's flesh may pass directly from its glory to a physical body, even one that is more human—yet the divine form and essence of my decomposed loves ends up as a carcass.

With the cessation of eroticization, while the flesh of the other becomes doubtful, my own flesh remains bounded to that which resists it (the object, the thing, the space of the world), without feeling (itself) (in) what would not resist it (the flesh of the other), such that it thus misses itself, too. To the point where I may doubt in general the phenomenon of the other, from the moment that the erotic reduction is lacking. What did I see? Did I even see anything? What happened? Did something truly happen? As in anxiety—where, once the wave has passed, I tell myself that, after all, it was nothing (which is true, because it was *the* nothing)—in suspended eroticization, I cannot not tell myself that, after all, this was no big thing; and in fact, it was a matter of no thing. Just as there are no true memories of dreams, because dreams offer no stable object to reconstitute, there is no memory of climax: it leaves no trace that I could take note of, describe, or interpret. So then, I must only recognize in climactic enjoyment a pure event, where the incident covers over and eliminates all sub-

stance, where the unpredictable arrival is imposed upon a submerged witness, and where no concept can articulate the intuition. It happens, and
there is nothing to see, nothing to recount—because no thing, no being
was involved there, and especially no body. Orgasm, the only miracle that
the poorest human condition can definitely experience—for it requires
neither talent, nor apprenticeship, but simply a bit of naturalness—nevertheless leaves nothing to see, nothing to say, and carries away everything
with it, even its memory. Thus it does not accede to the rank of a saturated
phenomenon [*un phénomène saturé*] and remains a simple *erased phenomenon*
[*un phénomène raturé*]. As soon as one claims to say something about it,
one can only come back to the play of physical bodies, of which one then
shows, at best, the contiguous contacts, the positions in space, the dis-
placements and impacts; but what one describes (by the lines one traces, or
by writing) remains perfectly foreign to the crossing of flesh; one substitutes for its radical invisibility a visibility in full exposition, public and prostituted; we thus name it quite rightly pornography, simply because of the
absurd attempt here at a "graphy" or writing. As if a body could climax and
feel (itself) feeling—and as if that could be seen.

All of that for this? Does the crossing of flesh wind up merely in this
disappointment? Not at all, for the disappointment arises not from the
crossing of flesh, but from its suspension, not from eroticization, but from
its (un)accomplishment, not from the last reduction, but from its stoppage.
The question consists rather in conceiving henceforward how and why the
crossing of flesh was bound to be suspended, eroticization to cease, and
the reduction to stop. In other words, it is a matter of conceiving of their
ineluctable finitude.

§ 27. The Automaton and Finitude

In the process of the erotic reduction, I the lover have thus leapt over two
gaps: first, the gap between the body that I imagined myself to be and my
flesh, and next, the gap between this flesh and its eroticization. But the two
gaps differ. Between my flesh and my body, the caesura proves to be total
and complete: no body has the flesh's property of feeling (itself) feeling—
not even my body, because in fact I do not have a body, except by an unwarranted analogy with bodies of the world; in fact, I originarily have the
rank and status of flesh and I only believe myself to be a body if I fail to
know myself. All flesh is born and dies as flesh, all bodies remain bodies.
But, between my flesh and my eroticized flesh, not only does the border

seem indistinct, but it does not cease to prove itself passable and passed; a borderline owing to its own eroticization, all flesh goes without stopping toward the flesh of the other and comes back, according to an oscillation between things that resist it and that which does not resist it—namely, another flesh. The first caesura is passed with a leap, the second, on the contrary, by a process that is alternating (the come-and-go of my flesh to the other flesh) and gradual (it grows and collapses suddenly). The eroticization of my flesh thus remains provisional, or even optional; it bears the mark and the burden of finitude, of my own and of that of the other. It remains to conceive how eroticization provokes finitude and attests to it.

Let us return to the eroticized flesh, or more exactly to my flesh on the point of eroticizing itself—of arousing itself. I say that it arouses *itself* or that it eroticizes *itself,* and not that I arouse it or that I eroticize it. Clearly, I have already noted that my desire remains ever intentional of the other; even if no real other attends it, my desire always depends upon at least a fantasy of the other, known or not (§ 24). Nevertheless, the other in her flesh is not enough to arouse my flesh: I can rest my flesh upon that of the other, and even experience its nonresistance, without for all of that entering into the process of eroticization; this may be because I have no inclination to advance into the flesh of the other; or it may be because I hold back this inclination, through censure, moral scruple, social interest, or simply a wish for relational efficiency; education, discipline, and willpower offer me ways to resist (at least for a time) the nonresistance of the other's flesh. In fact, I do not voluntarily eroticize my flesh any more than does the other flesh compulsorily eroticize it. The other flesh offers a necessary, but not sufficient, condition for my eroticization, and my will exerts a simple resistance but alone cannot start it up. This is confirmed precisely by the fact that I can always (at least for a time) resist this eroticization, resist the nonresistance of the other's flesh toward my own ("Don't touch me!"); and I would not have the freedom to resist it if the simple nonresistance of the flesh of the other were enough to eroticize my flesh, or if it only depended upon me to provoke (or not) my own eroticization. Thus there remains only one hypothesis, the one that we indicated at the outset—that my flesh is aroused, that it is eroticized *of its own accord.*

It remains to describe this spontaneity of eroticization, in the end as independent of my decision as it is of the nonresistance of the other's flesh. By experiencing the other's flesh, or more exactly by experiencing that here and nowhere else nothing resists it, and that on the contrary this flesh withdraws in order to allow the other's flesh to advance and to increase, my flesh does not first of all experience a new sensation, more delightful than any other; in fact, it experiences nothing (no thing), and its pleasure comes precisely from this void, where it experiences itself. For the first time, my flesh experiences itself without restriction or limit, and thus receives itself as such; it experiences in fact its own spontaneity, its autonomy and its free strength. It arouses itself as it lets itself go, drives into the opening and sinks into the first openness. It puts itself in movement, walks by itself and proceeds from itself. The flesh of the other only contributes by its non-resistance, through its very irreality, and my will can only contribute by not resisting any more, by lifting inhibitions and censures (rightly or wrongly, it matters little here). My flesh, finally delivered over to its unrestrained impetus, becomes, strictly speaking, auto-motive, in short automatic. My eroticized flesh becomes automatic, like dream-writing. It begins if and when it wants. It takes off, it starts up. What we call desire, namely the strength of my flesh eroticizing itself, consists in being able to engage one-self—to engage the flesh [like a pinion] in the rack of eroticization. It is enough for the other's flesh to consent not to resist (but the flesh of the other is defined precisely by that) and for my will also to consent (and I experience my will's yielding almost always), in order for my flesh to engage its eroticization. What we call "loving" is summed up most often by yielding to the automatic desire of my flesh, or the flesh of the other. And so, all at once, "Off we go!"

Off we go—which signifies that henceforward my flesh has no need of anyone in order to receive itself from the flesh of the other and to give without stopping to the other her own flesh. Henceforward I no longer control (no more than does the other) the crossing of our two fleshes, more inward to ourselves than our abstract wills, completely obsessed by their mutual increase, accelerating automatically the rhythm of their un-endingly renewed and restarted advances. We have seen (§ 25) this rhythm determine a new space and a new temporality, foreign to the world of things and to our wills. If my will by chance intervenes, either it truly takes things into hand again, but the process immediately disappears and I anticipate the suspension and reestablish socialization; or it places itself in the service of automatic flesh, as a simple auxiliary that is useful but not indispensable, in the service of an already victorious power, which it strives to follow and to reinforce, and, eventually, whose autonomous movement it strives to orient. My flesh alone decides the engagement of its eroticization, of its rhythm, and above all, of its end. For this very end attests, more than anything, to the automatism of eroticized flesh: for neither I, nor the other as will, wills that it end; we always will each to receive more flesh from the flesh of the other one; of course, we also will the final explosion, without which the crossing of flesh would not actually be attested. This contradiction, not willed by us, imposes itself nevertheless on our drowned wills, because the eroticization of the flesh is constituted there; even more, henceforth our wills involuntarily fear just as much to reach this instant (why finish and not pursue an endless course?), as not to accomplish it (which depends not upon the wills, but upon our flesh). It will be finished when the automatic flesh decides, without me or the other having willed it, since we have wished for it as much as we have delayed it, accomplished it without nevertheless having decided it. I eroticize myself and I climax by abandoning myself to the automatic eroticization of my flesh by the flesh of the other, above all by doing nothing, by allowing everything to be done in me without me—and the same goes for the other. If I acted, I acted as an automaton—the automaton of my automatic flesh. And if it must start again, our flesh will decide for us, just like the first time: if our flesh decides on it, when and each time it decides to put itself in movement.

In this way the finitude of the lover comes to light, a finitude that in fact has a false bottom. A finitude that is at first obvious, because my flesh eroticizes itself in me without me. Its radical passivity (receiving itself from another flesh, which does not have it, and yet gives it) arouses itself like a spontaneousness in me that is not me, stronger than my intention, which eventually takes over from it and serves it, but like a servant always on the brink of revolt, who takes initiatives and then presents the accomplished facts. Flesh that eroticizes in him without him, or indeed even against him, exerts a real violence upon the lover, who cannot begin without the flesh and must stop when it stops. The lover knows well this ascendancy over him of the flesh eroticizing itself, because he can sometimes yield to the temptation of turning it upon another: it is enough for the lover to provoke the flesh in the other, by giving flesh to the other through his own, even if the other does not at first consent; it is not a matter of sexual violence (such violence is produced in spatial grappling, where a body wills to violate the resistance of another body, to invade it or displace it in the world) (§ 31), but rather of a provocation to consent; I attempt to give to the other the flesh that she does not want to receive, to lead her to behave like eroticized flesh, and thus not to resist me, to yield to my own flesh with all of her own, while she would like to leave her flesh unscathed by any other flesh, or at least, unscathed by mine. The worst of rapes is doubtless accomplished when one extracts consent and one constrains the other to desire his or her own nonresistance. Gentleness violates more than violence, because it no longer lays hold of a body, but of consent—that is to say, of flesh. In fact, it's already like this between the lover and his own flesh: by being eroticized automatically, the flesh can arouse itself and let itself be received from another flesh even without the lover consenting; my flesh can be aroused by the flesh of another than the other of the oath, or without any oath at all, or even against my intention, without any advance, without myself loving first. For, while I can at least set my heart on making a decision with my mind (I have consciousness of it) and with my body (I make use of it), I nevertheless cannot make a decision about my flesh which constitutes me, and which I am, especially when it is eroticized. The *ego cogito* sometimes fears that a faculty unknown to it thinks within it and without it; the lover is always afraid that his or her flesh will be eroticized without him and without his oath—an indefinite flesh that cruises randomly. It is unquestionable that an unconscious inhabits me, and keeps me busy—my flesh that arouses itself.

In this way my first finitude emerges. It does not consist in my flesh, which, insofar as it feels itself feeling the things of the world, unfolds itself indefinitely, in all directions and at each opportunity, always setting off. Finitude consists exactly in my flesh eroticizing itself on its own initiative, itself provoked by another flesh, that is, in me, eventually without me. Finitude is not due to my flesh alone, but to my flesh eroticizing itself. Metaphysics assigns finitude to the sensible character of intuition, which is passive because purely receptive according to space and time, and not spontaneous, like an intellectual faculty, which is active; this thesis, correct in and of itself, nevertheless remains superficial, because derived. For the passivity of our sensibility does not allow only, or to begin with, the receptivity of various intuitions in space and time, but also the nonresistance of the other flesh to mine, and of mine to this other; receptivity of the intuitions of the world still only offers the index of a more originary and otherwise passive receptivity—that in which my flesh receives itself from the flesh of the other. This receptivity does not refer back to bodies, but to another flesh—and thus to the passivity without common measure of my flesh eroticizing itself beginning from another, and for that other. This passivity in its turn is not limited to a finitude of my faculties of knowing (and of knowing nothing other than the objects of the world), a simple, theoretical or contemplative finitude, but rather it is connected with a radical finitude—that in which, more inward to myself than I, the eroticization of my flesh, which deploys itself without me, or even against me, is engaged in the name of another who escapes me, and from whom I do not escape.

Thus we have an erotic finitude that the other exerts over me; the other borders me, sets bounds around me, because she approaches me; she overflows me, because she arouses me and is aroused by me; she defines me, because she precedes me at my core and there assigns me to her. Henceforth, I cannot even say, "I love first!" because I know that I am no longer first, that I am no longer even myself, but that originarily I am other than myself—I climax other than myself.

The lover discovers herself finite, because her automatic flesh alienates her from herself. But for all of that, she is not yet at the end of her finitude, which comes not only from the autonomy within her of automatic flesh (relative finitude), but also from the bounds of eroticization itself (intrinsic finitude). For the flesh proves itself definitively finite in so very far as it is aroused: however far the process of eroticization goes, there always comes a moment where it stops—the instant in which the flesh wears out, is accomplished, and thus suspends the unaccomplishment in which it was increasing. Flesh cannot be eroticized infinitely. It persists in beginning its eroticization again as soon as possible, because it must always end by ending. It is a matter of a fact which has the force of law: no more than the flesh can be confused with a body that is permanent in the present can it eroticize itself without end, as in a lasting state. Doubtless there is no sense in asking why: the fact of finitude has no reason, because it fixes the horizon even of thinkable reasons; at the least, I am able to distinguish what this intrinsic finitude allows and forbids, and thus find its meaning. If eroticization were to last without end, it would suspend the world, its time and its space—the erotic reduction would thus tear me definitively from the world. Suspension, on the contrary, keeps me in the world and prevents me from leaving it too quickly; it thus maintains an open history for me and for a possible other. This finitude does not condemn me to renunciation of the erotic reduction, but only to its endless repetition; it thus trains me to temporalize myself without end according to the eroticization of the flesh, or in fact according to the flesh of the other, who gives it to me. Eroticization's finitude thus teaches me, paradoxically, to be reborn without respite as a lover, and thus to live as a man—according to the advance, the oath, and the flesh given and giving. Eroticization's finitude assures me the infinite repetition of the erotic reduction itself.

§ 28. Words for Saying Nothing

I thus have at the same time the most extreme and the most disappointing experience of eroticization. I receive my flesh there at its maximum, but it escapes me at the very instant in which, an instant later, I was going to attain it. Climax and suspension nearly coincide, and yet the miniscule gap that stretches between them is enough to oppose them: I experience suspension as much as climax, missed by a mere nothing; in fact, I hold on to the memory of suspension more, much more than that of climax—missed by so little, climax succumbs beneath the evidence of suspension. Without a durable present, the phenomenon of eroticization leaves me in fact no memory, or at least an abstract memory—that of the most perfect consciousness, but a consciousness of nothing; a perfectly clear idea, but absolutely not distinct—a flash of lightning, but not definable or recognizable, without a sign to recognize it by, which thus becomes confused with every other void; so, unable to describe it or name it, one can only repeat it. It is not a matter of a saturated phenomenon, where the excess of intuition would call for an excess of conceptual hermeneutics and description. Rather, it is a matter of an erased phenomenon, where the excess of intuition over the concept does indeed invade all of the horizon of manifestation, but withdraws itself and disappears immediately, so that nothing, upon this beach without waves, remains to explain, to comprehend, and to put into evidence. Of eroticization, this erased phenomenon, one can say nothing, even to oneself, even from lover to lover. The words are lacking.

Where there is nothing to say, since there is nothing to describe, is it necessary to keep quiet? The philosophical vulgate, heavily armed with dogmatic skepticism, has no doubts: where there is nothing to say, nothing to predicate of anything, it is necessary to keep quiet. And anyway, isn't it necessary to keep quiet when any true agony is accomplished—doesn't the suffering of sports, of combat, of pain and of death escape discourse and description? Shouldn't we keep quiet when we watch it from the outside? And when one experiences it in the first person, doesn't it stop short our speech? Doesn't every great suffering, and thus every true climax, remain mute, and thus also unspeakable? Perhaps this is true for suffering (although one must remain prudent), but surely not for my climax. For my climactic enjoyment needs and has the right to be said and to let itself be said, because, in order to climax, rather than suffer, I need to turn to the other and address myself to her, and thus address her with speech and await her response. For—I had already understood this (§ 25)—climaxing, or what is called climaxing (to unite oneself with the other for the other herself) is distinguished from the simple using of the other (making use of the other for oneself) in that it is paradoxically a matter of the other herself, and not of me; or at least it is a matter of no longer distinguishing between what arises from me and what arises from the other; I climax, because I feel not only my own feeling (as when my flesh feels a body), but also the other's feeling (because my flesh is exposed to another flesh). Thus I climax: that is beyond debate, just as it is beyond debate that I only climax through the other. My climactic enjoyment gives me a flesh, because it comes from a flesh; now, as neither one nor the other arises from objects or beings of the world, I nevertheless enjoy nothing; or rather I take enjoyment from nothing, precisely because I take enjoyment from the other, who is nothing of the world. I thus have nothing to tell her, having in fact nothing to share with her, since we give to one another reciprocally only the possibility of *extracting* ourselves from the world by becoming flesh. This very fact—that we have nothing to say to one another, for we have nothing worldly in common—nevertheless designates us as inevitable interlocutors: we find ourselves, without visible faces, the partners of a privilege of worldly inexistence. My climactic enjoyment disengages me from the world, because it engages me toward the other. Thus, having nothing to say to the other, I have to tell her of this exceptional nothing, which I received from her and gave back to her. I can speak of nothing, but I can speak to her of this fact. I can even speak only to her of this exceptional nothing, because she alone knows it like I know it—each of us enjoying it with the other. The very fact of having nothing to say to her forces me to speak to her. In this way climactic enjoyment is distinguished from all agonies, which only concern me and cannot be told of to anyone. Precisely by virtue of that of which I cannot speak, I must speak to the other. Thus the erotic reduction redefines the rules of language.

When I climax, in effect I speak. I say nothing about nothing, but I address myself desperately to the other. I say only, "Here I am!" but I address it to the other in all her aspects, and thus in all of my own; in the future, I tell her, "Here I am!" by asking of her, "Come!"; in the present, I tell her, "Here I am!" by announcing, "I am coming!"; in the past, I tell her, "Here I am!" by begging, "Again!" (§ 25). In these statements, obviously I describe nothing, I predicate nothing upon anything, I demonstrate nothing; but I address myself to the other very precisely, very earnestly, and very intimately; she knows exactly what I ask her, announce to her, and accomplish; there is no doubt between us; she knows that I expect her to climax, that I am going to climax and that I want it all to begin again or to continue; never have we understood one another so well, so quickly, without waste, without ambiguity or reserve. We speak to one another, then, even though we speak of nothing—we speak to one another precisely because we have no recourse to any intermediary tale, which makes an obstacle or a distraction. Only suspension, which will inevitably intervene, will oblige us once again to speak of something, of one story or another, which will make itself the translator of our mutual addresses, henceforward indirect. But now, in the process toward climax, we address one another directly—statements without stories, speech about nothing, laid bare for us and for us alone. The address grows as predication is extinguished.

Speaking of no thing, never telling anything, we address one (to) another in what it is necessary to designate as *the thing*—in fact the non-thing par excellence, what predicative language paradoxically can only aim at as *the thing* par excellence. That which one can only say by not saying it or by saying exactly its opposite—the thing that interrupts the course of things, because it excepts itself from the world, of beings and of objects. The negation of the thing becomes the sole manner in which to say that we speak to one another without speaking of any thing in the world. And this negation does not so much invert the affirmation as it repeats it at a higher level; for it is abolished in a mode of language wherein there is nothing to affirm or to deny, because it is no longer a matter of predicates or of subjects, but instead of you and of me—who have only to speak to one another, for ourselves alone, outside of the world. Not in order to describe ourselves, not to know ourselves better, nor in order to meet one another (as the beautiful soul imagines it), but uniquely in order to arouse ourselves. To speak in order to arouse—to make ourselves go out of ourselves as flesh eroticized by words, above all by words. This is what our mouths are for, when they do not give themselves to kissing.

So we do speak in order to say nothing, but yet not in vain: here there is no failure, no silence, no solitude, since we speak in order to arouse ourselves—in order to give ourselves mutually the flesh that we do not have. For language does not always exercise a certifying function, categorically stating states of things. When it is not a matter of things, there is no longer anything to describe, anything to predicate of anything, nothing to affirm or to deny. If I say, "Here I am!" ["Me voici!"] I say nothing that may be known and transmitted as data; here the personal pronoun refers to whoever pronounces it and designates no one in particular; and the preposition [*voici*], which in fact has a verbal function ("vez ci, vois ici"),* commands

---

*Old versions of the modern French word *voici*—*vez ci, vois ici*—translate into English as "see here"; thus the current expression *Me voici* could be translated according to its etymological meaning as "See me here."—Trans.

only another who is accidentally concerned to envisage this *I,* who is also accidental. If I say or intend, "I love you first!" I cannot reasonably expect the least verification or invalidation, empirical or formal—no one could assign a truth value to this statement, except for the one who performs it and who, besides, first of all can guarantee nothing, except, in the best of cases, an intention that is private, subjective, uncontrollable, and always provisional. Nevertheless, no one doubts that to say or to intend, "Here I am!" or, "I love you first!" has some sort of effect, accomplishes an act, or provokes an actual situation. Thus it is necessary to conclude that these utterances have no enunciative, categorical, or descriptive role, but simply a performative function: they do not say what they describe, they make what they say. If I say, "Here I am!" or, "I love you first!" I announce myself immediately as a lover, because I effectively become one; even if I say it without thinking it or willing it, I still perform what I say; for the other will always take me exactly for what I perform, and I will be lying to her, precisely because what I say, I will be—I will have already made myself a lover. The lover makes love by saying it *ex opere operato,* without regard for his capacities or even for his intentions. My declarations—for it is a matter of declaring what is not yet, and not of stating a state actually already there—perform what they state. "I love you" or "I don't love you," "I believe that you love me" or "I don't believe that you love me," or "I believe that you don't love me," or even "We don't love each other anymore"—all of these declarations accomplish what they say, and that which, before them, was not. Once again, lovers declare love like one declares war: to say that one loves is equivalent to provoking it. Erotic language describes nothing, it stages the oath; or rather, as this scene makes nothing seen, erotic language puts eroticization into movement, where each flesh receives itself from the other without possessing itself. Language allows the flesh to be aroused— it allows each lover to take flesh.

We now understand that erotic language not only speaks in order to say nothing, but most often says anything. The lover addresses her- or himself directly to the beloved in the intention of arousing him or her, and of receiving his or her own flesh; the lovers thus experience no need to pass through the description of objects, to state the properties of beings or to refer to the states of things; or rather, the erotic reduction dispenses the lovers from all of this, and even radically diverts them from it. A love begins when each speaks to the other of the other him- or herself, alone, and of nothing else; and it ends when we experience once again the need to speak of something other than the other one—in short, the need to make conversation. Lovers speak to one another solely in order to provoke one another to eroticization; alone in the world, or more precisely alone outside of the world, they only use words in order to arouse one another, and never in order to know or to describe anything. Thus they free their words of every obligation toward the world and, first and foremost, of the duty to know it. What is more, they only use these words in order to free themselves from the world through its emplacement in the erotic reduction, and in this way accede to their respective flesh. By definition, their language is set free from the world and sets them free from the world (and doubtless, the erotic reduction and poetry are in league, such that all poetry, at its core, arises from the erotic and leads back to it). Lovers thus speak without saying anything in order to accomplish thoroughly the erotic reduction; they therefore privilege the lexicons that least describe beings, or even that cannot tell of them at all; and it so happens that these very lexicons incline more than others toward the performance of eroticization. The less I say of anything, the more I give the other her flesh; the less you speak to me of objects, the more you give me my flesh; you and I give our flesh by only speaking in order to arouse it. Erotic speech thus provokes a transgressive language—because it transgresses objectivity, transports us out of the world, and also, by simple consequence, transgresses the social conditions (the decency of conversation) and the public finalities (the evidence of knowing) of worldly language.

These transgressions thus privilege marginal, eccentric, or even senseless lexicons, which say and describe nothing and thus allow the flesh to arouse itself while speaking. First, of course, there is the language that is called obscene, the language that reduces each one to his or her sexual organs and only names him or her by their names; for, by thus taking the part for the whole, by designating the other by his or her sex (or any other organ, as in the poetry of the blazons of the human body), I say and describe nothing of the other, I don't even see anything of the other, because a sex remains abstractly a sex, indistinct from any other; thus, beneath these obscene words, I limit myself purely to invoking the other, to provoking her, to stirring her; in short, I give her her naked flesh while asking her for mine. Likewise the penchant for naming these sexual organs as trivially as possible is not at all senseless or out of place: the point is to rip, very intelligently and wisely, these organs from their status as worldly objects (from their medical, physiological, and biological names, from the litotes that render them socially acceptable, in short from their nonerotic neutrality), to render them definitively filthy—that is to say not so much impure as outside of the world, so as to make them appear as flesh pure and simple. Thus, my speech, descriptively null, becomes purely performative—performative of the performance of the other flesh.

Next we come to the lexicon that in appearance is most opposite, that of puerile words, of those words said by those who do not yet know how to speak correctly; for children, who at first say only their affections and their passions, their desires and their needs, spontaneously use a language freed from all its descriptive, enunciatory, and cognitive functions; they at first know only to speak in order to say nothing (nothing of the world) but their flesh; whether this flesh is already eroticized or not matters little here, so long as the children's language obeys and conforms to it. Thus lovers can address one another just as well and in turn with obscene words and with puerile words. Nothing is more coherent and pertinent, because in the two cases, their language directly reaches the flesh, without a worldly intermediary, and thus allows them to be aroused.

Finally, a third lexicon intervenes, also in apparent contradiction with the first two. Before identifying it, we should keep in mind that eroticization deploys itself as a process that should never, as such, come to its end—accomplishment without accomplishment, reciprocal increase of two fleshes that mutually restart one another from one excess to another, infinitely. Erotic speech provokes excess and wants only to tell this very excess—to wit, that every accomplishment must become a new beginning. Thus it must inevitably borrow words from mystical theology, which also, and first, tells and provokes excess—the excess of union, and thus of distance. All the same, the process of eroticization only lasts for as long as it says, "Again!" But what does "Again!" mean? I cannot say (and intend), "Here I am!" except by also intending (and saying), "Come!" which is, to the letter, the final word of the Book of Revelation and thus of mystical theology, which is rooted there. We must conclude that erotic speech cannot be performed without the language of spiritual union of man with God, any more than it can avoid the two other lexicons—the obscene and the childish.

These three lexicons equally and indissolubly support erotic speech. One can be surprised at this, but one can hardly contest it. One cannot object that they differ too much to come together, and that there is impropriety in mixing them. This impropriety only arises, as a matter of fact, from the supposed incompatibility of the objects to which philosophy and the natural attitude refer them: the disproportion between obscenity (supposedly filthy) and childhood (supposedly innocent), between obscenity and childhood (each supposedly imperfect) and divinity (supposedly perfect). But who will not notice right away that this disproportion and this impropriety depend only upon objects and their rank in the world, and thus presuppose yet again a descriptive and cognitive use of language? The erotic reduction excepts lovers from the world, and its language states nothing, but performs the eroticization of the flesh; words thus no longer say anything of being or that is objective, and they must not, so that the worldly hierarchies no longer matter to erotic speech, which can freely borrow all words, without accepting their worldly significations, so long as they arouse the other to give me my flesh, and arouse me to give her hers. The flesh remains the sole referent of all the lexicons employed by erotic speech. What does the worldly signification, meaning, or reference of words matter, once it is a matter of performing eroticization and the erotic reduction? One could even go further: not only do the three lexicons not contradict one another, but they are articulated by analogy with the three ways of mystical theology. The lexicon of obscenity would thus correspond to the affirmative way—where I attribute to the other what I can say that is most clear, most positive, most brutal, at the risk of petrifying her. The lexicon of puerility would eventually correspond to the negative way—where I erase from the other every fixed, definable, and assignable characteristic, at the risk of diluting her. And the theological lexicon would correspond almost to the hyperbolic way, where I aim at the other only through the process of excess endlessly taken up again, and of accomplishment without accomplishment, at the risk of never comprehending her, except to comprehend that this incomprehension alone is fitting.

Thus the lover has taken flesh, because he or she received it from the other one, who gave it to him or her without having it. The phenomenon of the other appears in the white light of eroticization. But, in its finitude, it disappears immediately. It is necessary to start all over again.

Concerning Lying and Truthfulness

§ 29. The Naturalized Person

The phenomenon of the other appears in the white light of eroticization. But this light is ineluctably extinguished in the very moment of its flashing forth, and the other thus disappears in his or her very apparition. Of course, we can begin again, and we will return to the task. But it will be necessary precisely to take everything up again from the beginning, starting from zero, without presupposing anything, even suspecting that nothing has been gained. Fastened to one another, endlessly having to begin again, we plough the sea. Eroticization implies a radical finitude, which inscribes us in an irrecuperable facticity—that of a process that is at once both powerful (more powerful than I) and automatically engaged (without me), even involuntarily (despite me), but which lasts for less time than do I (the lover and his or her oath). If one knows nothing of or underestimates this paradox—as do the unilateral doctrines of desire, of drives, of instinct, and so forth—not only does one miss the residual gap between the lover and his or her eroticization, but above all one sinks into a psychological and moral interpretation. But it is a matter of a formal difference, pertaining to the architectonics of the erotic reduction: the lover, whose advance is accomplished in the oath, wills the infinite ("once and for all," and may it last without ending, § 21), while the eroticization of crossed flesh remains in principle finite (§ 26). Even the liturgy, in which the other gives me my flesh (and individualizes me) and I give him his (thus individualizing him, too), must end by stopping without leaving a trace or fixing meaning. It gives and then takes back; it suspends what it accomplished precisely by accomplishing it; it closes what it opens. This gap is marked first according 151

to time: as long as the process of eroticization lasts, the other individualizes me by giving me my flesh and vice versa; but, as soon as suspension
intervenes, nothing remains of it and the whole carnal phenomenon of the
other disappears. Henceforward, the temporal gap is frozen like a spatial
frontier between my flesh, which once again becomes a body for the other,
and her flesh, which again becomes a body for me. Whence comes what we
will call *suspicion,* by which I ask myself if, after all, the eroticization of the
flesh truly took place, since it has disappeared without a trace, or if, supposing that it did take place, it changed anything between the other and me,
since everything seems exactly like it was before. Suspicion derives directly
from the temporal finitude of eroticization—I can no more escape it than
I can shirk my flesh.

The consequences of the paradox of eroticization risk weighing so
heavily that it is important to clarify completely its initial contradiction.
Suspicion arises first from the finitude of the eroticization of my flesh, or
more exactly from the temporality of this finitude: once again, I run up
against the fact that the process of eroticization must cease, that it cannot
last, even if I want it to. One will note that this inevitable interruption also
forbids assimilating eroticization to one of the vital physiological functions
(which are never interrupted: for instance breathing, or the heartbeat); or
indeed even to other physiological functions, also temporary and repeatable, but which respond to irrepressible biological needs (no one can live
very long without drinking, eating, or sleeping). For eroticization is in no
way obligatory, or permanent, or required, and experience proves that one
can go without it for long periods of time, or even completely, without dying. Suspension moreover does not interrupt only the process of eroticization, it defines its course—if this were not so, how would we understand
the puerile yet obsessive anxieties about orgasms that are too rapid or, inversely, the difficulty of attaining one? Suspension does not so much interrupt eroticization as it attests to its contingency—eroticization does not
last, because part of eroticization as such is that it is capable of not happening. By stopping outright, eroticization proves itself to be optional and
superficial—its suddenly dissipated power and violence only serve to reinforce disappointment. By ending, eroticization indeed traces a border
between a before and an after; but above all, the final void throws an irremediable suspicion upon the actuality of the beginning; between the two,
the manifestation of the other in person vanishes, and so too does the enjoyment of my own individuality that I received from her. For, once eroticization is suspended (§ 26), the other's flesh disappears, like that which

gave me my flesh; in this aftermath, my flesh no longer experiences the miraculous nonresistance of the flesh of the other, but instead the redis-covered resistance of a(nother) body. Not only does the flesh of the other withdraw, but I suspect that in reality there never was another flesh, only simply another body.

Suspicion goes even further. For, if the orgasm, this erased phenome-non, shows nothing, and leaves no memory and nothing to say (§ 28), how could it give me access to the other in person? The same orgasm, always without a clarifiable content, suits by right every possible person, because it manifests no one in particular. Indescribable and instantaneous, climax remains abstract, and thus anonymous; in and of itself, it bears upon no one. This impersonality is confirmed by two arguments in the form of ques-tions that are, moreover, rather sinister. First, does the other climax at the same time and with the same pleasure as I? I know very well that my sole eroticization will never teach me anything along these lines, and that it will be necessary for me to hold to the other's speech, and thus in fact to my confidence in her confidence, which reposes in its turn, in the final analy-sis, upon the oath; I am thus led back, in order to judge the climax of the other, to passing beyond eroticization. Next, supposing that we do truly share the same orgasm, is that enough to open for us an access to one an-other? If her speech does not confirm it, if mine does not acknowledge it, then eroticization alone will be able to do nothing; and even our crossed speech will be incapable of anything, if it does not ratify the oath, which thus is confirmed as more originary than eroticization. The intuition of eroticization does allow each of our fleshes to cross one another, but it does not allow us to meet one another in person—nothing less than the signification of the oath is necessary for that (§ 21). Thus neither of the two of us climaxes in person, nor with anyone else in person. The erased phe-nomenon does not go as far as that: the gap remains between the eroticized flesh and the person.

From this point forward, I can better measure the threat constituted by the automaticity of my eroticized flesh—its power to be aroused on its own in me and, consequently, to arouse me without me, or even in spite of me. Of course, I do not suffer this arousal all the time; sometimes, I exert it, when I attempt to give to the other her eroticized flesh in spite of her, against her will—a perverse gift, worse than rape, because I tear from her even the consent to my taking control over her. Thus the eroticization of the flesh does not always, or necessarily, reach the other in person, nor my-self, for that matter—it may subjugate us to one another against our desire, or in fact against our will; but, if the flesh can be eroticized against the will, and if no person can conceive of her- or himself without a free will (which we know at least negatively), we must conclude that eroticization never reaches the person. Eroticization does not take account of persons, and, out of lack and impotence, it sees no difference in so doing, because it never sees any person, and because it never puts any person into play. This conclusion brings with it another that is likewise negative. If, on the one hand, the finitude of eroticization forces it to stop, and thus, in the best of cases, it may begin again, just as, on the other hand, it never reaches any-one in person, but remains at the level of the pure anonymity of another in general, then we have no reason to exclude the possibility that repeatabil-ity results finally in the *substitution* of one other for another. If eroticization never reaches anyone in the first person, anyone can do the job; or at least, one could not exclude anyone from doing it. And in fact things happen in this way in the immense majority of cases: finitude allows, or even seems to demand, an infinite multiplication of others required by my eroticization endlessly beginning again; thus cloned (and yet clones of no original, since they lack all personality), these others are reduced henceforward to the hu-miliating function of simple "partners," thrown into eroticization but, par-adoxically, thrown out of the erotic reduction, where they become once again simple objects, instruments of which I make use in order to arouse my flesh. Since eroticization never reaches the person, or at least may never claim to do it or assure that it is done, no one any longer appears indispen-sable. And yet eroticization proliferates all the better now that, in this des-ert, no one holds it fixed.

Thus finitude—at first temporal (suspension), then formal (suspicion) —makes eroticization fall short of the person (substitution). I do receive from the other my flesh, and I do give her hers, but the white lightning of the orgasm blurs us, one in the other, jumbles us together, and finally no one, no person, appears. By "person" I here mean, in a negative sense, this heart of the other, whoever he or she may be, the disappearance of which would radically forbid me from loving him or her. Or, put positively, the last possible individuation (the *haecceitas* of the philosophers), no longer de-fined by form or matter, number or quantity, in short by the world and na-ture, but, instead, by the pure aim of the lover in the erotic reduction. Or again, the function of the person is to avoid the other's reducing him- or herself to a simple role in eroticization, or in other words to require un-substitutability—thus the person precisely does not equate to the *persona,* the mask and rôle of theater. We must conclude that eroticization neutral-

izes the person, placing the person back beneath the yoke of the world and
lowering him or her to the anonymity of the orgasm, or in short, naturaliz-
ing him or her. To naturalize in effect signifies the embalming of a cadaver,
in order that it may be conserved as an object and give the illusion of remaining there in person, while in fact it belongs to death. To naturalize the
person thus postulates the deepening of the gap between a person's appearance and this person him- or herself—which allows the site of the
erotic lie to open. Henceforward, it is no longer only a matter of the suspension of the eroticized flesh and of its return to a body (§ 26), but, more
radically, of the retrospective suspicion that in the midst of eroticization I
in fact enjoyed no one in particular (although I always enjoyed someone in
general). And what if, I ask myself, in eroticization itself no one ever appeared to me in person?

From erotic auxiliary, the flesh becomes an intermediary between me
and the other, and then, for lack of any person, a screen between us. Whence
there comes a properly erotic suspicion, which increases the gaps between
the other and her flesh, between my flesh and my person, and finally between lovers. This suspicion does not attack certainty only, it rises up against
assurance itself (§ 3); it is not a matter of a doubt (epistemic, about objects),
but of a *suspicion* (erotic, about the other). Henceforward, I suspect that, despite the radicalized erotic reduction, or rather because of it, it may be that
I do not love in person, since I can receive my flesh *in spite of* myself; and
thus it may be that the other does not perform in person, either, since she
too can make the other receive his flesh *despite* that other (well do I know—
often I impose the other's flesh upon her!). Henceforward, instead of reinforcing the oath, eroticization substitutes itself and disqualifies the oath,
because it compromises the possibility for each lover to say, "Here I am!"—
since no one any longer plays the lover in person, nor manifests his or her
person. The erotic reduction undoes itself with an ineluctable defeat, one
that results from its very radicalization. The fault falls to no one—no one
has gone astray: it is precisely a matter of a lack of any persons.* The apo-

---

*Throughout this fifth meditation, the author plays on the double meaning of the French
word *personne,* which he sometimes uses positively, to mean "a person," and at other times negatively, to mean "no one" (an example from the end of the previous paragraph: "personne ne
m'apparaissait jamais en personne . . . "—no one ever appeared to me in person). In the particular sentence here footnoted, the French reads "il s'agit précisément d'un défaut de personne";
"personne" here means "no one," but at the same time echoes the positive meaning of "a person." Thus a literal translation of the phrase would give us: "it is precisely a matter of a lack of
anyone," but I have rendered it as "a lack of any persons" in order to communicate the echoed
positive meaning as well.—Trans.

ria results from the very finitude of the erotic reduction: eroticization ends up by ending, and—this is the horror of it all—one does not die. One does not die of love—that's the horror. One starts over again with love, just as one "starts a new life"—that's the horror. If we survive the end of eroticization, then love does not have the rank of an absolute.

§ 30. The Gap and Deception

For the moment, I cannot surmount this disaster, but it remains possible to describe it. In truth, we are concerned here with a disaster and not only, or first of all, with a contingent failure. Before any moral or psychological consideration, we must recognize here an aporia in principle, which hinders us: if we remain apart from one another, if I do not succeed in manifesting myself in person to the other, nor she to me, this is not the result of a bad or weak will, but of a more original gap—the gap that each of us has within ourselves. For my eroticized flesh remains apart from me myself in person, as does hers from her person. Each of us must remain, whether he wants to or not, short of the person of the other, because first of all, our eroticized flesh keeps each of us short of our own respective person. And I know quite well this impossibility, which results from my very finitude: on the one hand, I identify myself with and through my flesh, which individualizes me in the final instance (§ 22); on the other hand, my flesh, when it is eroticized in contact with another flesh, engages automatically (§ 27), until the process is suspended of itself (§ 26)—my flesh thus escapes from my decision and my will in two ways; now, every person comprehends free will (or at least the will to act as if he or she enjoyed liberty, § 19); thus eroticized and finite flesh contradicts the person in me. If a person must be able always to resolve to . . . in order resolutely to attain him- or herself, then the eroticization of my flesh mortgages my own access to the person in me. Lacking resolution, I become suspicious of my own flesh. And if the other happens to fail me, how could I seriously hold it against her, since I, first, escape myself by dissipating my own person in my eroticized flesh?

Can I even speak here of a lie? Doubtless no, unless one admits that it is first a matter of my lying to myself and not to another. Doubtless no, except if we recognize that it is a matter of a formal lie in an extra-moral sense: I do not lie (to myself) in a moral sense, because it is not up to me not to lie (to myself), or more exactly to abolish the gap between my eroticized flesh and my inaccessible person. I do not possess the possibility of abolishing this gap; my erotic finitude imposes itself as the phenomeno-

logical impossibility of accomplishing in person the *me* that would in truth
say, "Here I am!" Once again, inauthenticity precedes authenticity originarily, or—which amounts to the same thing in the erotic reduction—the
lie (in the extra-moral sense) precedes and determines truthfulness. Let us
note that the erotic alternative between lying and truthfulness substitutes
itself for the metaphysical couple truth and falsehood. But with this addi-
tional difference, that henceforward the order of priority is inverted: far
from the truth also manifesting falsity by first manifesting itself (*veritas index sui et falsi*), here lying offers itself right away in full intelligibility (following the contradiction between automatic flesh and the person's will),
while truthfulness is only comprehended by derivation, so often does it remain problematic. Indeed, truthfulness seems problematic at the very least
because it implies authenticity, and therefore a pure transparency of self to
self (certainly for the other, but first of all for me), which the automatic
eroticization of the flesh compromises on principle. Who, in the white
light of orgasm, can claim to have experienced (let us not say to have seen)
any person unsubstitutable as such? Who can assure (or assure oneself)
that a person is distinguished there as such, and manifested there in his or
her individuality? Can I myself claim that I manifest myself as such there,
in the evidence of my final individuation? Without a doubt, no one can
claim *here* the status of a person. On the contrary, I have always, if for only
an instant, and even in the greatest outbursts, experienced the residual and
heartbreaking gap between the other and I, the simple double of a more
awful gap—that between my own flesh and my own person. I await the
denials.

From this we have to conclude not only that lying must be described
first, because it is conceived of alone, while truthfulness remains problematic and therefore not very describable, but that lying attests to more honesty than truthfulness. Indeed, truthfulness wants to trick us, just as it
tricks itself, when it claims not to lie when saying "Here I am!" or, more
commonly, "I love you!" when it knows (or has the feeling) that, erotically,
no one can accomplish these things—precisely because only a person
could do these things, while no eroticized flesh accedes to personhood. If
truthfulness wanted to merit the name, it would not claim, "I say 'I love
you!' I am sincere, I manifest myself in person"; it would recognize on the
contrary that, even with the best intentions in the world, erotically I never
manifest myself in person, because the person escapes the automatic eroticization of my flesh. Truthfulness would only become credible by *not* claiming to act on the authority of its inner sincerity in order to tell an inacces-

sible truth, but by playing honestly at whoever lies wins, so as thus to find once again a phenomenologically solid ground—that of an initial inauthenticity, where I know myself originally as apart from myself. It is necessary to draw from this paradox an unavoidable conclusion: the lover, who knows himself as lover and above all in the situation of eroticization, should never claim to say, "I love you!" or, "Here I am!" because he knows his gap within himself. The lover should only say, "I will love you again—afterward!" (§ 19). His truthfulness surpasses, by far, sincerity, which is always suspect.

Against the background of such an extra-moral determination of the gap between the person and eroticization, I can now examine the immoral conduct that chooses to lie in the moral sense and make use of the possibility of deception. What happens here, and by what right may one condemn it morally? It is necessary to distinguish, but in every case the issue is the same deception: to claim, by giving to the other his or her flesh, to also give my person; the issue will be, strictly speaking, that of a deception regarding the person.

In the first case, there is no mystery: one cruises fast and furious, with the least possible amount of talk and preliminaries, without even the pretence of an oath; "Here I am!" is reduced to "Let's go!" (or even "Where should we go?"); in principle, each party says that he or she gets something out of it, but in truth one must of course pay the price of eroticization thus reduced to itself: the renunciation of reaching the least personhood of the other, and thus, first, the renunciation of manifesting one's self in person. In this double depersonalization, not only do I deal merely with equivalent, indifferent, and disconnected "partners," but I myself am nothing more than a "partner," too, without a name or a meaning. Indifference, which buries the other in the fog of anonymity, holds me back, short of myself. Lying consists here in not even pretending to wish to accede to the phenomenon of the other, nor, therefore, to one's self. With *cruising*, the crossing of flesh is inverted: it serves only to prohibit us the status of lovers, to separate us from one another, to isolate me. Or no, not even to isolate me, for solitude still implies individuation, while the equivalence of "partners," which renders them indifferent to me, also renders me anonymous. I don't even have the means any longer to remain alone, because I am no longer anyone.

More often, a different situation is presented to me: active seduction, where a little mystery remains, or at least some claim to a little secret: I want to convince the other, and thus, to begin with, myself, that we very well could, perhaps, one day, why not? end up by drafting an oath. In fact, I don't at all believe that I will ever be able to go that far (and this protects me from the risk of getting myself caught in the game, and so leads me to push the affair further along), but I try to make the other believe it, so that she abandons herself to what I will never give her (myself, in person), and yet gives me what I am looking for—my own flesh. With *sweet-talking* (as it is called), we both speak in bad faith; I because I claim to sketch out an oath when I actually want eroticization without an oath; the other because she knows perfectly well, but pretends not to suspect my lie. This bad faith takes two shapes that are distinct, but converge. Either the other wants the same thing as me (her flesh without an oath) and lies to me in return; this shared lie, an honest lie, so to speak, brings us back to the previous case— cool, blithe cruising, like all dirty wars that never end. Or, one of us (for the sake of simplicity, let us say the other) guesses the lie, but prefers to run the risk; not that she loves me in advance as a true lover, but simply because she prefers to receive her eroticized flesh from me, even without an oath, following the principle of good sense that it is better to have something than nothing; the other thus lies to herself by hiding my lie, which is nevertheless visible enough; she makes her own my bad faith and ratifies our common refusal to say to one another, "Here I am!" and to risk ourselves in person. By a logical consequence, she will indeed receive her eroticized flesh, but with nobody [*personne*] to give it to her, nor (herself as) anyone [*personne*] to receive it. The immorality of sweet-talking derives, then, first from my lie (making believe that I manifest myself in person and want to see a person, when in fact I only desire to augment my own flesh without owing anything to anyone); then from the lie (implicit or explicit) of the other, who ratifies mine. Under these two forms, lying consists here in our claiming to be the lovers that we above all do not want to become. In sweet-talking, we become vaudevillian lovers, or put otherwise according to the rules of the erotic reduction, semblances of lovers, lovers' lies.

But this figure (sweet-talking) suggests a new possibility, doubtless a major one: if lying consists in attempting to receive one's flesh without putting oneself in play as a person (by oath)—just as, in another way, I can scarcely receive my flesh correctly from the other without simultaneously giving her hers—I ask: would it be necessary to conclude that I can truly give another her flesh only if I really put myself in play in person? Wouldn't truthfulness then lead to the inverting of the relation between the oath and eroticization? Instead of only supposing that the oath must be reinforced by eroticization, or indeed that it must be resolved there (as we have admitted up to this point, § 22–24), shouldn't we also consider the opposite possibility? The possibility that eroticization only succeeds in *truly* accomplishing the crossing of flesh (meaning, that each gives to the other the flesh that he does not have, and vice versa) if each one gives it and receives it in person (without stealing mine by refusing the other his or her own), which is to say under the condition of the *truthfulness* of the oath. In this hypothesis, the oath would pose the condition of accomplishment for the crossing of flesh, because it would precede it, would free itself from it, and could go further than it—that is, suspend the suspension. But then, could the oath deploy eroticization as it pleases and according to its will—an eroticization that is free (§ 35)?

Next there comes the case of a pure, radical, and dangerous lie: *infidelity*. The purest, because here, for the first time, I lie in words to someone explicitly, openly, and thus sincerely. Sincerely, for the liar always ends up by having to convince someone that he is not lying, by telling him or her face to face, straight in the eyes, as sincerely as possible, "I am telling you the truth"; moreover, a true liar recognizes himself most often in that he knows how to lie; and knowing how to lie consists in knowing how to say, "You know that I don't know how to lie," or, "Trust me." In the preceding cases (cruising and sweet-talking), the lie required nothing of the sort, it was enough to say nothing in order to have already perfectly perpetrated the lie; here, it is necessary to do it without stopping, to continue it and confirm it. Once again, sincerity gets along perfectly with the lie, and is absolutely opposed to truthfulness.

The same goes for the most radical lie: I do not only add one of my intentions to another, for example the apparent and lying intention (the pretense of the oath) redoubled by the real intention (the desire to steal my flesh); here, I redouble a person, the one that I continue to claim publicly to love, with another, the one that I claim to begin to love in private. In fact, I do not redouble one with the other, as if they could be added to one another so as to give me two for the price of one, with the difficulty of a choice, to boot; I do not redouble them so much as double-cross one with the other; in fact, I betray one with the other, in the way a double agent betrays each side. This other that I claim in public to love I do not love, because I want neither to attain her in person, nor to manifest myself in person before her. And as for the one that I claim to love in private, I do not love completely, because I cannot do so; because I must hold myself back for the other lie, I cannot advance without reserve in person, and thus I do not manifest myself as such and I lie yet again; this lack of truthfulness for-

bids me from requiring that the other advance in person; I can only negotiate a compromise with her—my half-measure against hers; but these two
half-measures at least produce a full lie, if not two, between us. I find myself caught between the public lie and the private lie, eventually doubled
and doubling. I lie doubly. And there's something worse: since I must play
my double role leading ineluctably to a double lie, I can no longer reach any
person (the one remains too close, the other too far), nor can I show myself in person.

Whence comes the extreme danger of this lie, which doubles the other
and me: there is no longer anyone in front of me and, above all, I am no
longer there for anyone, because I am not even a person anymore. And this
lie can no longer be stopped, much less made up for: it is necessary to dive
into it, invest oneself and lose oneself there, without hope of return. For,
in order to elude the two that I deceive, I must not only conceal from them
my person, but also construct for myself a double personality for a double
life; but by acquiring two personalities, I lose myself as such, precisely because I no longer have anyone to lose or to save. The most dangerous lie
requires that I *truly* lose myself in person. Contrary to the two preceding
cases, the lie does not conceal the true person, it kills him. Under the mask
of the lie, I am no longer anyone. And here we come to the only truth at
the end—I am no longer anything but a mask, which no longer hides anyone [*qui ne cache plus personne*].

In order to get out of this tomb, we cannot imagine that it is enough
to "have the courage" to "tell the truth" to one's "partner," by telling him
or her that "It's over!" and thus assigning him or her the status of (yet another) "ex-." These trivial formulas conceal badly the inanity of this attempt. For through this final violence, I merely admit to one of these others that I have lied to her—which obviously in no way abolishes the lie, or
reestablishes the truthfulness that I owed her in the previous oath. As re-
gards "honesty," far from getting out of my lie, I instead consecrate it in its
factuality and its evidence: I admit that I have lied, but I reestablish no
truthfulness or truth whatsoever. What is more: even if I could make the
deceived other disappear and make her undergo profits and losses, as if she
had never said, done, or loved anything, my lie would remain to endure; for
I will not be able to lie to myself enough to stop knowing that the oath that
I claimed to accomplish in the past today is no longer worth anything; I
know that I deceived myself—I told falsehoods, I disappointed the expectation of the other, I deluded myself. Even if I do not deceive another
person (and nothing is less sure, in fact), I still deceived *myself;* my lie has

indeed infected my past, and never again will my present recover its truth-fulness. From this point forward how will I be able to apply today for a new truthfulness—if it runs the risk in the future of turning into a real lie? I can sincerely call myself truthful—but that proves nothing, since formerly I lied sincerely; my protest does not fool anyone—because I already fooled someone. I began by deceiving myself, and then by deceiving, pure and simple; if I was able to lie even the first time, even with a single other, why would I not do it again?

Lying thus proves itself to be the horizon of eroticization, which is first extra-moral (the gap), and then moral (deception), once the person has been naturalized (§ 29). Should I the lover, then, put up with lying, or can I hope to pass beyond it? In any case, I must confront it, for the erotic re-duction plays out nowhere else.

§ 31. Abduction and Perversion

Though I practice it so often and so easily, in fact I cannot put up with ly-ing. No one can tolerate it, at least in the erotic reduction, when another lies—to a false oath, I prefer, by far, that she declare that she does not love me, or even that she hates me. Most often, I myself lie out of cowardice, and not with a firm intention or according to a carefully weighed stratagem; nor do I hardly ever lie straight to someone's face, because that requires character and even a perverse courage; I never admit having lied without embarrassment or shame; and even in order to say it to myself, I still must look for excuses. Why can't I face up to what I so often do discreetly? Doubtless it is because eventually the lie will annul the erotic reduction in its entirety, since the lie is directly inscribed there and is only conceived be-ginning from the erotic reduction. But above all, it is because no lover—the person having paid the price of the advance and of eroticization—can tolerate calmly and indifferently another playing with what the advance and eroticization cost, and what they reveal, and surely not the other lover, the other of the oath and the orgasm. For her lie not only steals her away from me, but also what I have received from her—my eroticized flesh, and thus in an essential measure, myself. If, in her lie, the other only took back from me her self, I would survive after all with a counter-lie, by a substitution. But also and above all, the other takes back me, myself, since she no longer gives me my flesh, this flesh that I cannot give to myself and that I obtain only from her. And what is worse, by suspending the gift of my flesh, the other also annuls all of my past flesh, since this gift leaves no trace or memory (§ 26); by suspending the source-point, she destroys the retentions. If the other lies to me, she has therefore always lied to me—not only do I no longer have my flesh, but I never had it. Thus it goes without saying that no lover can tolerate, even for an instant, the bald-faced lie of the other; a lover will even go to the point of preferring any absurd denial, or indeed lie to him- or herself, in order not to have to look this lie in the face. But what can the lover do, if he or she is no longer satisfied with this delusion and wants actually to surmount the deception—to reduce the gap between him- or herself and the other, that is to say between him- or herself and the eroticized flesh that he or she has received from the other?

First, the lover can claim actually to restore truthfulness from the moment of the crossing of flesh, by insisting that my person as lover and that of the other manifest themselves and be accomplished directly in the eroticized flesh. Put another way, I claim that, *for me* at least, I accomplish perfectly "Here I am!" in my flesh; and, what is more, that my flesh, by being eroticized, puts my person in evidence; in short, that I have personal, transparent, and sincere eroticization. This delirious ambition ineluctably produces the inverse of what it promises: it reinforces the lie by not keeping its promise. It deceives first because it promises sincerity, which remains an illusion of metaphysical subjectivity—that I may make myself equal and transparent to myself—and which contradicts the lover's advance in the erotic reduction. Next, it deceives because the finitude of eroticization (no one can climax endlessly) always makes me disappear at the completion of eroticization and be there no longer for the other, or even incites me to substitute another other for the first one. Finally and above all, this delirium of sincerity deceives because it presupposes as realized that of which the very possibility is compromised by the lie—that my flesh accomplishes our oath or puts my person on stage. By insisting upon sincerity in my eroticized flesh, I not only rave madly, but I lie all the more, because I lie to myself.

Consequently, the lover very quickly endows him- or herself with another tactic; seeing as he or she cannot claim to produce for him- or herself truthfulness according to the eroticized flesh, he or she demands it *on behalf of the other.* And, as the raving lover assumes that flesh can accomplish an oath or put a person on stage, he or she imagines that taking hold of the flesh of the other will suffice to assure him or her of the person. We will call this erotic absurdity *abduction,* inevitable though it is at this moment in the logic of the amorous phenomenon. Clearly, abduction contradicts itself and also accentuates the lie. First of all because abduction supposes that the flesh makes one accede to the person, when in fact it obscures the person. And also because abduction misses this person all the more, because it exerts upon his or her flesh a constraint and suspends the least of his or her free will. Abduction, when it exerts itself paradoxically without recourse to physical violence, attempts to annul the will and, thus, suppress the personhood of the other; one can actually lay hold of the flesh as flesh, and against its will; it is enough to make use of one of its essential properties — its automatism, its arousal without or in spite of the other; in order to lay hold of it, it is enough therefore to constrain the flesh to arouse itself and climax in spite of itself; or rather, since as such it is aroused automatically (without, or even against every free will), there isn't even anything to constrain, provided that it spontaneously follow its irrepressible movement. There is no need to impose a consent upon the flesh (it has always already consented), since it only consents to its own automaticity. The absence here of physical violence opens the arena to a worse violence, violence directed toward the will, which properly denies the person.

If, on the contrary, abduction is exercised with physical violence, it doesn't contradict itself any less, by accentuating another lie. Let us suppose that a lover, in order to reduce the lie, exerts violence upon the other; he thus no longer counts upon her automatic flesh to lay hold of her person; he renounces passing through her climax and even dispenses with her flesh; there only remains one flesh in play, that of the lover, who tears his own flesh from the other, without giving her any at all; thus it is a matter of only a half-eroticization, a unilateral eroticization, in which the other is robbed not only of her climax but also of her flesh; the abduction becomes a rape accompanied by theft of climactic enjoyment. But then, what does the violating lover lay hold of? Not of the other's sincerity, since he denies her her will and her personality (the first lie, that of the abduction). Nor of flesh, either, since by depriving her of eroticization, he no longer gives to the other the least flesh (second lie, that of the rape). In fact, there remains only a physical body, all else (flesh, eroticization, will, and personhood) has already disappeared; there remains a final step to take in this logic — the only good body is a dead body (or eventually, a body bought and sold). Abduction thus ends up at its final contradiction: "I loved her too much, I killed her." Sincerity (that is, the delirium of sincerity) kills, because it claims to exert itself directly upon what forbids it — the automatic eroticization of the flesh.

Another route remains, deviating, or rather deviant — *perversion*. A smarter route: in order to claim to reach the person in his or her flesh, one appeals no longer to impracticable truthfulness, but instead directly to the perfectly practicable lie. As lover, I thus cannot put up with the fact that the other's eroticized flesh endlessly becomes a body again, nor that its eroticization closes the access to her person; I will therefore strive to force her flesh to remain flesh; I will use every means to do so, even pretence. In order to keep the other's flesh, and thus mine, too, alive, I will begin by keeping it in sight, even if, in order to make this work, it must pretend and lie about its status as flesh. I will constrain the flesh of the other as well as my own to remain flesh at any price, through every trick and every convention: make-up, disguise, masks, play-acting, etc. I will make use of the resources of bodies, even their illusions, in order to capture the flesh. And, since I only have an advantage over bodies when I seek to capture the flesh of the other, it is necessary that I push bodies, and thus their naturalness, to their limits, or even beyond these limits: thus I will play the nature of bodies against nature, without scruple or restraint, risking all in order to maintain the miracle of eroticized flesh in sight. Thus I will transgress the borderline of excitations, passing from pain to pleasure; I will transgress the borderline between the sexes; I could almost end up—why not?— transgressing the borderline between species. But I will always be deluding myself, I will deceive myself and lie yet again, because here too I will confuse degrees. Suppose that I do succeed in keeping the other's eroticized flesh as well as my own in sight by sheer force of hard work on bodies (the first confusion); suppose even that I succeed in prolonging the process of eroticization to the extreme, or even that, by force of hard work and substitution, I imagine myself erasing its essential finitude (second delusion), it will remain the case that nothing—whether I make a flesh shout or cry, whether I make it give up its spirit or ask for mercy—will allow a person to be made manifest. On the contrary, all these efforts to accomplish this "making," regardless of whether it is with or without the other's consent, prove that it is always and only a matter of staging the other from the point of view of my gaze, and thus in no way and by principle a matter of a manifestation of the other as person. No object will ever phenomenalize a person (the third contradiction). The other remains apart.

Lying thus remains intact for as long as one wills to surpass it by force. Abduction and perversion confuse everything and succeed at nothing, because they seek the person in the realm of the impersonal. A person does not possess himself any more than does one possess an eroticized flesh— one only possesses a physical body or an object. One only possesses that which cannot love. And as soon as one realizes that one does not love it, one kills it—in fact, one discovers that it is already dead. Like Orpheus's complex: Eurydice is found everywhere, except in Hell (wherever a person is found, there is no hell, not even Hell); or else, under the name of Eurydice, Orpheus was looking for something else entirely, something less avowable.

§ 32. The Street of Darkened Faces

The aporiae through which we have just traveled all result from a single confusion—consideration of the eroticization of the flesh as an access to the other in person. Thus they all result in the same disaster—far from being accomplished in a person, the other's flesh thus falsified ends up in the rank of a body pure and simple, where one may kill the other's person. If a way out remains open, it thus must be first to explode this confusion, by detaching the face from the glamour and trickery of its eroticized flesh. Inevitably, a question will be posed: eroticization can encompass even the face (§ 24), but does it follow that it should? In order to accede to the person, is it not necessary to come back to the proper function of the face—to assure to the phenomenon of the other its signification (§ 20), before the crossing of flesh (§ 23)? Thus the face, taking up again its autonomy and finding once again its privilege, could give me access to the other in person. This tactical movement seems almost to go without saying, and yet it offers more difficulties than it resolves. Indeed, I find myself firmly within the situation of eroticization, without possible return, because without the eroticization of our flesh, our oath would remain formal and incapable of individualizing its actors; far from compromising the erotic reduction, the passage to my flesh, and then to my flesh receiving itself from the other, has alone allowed access to a true phenomenon of the other. True, the crossing of flesh is, for the moment, stuck in lying (the gap and deception); true, the truthfulness of the person remains inaccessible at this point on the path. But for all of that, I can no longer go back, first of all because I would move away from the other to whom eroticization has undeniably brought me closer than did the oath; and next because, once eroticization has been attained, I can no longer consider myself apart from it—even its suspension makes it more irremediable to me, because it reveals to me my utmost finitude. If I thus cannot go back upon eroticization for the sake of the face, it remains for me to go back to the face within the very horizon of eroticization, in order to ask if, in this irrevocable situation, the face can still manifest the other in person, and not only in the glory of his or her flesh. This amounts to asking if a truthful face can manifest itself. Put another way, what becomes of truth under the rule of the erotic reduction?

Even before the erotic reduction, the face distinguishes itself from the simple facet. The facet shows a surface, without reserve or withdrawal, like an object or a subsistent being; its absence of depth dispenses it from showing itself as such, since it lacks the dimension of this "as such"—the most beautiful façade in the world can only give what it has: a surface effect. The face shows itself all the better because it allows a glimpse of the withdrawal from which it issues; through this place of issue, it opens a depth, beginning from which a gaze can come to us from elsewhere—a gaze that is older and more distant than our own, upon which it comes, and weighs, and which it contradicts; the face as such addresses me with a gaze that exerts right away a call and a command. The face envisages from afar, it takes hold of me from above, so that it cannot refrain from emitting a demand. The entire question becomes—what is it demanding of me? A response is clear: the face charges me verbally with (or silently intimates) the ethical commandment, "Thou shalt not kill!" It remains to know what this ethical commandment can do once the erotic reduction is accomplished (§ 20) and even once this erotic reduction is radicalized by the crossing of flesh: does it impose itself without question, like an absolute imperative that one can only transgress de facto by confirming it de jure? Clearly the answer is no. For in the erotic reduction, the face no longer commands me only with "Thou shalt not kill!" but demands, "Thou shalt love me!" or more modestly, "Love me!" The difference does not consist first of all in the face's passage from a negative demand (an interdict) to a positive demand (that I will never be able to satisfy, because it exceeds all measure); the difference lies above all in that the first requirement applies unconditionally for every face, because it does not depend on an individual, his or her qualities or intention, but rests upon a negation of the particular person and upon the absence of his or her individuality; while the second requirement demands that I love such and such a face, such and such person individualized by his or her singularities, just such and none other. For love requires the personalization of the face, for two reasons; first because I can only love in an oath, where just such an other will say to me alone, uniquely and in the first person, "Here I am!"; next, because I can only love if my flesh is eroticized to give to the other her or his own flesh, but with a finite eroticization, limited to a single other in a given time—I can give only one flesh, and thus I can only give it in particular. Once within the erotic reduction, the face thus can no longer demand unconditionally, universally, in silence—it is necessary that it speak in person in the oath; it is also necessary that it pay with its flesh individualized in eroticization. The face must be individualized and manifest itself as such, which it cannot accomplish without making its truthfulness recognized. The question is once again transformed: it is a matter of knowing if the face, under the rules of the erotic reduction, cannot only tell the truth, but also show that it tells the truth (show itself to be truthful), in short phenomenalize itself in such a way that I see that it does not lie. In a word, can it escape from lying, which compromises the eroticized flesh, and justify its claim to open access to the other in person?

As much as one can agree that the ethical face does not lie—because it remains too universal to have the means to do so—so too must one admit that the face has no particular privilege of truthfulness in the radicalized erotic reduction. On the contrary, the lie, which yet remains extra-moral with eroticized flesh, becomes truly moral when played, or possibly played, by the face. Paradoxically, the flesh does not lie; only the face can lie in the strict moral sense, because it alone has an ethical status. And the first lie consists in claiming not to lie, and then asserting innocence and goodness. Not lying: the face of the seducer, who does not love but makes himself love, shines indeed with a perfect sincerity: in this way he can calmly betray with a kiss. Goodness: the faces of the worst murderers, terrorists, or torturers can often give the appearance of a childlike innocence or an angelic beauty; without a doubt, their ignominy would be attenuated a bit, if some ugliness made them visibly bad; but in the erotic reduction, precisely, beauty has never become the placeholder of goodness or retained an analogy with it (metaphysics is almost alone in supposing it). Innocence: only an innocent face can lie well; it would not lie if it allowed its dishonesty to be guessed at; there would already be much honesty in presenting the face of a liar, a scoundrel, or a used-car salesman. Lying prowls everywhere, especially there where one expects it—on the face. Indeed, in the erotic reduction, faces (one can no longer say "the face" because we must individualize when it is a matter of loving) become inevitably the instance of a possible lie and of a compromised truthfulness, precisely because they no longer are limited to demanding universally and negatively ("Thou shalt not kill!"), but must also respond to my face—positively and in person ("Here I am!"). Every face begins to be able to lie the moment that another face asks it to tell it in truth that it loves it—that is, from the moment of the oath. How would a face not continue to be even better able to lie, seeing that the crossed eroticization of flesh repeats and accomplishes the oath? The lie blurs the truthfulness upon faces as soon as the erotic reduction reckons that they will become lovers. Lying does not so much disrupt truthfulness in love as the one and the other signal to us the third dimension of the face: the invisible depth that the face takes on when the erotic reduction illuminates it.

In love especially, faces allow themselves to be caught in lying, like a swan in ice. I can gauge this in at least two postures, according to the oscillations between dissimulation and opening. Let us suppose that my face opens without holding anything back (or at least that I sincerely think so), because I believe that I am exposing myself to another face that is also open without holding anything back, but that in fact this face holds itself back and dissembles, offering nothing more than a façade. Thus I let myself be envisaged or faced openly, without envisaging or facing anything in return; I find myself seen without seeing anything; I came, I was seen, and my hopes were frustrated; I am able to go have myself seen, but I got myself had; indeed, I was had, because I didn't see anything, not even the shots that were fired. I discover myself seduced and abandoned. Seduced: I believed I was seeing the other in her face, I believed that the openness of her gaze led me to her person, when she was looking me straight in the eyes and lying, in order to lead me far away from her; she asked me to "go look elsewhere to see if I am there"—and I went. Abandoned: come to the edge of her gaze, having almost already entered into her inner personhood, I was gathering my momentum when I discovered that I was leaping into the void, without anything to receive me; she asked me not to abandon her but, when I wanted to shelter her, she had disappeared; in contrast to the gifted (who receives himself from what he receives), I find myself as one who is abandoned (one who loses himself by losing the remainder). And, if I hold to it, it remains for me eventually to find some erotic pleasure in this injustice done to my face.

Inversely, let us suppose that my face holds back and dissimulates itself, offering nothing more than a façade to another face (which imagines itself at the least as) open and not holding anything back, in person. Thus it is I who seduce this time, without letting myself be seduced; I envisage without letting myself be envisaged; I see without letting myself be seen; I take hold of a face without exposing myself open-faced. I do not want to declare my face open, as one declares a city open because he has given up its defense and placed it under the supposed benevolence of the victor. As seducer, I want to guard it; so I close my face, just as one closes a door, a discussion, or a possibility—in order to be done with it and to remain the master of myself, or more exactly, of the other. Seducer indeed, I keep my guard only in order to regard or gaze upon the other, to let her come forward unprotected, to lay her bare, and then to make her wait as I decide how to betray her. Either I do not give her her flesh in the end, and I climax alone; in this case, she will learn of her frustration and, moreover, I do not take her for my other and, thus, she is no one. Or I eroticize her completely, give her her flesh and make her feel its automatic power, which plays without her and against her, but I forbid her to give me my flesh; she climaxes alone, without my consenting to climax through her; this would give her too much pleasure, when on the contrary I want to convince her that I do not climax automatically, despite myself and through her; in my refusal to climax through her and through the flesh that she would give me, I want her to realize that it is I who accede to personality, and not her. And I can even find some erotic pleasure in making for myself such an unjust non-face.

These two facets of the face within the situation of lying (in short, masochism and sadism) nevertheless rest upon a rather fragile parallelism; can a non-face (a façade) envisage or face a face in the same way that a face can envisage or face a non-face? Who would doubt that a face can deny to another face its dignity as a person? The history of the century that has just passed—the darkest of all (notwithstanding the performances of the new century)—forbids us from doubting it. But, by denying to the other face its stature as face, by thus rendering the dignity of the other debatable, does not the supposed seducer's or persecutor's face (they are the same) become debatable, too? The one who kills by de-facing thus no longer faces anything, for he has destroyed every other face that would recognize him as a face; he knows, too, that nothing prevents him from being de-faced as well, since he succeeded first in de-facing others. The seducer and the executioner thus strain to lose, for themselves, the dignity of the face that they destroy in others. The non-face of educated bestiality and of ideological totalitarianism share the negative privilege of the seducer—he no longer hears anyone, he can no longer speak to any person, and must commit suicide.

Thus the face is not an exception to the nullity of the concept of sincerity, but instead confirms it. The face cannot set itself up against lying simply by priding itself on its truthfulness, for the lie itself appeals to sincerity, and only sincerity allows the face to flout truthfulness. We must conclude that neither eroticized flesh nor the sincere face allow lying or truthfulness to appear; since lying and truthfulness are not phenomenalized, it would be necessary to conclude that they do not form part of the phenomenon of the other. So where do we situate them? Outside of erotic phenomenality, as its conditions of possibility? In this way, lying and sincerity would, under the rule of the erotic reduction, take back the transcendental function that truth and falsehood assume in metaphysics. But at the same time, if lying and truthfulness cannot be phenomenalized, the person, who puts them into play and cannot be described without them, also will not be able to appear under the rule of the erotic reduction. Nevertheless, this is precisely what jealousy, in a brutal and unexpected manner, will contest.

§ 33. Jealousy's Honor

Jealousy—I can hardly dare to evoke it, so much has it been disparaged as a passion of possessiveness, selfish, to be sure, but above all contradictory and in the end ridiculous. Nevertheless, I am going to take it seriously, for it, at least, confronts shamelessly and straightforwardly the heartbreaking aporia in which I find myself stuck: in eroticization, the other does not appear as a person, above all if she claims to be sincere, such that she cannot not lie to me, and always ends up by lying to me (or me lying to her). Jealousy endures this aporia as the worst of possible sufferings—the other appears to me just enough to signify that she will never phenomenalize herself in person. Jealousy knows this better than anyone, and knows that of which it speaks. So we must let it speak, even if it does not always know what it is saying—for perhaps I will be able to learn more from its delusion than from all the soothing denials of those who believe themselves beyond it, simply because, having never been able to become lovers, they have never given in to it.

And yet, how can it not be admitted that, in the deplorable figures that it assumes as its own, jealousy contradicts itself and in appearance demonstrates its inanity? To be convinced, it is enough to listen to it speak.

First figure: I love another perfectly (so I claim, or brag), and she, for her part, does not love me in return; I see an injustice in this; I conceive a lively resentment, which we call jealousy. But what does love signify here? Nothing but a shapeless desire, which has not yet acceded to the erotic reduction, has no knowledge of the lover's advance, and becomes exasperated by blindly laying claim to reciprocity without ever supposing that, perhaps, it is not so simple. Jealousy's demand leads to a dead-end. If I persist in laying claim to something that no one owes me, this puts into question my intelligence, lucidity, capacity to please, and charm, but it does not concern the other, who by definition owes me nothing. Thus there is a misapprehension of the duties of the other, of my rights with respect to her, and, above all, of the very notion of love itself.

Another figure remains, one that is more current and tougher, as well: I love a certain other, who claims to love me (or who lets it be believed), but who in fact betrays me, either because this other simply doesn't love me, or because she loves another in my place. It goes without saying that here, too, to love has no meaning, and neither is it inscribed within the erotic reduction. In this figure, jealousy is better comprehended, since an explicit lie plays a role; the evil that it inflicts upon me increases, too, since there may appear here a third party, a mimetic rival, who condemns me to exit the game. Here my situation appears clear and simple, but the position of the other becomes completely incomprehensible, because contradictory—she loves me and she loves me not, in the same moment. Of course, this contradiction reveals itself most of the time to be quite apparent; in fact, I produce it myself in order to delude myself and to hold on to a false hope; I want to imagine that the other loves me (a little bit) and does not love me, while clearly she does not love me. As soon as I will have found the courage to admit it, the contradiction will vanish and I will come back to the figure described previously. But sometimes, it is a matter of a real contradiction, which actually structures the conduct of the other in opposition to me: the other loves me (or at least "likes" me "well enough") and, at the same time, does not love me. And what is more, this contradiction can sometimes also be understood in two ways.

On the one hand, the other alternates between love and rejection in order to keep two irons in the fire, to hold me there with the tongs and have me be consumed; this malicious game has no other intention than to cause me pain and to get a kick out of it; though rare, this tactic has its logic— the logic of darkened faces, which mask at any price the person within them, to the point of taking hold of the personhood of others (§§ 31–32). On the other hand, the other lies to me out of simple weakness: she doesn't know how to tell me no, any more than she knows how to say yes to the third party, to that other one, to the supposed rival; this conduct is met with all the more often because it results directly from the anteriority of the lie over truthfulness; it confirms the difficulty of making the least decision in general and, in particular, of saying, "Here I am!"; above all it stigmatizes the problematic phenomenality of the person (§§ 29–30). For all of that, even though intelligible, these two contradictions remain untenable; for I claim to love an other who either wishes me ill, or who does not know what she wants, and thus I claim to love either a person vitiated as such (by a bad will), or a weakening person (by lack of will); in both cases, I ought simply not to continue to love the one that one cannot seriously love, nor desire her, simply because she is not worth it. Since I am not dealing with an other in person, there is no cause to love, and thus no place for the least jealousy. Logically, to extinguish immediately the least spark of jealousy within me, it should be enough to see that there in front of me, in fact, there is no one—no person.

Thus jealousy is not so much disqualified by its contradictions, as evident as they may appear, as it is by its blind ignorance of the erotic reduction and of its successive moments. For jealousy, when it complains that the other does not love me, doesn't even see the deep injustice of what it is thus presupposing—that the other should love me, that she must do it all the more because I love her already and, above all, because love requires reciprocity; jealousy implies, then, that I *not* accomplish the erotic reduction, that I *not* substitute for the question "Does anyone love me?" the question "Can I love first?"; in short that I *not* make love as a lover, that I *not* practice the advance, but that I demand reciprocity; in short, that I not love. Understood according to these meanings, jealousy only proposes a regression to the inferior stages of the erotic reduction. All I can do is thrust it aside from my path, where it would only add one more aporia.

Nevertheless, I cannot get rid of it so easily. In its delusional, unjust, and pathetic plea, I divine that another speech is trying to express itself, and that it has much to say. Fools usually reproach God with, among a thousand other crimes, giving in to jealousy, a sentiment that is too human for him. This is a strange and ridiculous grievance. Ridiculous, because an excess of humanity does not seem to be the danger that threatens us the most: rather, it is lacking humanity that we have to fear, and falling into bestiality. And strange, because, if God asserts his right to jealousy, this does not imply that he accomplishes it in the sense found among us humans (an infra-erotic regression), but that, if necessary, he makes use of it in a more radical and edifying sense—I mean, one more advanced in the erotic reduction than are we. If we managed to understand it in the sense in which God himself condescends to exercise it, jealousy might not only not lead us astray, but help us to get over the aporia where we are marking time—the aporia of a phenomenalization of the person. What, then, does jealousy wish to say, taken in its erotic essence? It is never a matter of willing to make myself loved by the other in spite of him or her, nor of imposing a duty of reciprocity upon him or her, nor even of demanding his or her fidelity—but instead of asking that he or she remain *faithful to him- or herself.*

The jealous thoroughly merits the title of lover because he clamors for the other to become or remain a sincere lover, and to accomplish, finally or once again, the advance, the oath, and the crossing of flesh; in short, that he or she make love or, having made it, not unmake it. She who is jealous does not stigmatize the other's infidelity toward her, but instead his infidelity toward himself and his status as lover, in short toward the erotic reduction. I become jealous of the very love that the other claims to accomplish and does not accomplish. I become jealous not of the other as such, but of the other as lover. I become jealous because I defend her own failing sincerity against her—not her sincerity toward me, but first and foremost toward herself as an avowed and failing lover. I enter into jealousy in order to defend the lover within the other and to defend the other against herself, less so that she does not betray me than so that she does not betray love itself. Thanks to jealousy, I take charge of the honor of love and defend it against the lover's lie. For the lover, when he or she fails, provokes a triple dishonor. First, she dishonors me by lying to me, and thus by denying our oath. Next, she dishonors herself by regressing to a point short of her status as lover, by obscuring her sincerity. Finally, and above all, she dishonors love itself: indeed, the advance—this decisive paradox that provokes the lover—only consists in surmounting the requirement of reciprocity and in loving first, without preliminary conditions, thus freely and without limit; and so, the true lover, who makes what he or she says and says only what he or she makes ("Here I am!"), is characterized by his or her unconditional advance, because he or she loves without asking for anything, or, in short, because he or she wins even and above all when he or she loses. Love is capable of all things, endures all things, hopes all things—because, even if it loses everything, it still wins what alone matters—loving, precisely (§ 18). Following this paradox of the erotic reduction (against economy and the natural attitude), he who loves the most, or even alone and without any return, does not lose, but wins. What does he win? The status of lover, the endless increase of love, in short, the advance itself. The lover gives honor to love by thus remaining faithful to it—faithful to the originary paradox of the advance. If I stand up to defend the honor of love by reminding the other of her failing lover's resolution, then, in this precise sense, I can legitimately become jealous and find in that jealousy my own honor. For in the end I reproach the other for nothing other than not loving to love, as a result of losing her title as lover—and all truthfulness. Through jealousy, I defend the honor of love and the truthfulness of the other.

Jealousy asks the other to accomplish him- or herself as a lover, from whom it demands truthfulness. It claims to see the other as a person, despite erotic finitude, despite the inevitable lie, despite the limits of phenomenalization through the flesh. Jealousy thus expresses a properly phenomenological requirement: that the other appear as *a* person, and no one *else*. So why does it remain misunderstood, seen at once as both pathetic and ridiculous? Because it does not know how to obtain what it requires, and even does all it can in order never to obtain it.

§ 34. Hatred's Way

Jealousy shares this contradiction with the hatred of the other, to which it sometimes ends up leading. If jealousy helps to describe the erotic phenomenon, wouldn't hatred allow for the same thing? There is nothing absurd about such a hypothesis. For, in the erotic reduction, love has already been in league with the hatred of everyone for himself (and of all for all), from which in a sense it emerges directly (§§ 9–14); neither was love able to avoid the suspension of eroticization (§ 26), which imposes upon it the gap and deception (§ 30), exposes it even to abduction (§ 31) or winds up by darkening faces (§ 32). In the end, one could ask oneself if the enterprise of phenomenalizing the other does not owe as much, or even more, to hatred than to love itself. More exactly, doesn't what we have described up to this point under the name of love in fact depend upon its dark side, hatred, which, less than inverting it, reveals its severity? At the point at which I have arrived, couldn't I suspect that I accede (or not) to the other through the erotic work of the negative, rather than through direct sight of her— that I see the other more if I hate her, than if I love her?

In the first place, is not the erotic reduction accomplished just as well if I hate as if I love? As we have seen (§§ 3–5), it is a matter of bringing the space and time of the world back to the unique point of reference of an other, who is not only privileged among others that she disposes around her, but who obscures them with her unique brilliancy, to the point where I see only her. Now, when I allow myself seriously to hate someone, he or she takes such a powerful stature in my eyes, arouses such an exclusive attention and obsesses me so profoundly that not only do I accord him or her a privilege of unique alterity, but in society I see only him or her—to the point where he or she and I are alone before the world, exactly like lovers on a public bench. This focusing upon an other because I hate him does not only individualize him to the extreme; it also makes me live; it also and above all assigns me to myself even more than to him (§ 13). The hatred that he accords me, with which he privileges me, or in short, that he *gives* to me, sometimes awakens me and obliges me to become what I was, without yet knowing it, or willing it. Reciprocally—through a reciprocity of which love seems necessarily incapable (§§ 15–16)—the hatred that I render to this other compels him to push to the very limits all that he can do to harm me. In fact, a nice reciprocal hate unites more thoroughly, for a longer time, and more solidly than an alleged love; at the least, in many cases, it lasts longer than a would-be love. Since as much as love, my hatred of the other leads us each to our accomplishment, I even receive myself from this other that I privilege by hating, as if in spite of him, and he receives himself by hating me. Our hatred individualizes me and individualizes him, too—more surely and more quickly than can the erotic reduction. Couldn't I, then, dispense with loving?

Indeed, it could be that hatred not only is not equal to love, but surpasses it. According to the erotic reduction, I only accede to the phenomenon of the other by passing through my flesh, and thus through the other's flesh, and their crossing. For, as we have seen (§ 23), the flesh exercises the double privilege of feeling the bodies of the world and, indissolubly, of feeling itself feel them; it feels itself all the more because it can feel without restriction and affect itself all the better when it feels less resistance; it thus feels itself all the better when it not only feels bodies of the world that resist it in space, but above all another flesh that has the property of not resisting it. My flesh advances and experiences itself for as much as another flesh yields precedence and allows it to advance. Whence comes the gap between our two fleshes, which is born from the withdrawal that they arrange for one another reciprocally, and which joins them together as such. If I do not directly see what I love, I nevertheless recognize it immediately as flesh—by the resistance that it does not oppose to my flesh and which attests to its also being flesh. We phenomenalize one another, because we each give to the other the flesh that we do not have—she mine, I hers. We cross our flesh. But this crossing separates us as much as it binds us together; for, while we indeed make love or, rather, because we make it, we nevertheless never make one flesh; we experience, on the contrary, and well before bumping up against suspension, that each flesh remains irreducible to the other, that each climaxes alone, although each gains full enjoyment from the other, and that the crossing of flesh never merges or exchanges it. Whence comes the aporia of eroticization, which immediately distinguishes what it joins.

Hatred, on the contrary, leaps over this aporia without difficulty; more accurately, it frees itself from it without even considering it. For hatred dispenses with the flesh, while love must pass through it. When I hate, I have the privilege of hating without flesh, neither the flesh of the other, which I would like to destroy as a body, nor my own, which I annul by making it resist bodies; no longer is it a matter of allowing myself to be affected, or of experiencing myself in this affection; on the contrary, it is all about *not* allowing oneself to be affected (not allowing oneself to be run over), gaining a toughness and a resistance that allow me to affect the other as harshly as possible and to resist him or her like a body resists another body—by repelling it. Because here I cannot "feel" the other, it is a matter of making him feel it; thus, first, *not* to experience him, then to repel him as far as possible, to chase him away and deport him, to make him disappear from my sight, or even in the end to annihilate him. Henceforward, delivered from the immediate mediation of the flesh, I take aim at him with a pure and transparent intentionality, not only as a simple object, but as an object that I sight for as long as possible, like an objective at which I take aim in order to shoot it down. Clearly, I aim at the other, but no longer in order to see him or her (I can no longer see him or her), but on the contrary in order to bring him or her down. I aim at him, but in order to destroy him, in order to be done with him. I "touch" him, but so that he will no longer touch me. At the same time, if I do not feel him, I no longer feel myself in him, or because of him (even my *ressentiment* only feels itself, and never the other); indeed, if I annul his flesh, I also annul my own, because I increased it by experiencing the nonresistance that his flesh offered to me; by denying the other his flesh, I thus deprive my own of its only opportunity to grow. By hating the other, I end up by hating myself, and his or her murder leads me, at first without my knowing it, but soon more and more clearly, toward my own suicide. Or, more exactly, toward my disincarnation—I will reduce myself to a consciousness so transparent to itself that nothing will come to trouble its empty purity, no feeling of self, no auto-affection, no flesh. We petrified ourselves into two bodies without flesh—and this dead bodily combat opens for me a more direct access to the other than love, even though—or no, *because*—I close up myself to myself by tearing away my own flesh. It is not necessary to imagine hate as enjoyable—it no longer has enough flesh to come to that. We must imagine it dry, like a desert—a place deserted by the other, of course, and, finally, by all flesh. Hatred's most perfect individuation thus has a cost—the diminution of my flesh, or even its disappearance. I hate, but in the state of a cadaver.

Thus hatred does reach the other as individual (and me, too)—in this sense, it is incontestably equivalent to the erotic reduction. However, it only succeeds by destroying the flesh of the other and my own at the same time: in this sense, it does travel the path of the lover, but in the opposite direction, by going from the crossing of flesh to the hatred of each for himself (§§ 12–13). Thus, even if it cannot claim to open an access to the phenomenality of the other, nor substitute itself for the erotic reduction, hatred teaches me a decisive phenomenological fact: it proves that the other appears to me even when eroticized flesh—his or hers, my own, and their crossing—no longer interferes. For, in hatred, the other still sticks out and pierces through: I want to repel her, she no longer affects me, she suspends her flesh and I mine, but she obsesses me, summons me, individualizes me. As disincarnated and empty as she may become, she still imposes herself in the horizon of my phenomenality. What status does the other retain here, where she seems strangely to appear outside of eroticization? Evidently, the status of that which the eroticization of the flesh acknowledges itself never able to attain, or better, that which it recognizes in order to forbid: the status of the person. The other, without and beyond the crossing of flesh, can only allow him- or herself to be sensed (if not make himself be desired) as a person, as no one.* A person, no one—doubly, because the other as no one shines by his absence, either because he grows weak (jealousy) or because I destroy him (hatred); nevertheless, even missing (there is no one), he sticks out as person. *The other as person / as no one*: I will hold here to the ambiguity of this formula—the other intrigues me still as *a person,* even if there is *no one* to assume the role or the phenomenon. The other, an urgent person in so very far as he or she is missing. The other, whose phenomenon survives even its automatic eroticization, its glory and its suspension.

Through hatred, I thus have confirmation of what jealousy already suggested. For love's two widowers—the jealous man and the hateful man—stubbornly persist in demanding the other in person longer and more faithfully than many lovers, who get mired in automatic eroticization

---

*See the note toward the end of § 29 explaining the meaning and translation of *personne.*— Trans.

and disappear with its suspension. Contrary to their declared intentions, the jealous and the hateful prove that, even if the eroticization of the flesh inevitably ends up at its suspension and hides the other in a necessary deception, I still have no motive to give up on reaching the other in person. And besides, this person yet appeared to me through the eroticized darkness of her face, precisely because I missed her; and I have a presentiment of her exactly in the same way that I ask for her—as missing. It is neither a matter of nostalgia (for I still have never reached her person), nor of a delusion (for I know and recognize this lack, with a precision that makes me suffer). No, the person is decidedly missing, and this lack itself is not lacking. It superabounds and obsesses me. Moreover, there is nothing surprising in that the person is first phenomenalized upon the figure of a lack, for this ambiguity attests once again to the constitutive duality of the person—the other already intrigues me as *a person,* even if there is *no one* to play his or her role.

§ 35. Free Eroticization

Thus, while conducting my whole meditation upon the lie and assuming that one cannot phenomenalize the personhood of the other (nor, for that matter, my own) in eroticized flesh, I learn to my surprise from the most resolute actors in this aporia (the jealous and the hateful) that the person still remains, if only negatively, on the horizon of eroticization, and thus of the crossing of flesh. I also verify this lesson directly, since the personhood of the other summons me insofar as I miss it—and I miss it because of the erotic reduction (§ 6). This reversal suggests that the alternative with which I struggled—either eroticized flesh, or the other in person—could not hold: it was too abstract, too conventional, simply inexact. Indeed if, having to choose between the flesh (and thus the eroticized flesh) on one hand and the person on the other, I opted for the person without the flesh— what would I be left with? Very little, without a doubt; in each case, nothing that allows for the phenomenalization of the other; without his or her flesh (and without mine), what will the person show? Without my own flesh that experiences hers and her nonresistance, what intuition could I still have of the other? If I gave up on the flesh and the crossing of our flesh, I would lose not only the flesh, but also all possible phenomenality of the other, in fact every possible path toward her personhood. Thus it is necessary to find, inside the very field opened by the eroticization of the flesh, a new way of making use of it, one that this time does not obscure the faces or the persons of which I there gain a presentiment. As if eroticization could give more than what it appeared to give.

To eroticize the flesh without, however, ending up by missing the person: this would signify that eroticization does not always result in the suspension that holds us back from advancing toward the person. But wouldn't claiming to avoid suspension amount in its turn to deluding with the thought of surpassing the erotic finitude of sensibility? And that is not possible, for finitude is not debatable, it is established, especially this finitude. All true, doubtless, but on the condition that we specify the nature of this finitude. Certainly, something in the eroticization of my flesh attests to its being definitively finite: it always finishes by stopping at one moment or another; this is certain, but what exactly is it that stops? Does the crossing of our flesh, which gives mutually what each does not have, have something to do with it? Not exactly, because we will with all our might this crossing and its continuation; the stop thus does not result from the crossing of flesh, but imposes itself upon it. What sudden stoppage, then, necessarily stops, in spite of us, the crossing of our [two] fleshes? Precisely not the fact that they cross, give themselves to one another, and arouse one another—we will all of that. What do we not will? Precisely that it stop. So why does it stop? Because our two fleshes cannot go on, or rather because they cannot go on and no one can make them able to continue. Here is the point: eroticization stops, and must stop, because it ceases without our wills, just as it began without them; it finishes like it begins; or rather, it finishes on its own *because* it began on its own. It is interrupted in spite of me (I give in, "I let everything go!") because it was engaged without me (I give in, "And off we go!") (§ 25). The finitude of eroticization is accomplished in the fact that I cannot slow its end any more than I could slow (that is, advance) its start. Finitude thus does not characterize eroticization as such, but rather the *automatic* eroticization of the flesh, which stops just like it began—automatically, without having been able to approach the other in person.

With this distinction made, the question becomes: can I conceive of an eroticization of the flesh that is no longer automatic, but free? Formally, the response leaves no doubt: such a free eroticization can be perfectly conceived without contradiction; it is clearly defined as a taking of flesh, where I would eventually not abstain from abstaining from receiving, without or against my liking, my flesh from the flesh of the other and from her nonresistance, where I would not resign myself to simply registering "Off we go!" in order to finish by verifying the suspension, without being able to do anything about it. The possibility of a voluntary eroticization, at least through abstention from giving in to it automatically, is thus not a difficulty. But its actuality confirms itself to be problematic: for, just as eroticization always plays out between two people, my flesh only receives itself by experiencing the nonresistance of another flesh; it receives what does not depend upon it and which affects it all the more because it is precisely a matter of what it most desires and can accomplish the least on its own— its spontaneous advance into the nonresistance of the other flesh. Does not the contact of my flesh with the other flesh, which thus places it in complete dependency, render absurd every claim to erotic independence, and thus every voluntary eroticization?

Unless I might touch the other flesh and let it touch mine *without contact*. This hypothesis only seems absurd for as long as one imagines that our two fleshes cross one another like two physical bodies enter into contiguous contact—by coincidence in space, just beyond the small gap that would still separate them, but just short of the porousness that would already merge them. Now it is enough to consider, first, that a flesh cannot in principle be explained by what it has in common with a physical body (supposing that it had even the least point in common with it). Next, we must consider that I find myself outside the world in the erotic reduction, and thus totally foreign to the spatial contiguity of things, and instead in the distance of lovers. Finally, consider that my flesh does not, exactly, enter *into contact* with the other flesh, since on the contrary it invades it, penetrates into its place and comes *into* it as it withdraws little by little in order to draw my flesh further forward. In the distance between one flesh and another, it is not a matter of one sticking to the other, as if space were lacking, nor of a juxtaposition, as when two physical bodies assemble together; when our two fleshes give themselves to one another, it is a matter of making love to an other, and as such. The question of eroticization would absolutely not be posed if it were only a matter of contact, however narrow it might be; the question is only posed because my flesh experiences itself by receiving itself from another flesh (which does indeed render it), such that we make ourselves each lovers; we touch one another, certainly, but being touched does not signify here simply entering into contact; it signifies nothing less than making love—meaning strictly this: giving one's flesh to the other and receiving it from him or her. And, just as it is not enough to enter into contact to make love, in order to make love I do not always, or first of all, or necessarily, need to enter into contact with the other; I can just as well give her her flesh, and thus have her experience my nonresistance (and reciprocally), by speaking to her. I make love *first* by speaking: I cannot do it without speaking and I can do it by doing nothing but speaking—incidentally, former French usage intended *faire l'amour* in this way.*

Certainly, it is a matter of a rather particular kind of speech (§ 28), which speaks of nothing, or at least of no thing, of no object of the world, or indeed of no being; it says nothing of nothing, predicates no predicate of any substratum. Indeed, it only speaks to the other of the other him- or herself, in the other's own right, as an unsubstitutable person, first and last; addressing the other thus, my speech only aims to touch her, to affect her in the strictest sense, so as to make her feel the weight, the insistence, and the nonresistance of my flesh; afterward, my speech will no longer speak to the other only of herself, but, little by little, of the interval between the other and me, of what is between us [*l'entre-nous*], of this non-thing, unreal and invisible, wherein we stay with one another, live, and breathe. With this conversation alone, the other will nevertheless able to experience not only my eager flesh, but above all that this eagerness does not want to resist her, wants only not to resist her; the other, finally, will, in listening to me, experience the expansion of her own flesh—enjoy herself through me. My speech, which speaks to her of what is between us, alone knows how to touch her heart and give her flesh in its completeness—without any spatial contact, which will only possibly become licit afterward and through this very speech. Speech is the first to give one's flesh to the other, within distance. But if I touch the other and give her flesh only by speaking to her, then I make love to the other *in person*. It depends upon me to speak or to stop speaking, to listen or to turn away; I remain free, while it does not depend upon me alone to suspend the contact of flesh with flesh, nor to abstain from their nonresistance. In order to resist automatic eroticization, I must do violence to myself and, sometimes, I must even do violence to the consent of the other to my nonresistance (§ 31). On the contrary, I can, alone and of myself, begin to speak, continue, and stop myself—I can do it, because this remains my responsibility. In a sense, in this case I do not even depend upon the other, because it falls to my speech not only to make love to her, but, by giving rise to her as the other of the lover that I become before her eyes, to make her enter, as well, into the erotic reduction. Because I do indeed will it, there opens the possibility that my erotic speech will reach the other in person.

*The same is true in English.—Trans.

The possibility opens all the more because, considering it well, the speech that I speak in order to make love can never lie, and attests a flawless truthfulness. There is no paradox here. First, just as this speech says nothing of anything, attributes no predicate to any substratum, and describes not the least state of things, it can express nothing false. Next, just as this speech only speaks to the other of the other herself, and then of what is between us, the other knows perfectly if what I say responds to what she experiences: it is enough for her to verify in herself whether or not my speech, which says that it gives her her flesh because my flesh does not resist her, really does provoke the expansion of her flesh; if the other in fact receives her flesh from mine, which speaks to her, then my speech speaks truly and attests its truthfulness; if not, it becomes apparent that I do not speak as a lover, that I do not know how, cannot, or even do not want to make love the right way—by first saying it. Please do not object that I can make love here by having the intention to lie (sweet-talking) (§ 30). For either what I say—even with the opposite intention—does not give the other her own flesh and it is a matter of a lie by default; or what I say actually gives the other her own flesh—what I was looking for—and then my eventual lie will become untenable and dangerous for myself: either I am going to be able to destroy what I gave rise to (the other's flesh), or, more readily, I am going to discover that the flesh that I in fact gave rise to has already given me my own; I thus find myself a lover without having willed it, or even seen it. In the two cases, my intentional lie did not resist the irrevocable truthfulness of my speech, which, whether I know it or not, has truly made love and given a flesh to the other. So, if I speak in person, with speech that is necessarily truthful, how would I not love anyone in person?

It remains to measure the extent to which free eroticization can be extended and applied. Evidently, since it succeeds without giving in to automatism (and without undergoing suspension), it is not limited to the sexual exercising of the crossing of flesh. Thus there opens before free eroticization an immense field of activity—it allows one to give (and to receive) an eroticized flesh there where sexuality does not reach. From parent to child, from friend to friend, from man to God (§ 42). Doubtless, we also recognize in free eroticism *chastity,* the erotic virtue par excellence.

Concerning the Third Party, and Its Arrival

§ 36. Faithfulness as Erotic Temporality

The intermittencies of the flesh themselves have led me to recognize for the first time the possibility of acting as lover in person. Even jealousy postulates it in the mode of absence (§ 33) and hatred confirms it by contrast (§ 34). The possibility of making love without touching any flesh, solely through the taking on of discourse (the taking of flesh through speech, § 35), sends me, the lover, directly back to my status as person. The link between the lover and the person, which does not go without saying, remains to be comprehended: there is already much difficulty in conceiving my final individuality—that which I do not share with anyone, and which falls to me in person—and there will be yet more difficulty in deducing it from my sole status as lover. Let us return, then, to the lover. He is accomplished when his advance—his decision to love first and his amorous intuition—finds its validation in the oath, wherein the signification that has come from the other becomes one with his own—"Here I am!" (§ 21). However, this unique erotic phenomenon unfolds in common for the two lovers—two intuitions for the single and same signification. The lover only becomes himself because the other, the other lover, assures the first lover his own signification through hers. The lover is accomplished in a filled erotic phenomenon, beyond the simple advance that was still manifesting nothing, so much did it remain unilateral (§ 18), in the measure in which he makes the oath endure—or rather, in the measure in which the oath makes him endure. Thus, the oath's endurance or, in a word, faithfulness, becomes the condition for the persistence of the erotic phenomenon. More precisely, the actuality of the erotic phenomenon depends upon its temporality, itself defined by faithfulness: not only does the faithfulness of the lovers in the unique oath (a signification of "Here I am!" for two) allow the erotic phenomenon to prolong itself, but this prolongation of the oath, or rather the oath as prolongation, defines reciprocally the sole temporality appropriate to the erotic phenomenon. It cannot last or even simply be temporalized in another mode and according to another process than faithfulness. Faithfulness here does not have a narrowly ethical, optional, and psychological status, but rather a strictly phenomenological function— to allow the temporalization of the erotic phenomenon, so as to assure it a visibility that lasts and imposes itself. Without faithfulness, the erotic phenomenon becomes again a simple instantaneousness, disappearing as soon as it has appeared, a phenomenal intermittence.

The erotic phenomenon, demanded by the lover, requires long and deep faithfulness. But faithfulness requires nothing less than eternity. As I have already experienced it, namely in the moment in which I love (§ 22), as soon as I say it and claim it (§ 28), and again in the moment in which I love according to the eroticized flesh (§ 25), I cannot give myself over to loving if I restrain my intention and its signification ("Here I am!") in a finite lapse of time; if I claimed to love for an allotment of time determined in advance, planned up to a certain date but not beyond, my love would not be annulled at that date of expiration, but rather from the beginning. Loving for a predetermined amount of time (and a mutual agreement would change nothing here) does not signify loving provisionally, but loving not at all—not even ever having begun to love. Loving provisionally—this is nonsense, a contradiction in terms. Without a doubt, one can say, "I love you!" without having the intention of faithfulness; but in this case it is only a matter of a lie, which may fool the other (if he or she wants to be blind), but clearly not me who utters it. In this situation, I experience that in fact I cannot say what I say and, at the same time, exclude the obligation to faithfulness; if, then, I persist in this performative contradiction, I will have to pay the price—contradict myself, become a real contradiction, in short make myself unfaithful to myself, because I do not want to remain faithful to the other. This contradiction of self defines, precisely, the true lie, which does not consist so much in lying to the other (which I may hope to conceal), as in lying to oneself (which I cannot hide from myself). And so, loving demands not only faithfulness, but faithfulness for eternity. Faithfulness thus temporalizes the phenomenon of love, by assuring it its only possible future.

Moreover, contrary to received opinion, the difficulty lies less in think-

ing the possibility of faithfulness—this *a priori* condition of the erotic phenomenon's temporality—than that of infidelity, precisely because it renders the erotic phenomenon impossible. Indeed, how can I, and apparently
so easily, settle into infidelity, and thus into erotic impossibility? How can
I not see that my acknowledged intention—to remain forever "free" for
new "encounters"—contradicts itself, since this "availability" implies either that nothing has lasted from preceding "encounters," or that I have
several "encounters" going at the same time, without any hope of them
lasting precisely because none even has the right to a whole present? In
short, whoever sets up infidelity as a principle by that very fact forbids
him- or herself access to the least erotic phenomenality, and denies its least
accomplishment. This is generally agreed, since one rarely proclaims infidelity as a declared principle of the erotic attitude; rather, one falls back to
an adaptable logic: the multiplication of successive fidelities, each with a
sincere intention, but all of weak resolution, and thus of short duration;
each time, I (almost) truly throw myself into "Here I am, the first!" and I
attempt (a little) to maintain my headway at least for as long as the inertia
of my short initial advance allows me; each time, the oath is accomplished
for a time, and, with it, the erotic phenomenon sketches an apparition; but
I cannot hold the common signification for long, because my living experiences of consciousness, like those of the other, pass; and they each pass
with their own rhythm; thus the common erotic phenomenon, under this
lag, becomes distended, tears, and ends up crumbling apart. I no longer
love and I forget that I attempted to love; I even end up no longer missing
the lack of the other. Consequently, as soon as possible, that is, as soon as
the erotic reduction disappears and I notice, I will start over, or try to start
over—by assuming again the same faithfulness *a minima,* again employing
the same already-used lived experiences, recycling a decrepit "Here I am!"
for a brief try that is vain in advance, because it lacks an advance without end.

However, we should not speak too ill of this often comic and always
sinister exhibition. First of all, because the premature interruption of the
erotic phenomenon does not put into question its definition by the oath,
and thus the requirement of faithfulness; it only illustrates the constraint
that the suspension exerts upon the weak lovers (§ 26), and thus the finitude of their eroticized flesh (§ 27). For the intermittencies of the failed
lover result first and above all from his or her relying unreservedly—na-
ïvely, out of cowardice, or stupidly—upon automatic eroticization, which
is in fact inexorably finite, in order to make last the advance of the oath,

which is properly without end. This contradiction between the ineluctable suspension and the demand for eternity is made so clear that it consecrates what voluntary eroticization (§ 35) already allowed us to see: it is patently obvious that the lover's advance is extended much further than the automatic eroticization of the flesh. Just as automatic eroticization can never hold the oath for very long (like a singer cannot hold a note that is too extreme for her register), and, in the best of cases, must constantly take it up again where it left off; just so does the lover's advance claim to accomplish itself once and for all, and demand for itself, and thus from itself, eternity. Thus infidelity is summed up, in most cases, as a succession of short fidelities, all provisionally sincere, all prematurely aborted owing to a lack of power, or desire, and a lack of advance. Faithfulness remains the basis and the condition of possibility for infidelity—which never stops reviving nostalgia and involuntarily rendering it homage. Thus, even in its lackings, faithfulness still defines the temporality of the phenomenon of love and its unique future.

Faithfulness constitutes at this point the temporality of the erotic phenomenon, assuring not only its future, but also its past. Indeed, it also takes the figure of the irrevocable. For I also remain faithful, sometimes in spite of myself, to my past lovers, as much to the one that I have already loved as to the one that has already loved me. The fact of having attempted, even if only for a finite lapse of time, to accomplish a "Here I am!" and, above all, of having experienced the other making the same "Here I am!" hers, so that we each shared the same signification, marks me and transforms me forever; this mark imposes upon me a new figure, and thus a kind of faithfulness to what the other has made in me, and has made of me. Every erotic phenomenon, including the least, remains my inalienable attainment, even if I let it get lost.

Let us consider first the loves that I loved for a time, before betraying or abandoning them. I nevertheless remain permanently faithful to them. Clearly, not by virtue of efforts of memory, which the work of mourning or a censure of spite may on the contrary want to abolish. But rather because, the more I convince myself that "I don't want to hear any more about it," the more I recognize, by this very denial, that I made myself the lover of this one whom, today, I claim to have forgotten. It is not a matter here of the memory of a certain face, nor of such and such flesh, nor of such and such other—all of that very well may disappear without leaving a psychological trace (§ 26 and § 29). At issue is the fact that I once declared myself for this one who has perhaps disappeared from my memory, and that I made myself her lover; that today I have forgotten everything about it in no way abolishes the fact that I did indeed accede, in order to love this departed person, to the status of lover, that I did indeed love her in advance, following the principle of insufficient reason, and that I did indeed receive from her my flesh (which she did not have) by giving her her flesh (which I did not have). From that moment forward, even if the oath did not know how to, couldn't, or didn't want to last, even if the other disappeared with the phenomenon that manifested her, I nonetheless radicalized the erotic reduction, the seal of which signs me forever. All that I did, said, and experienced through love within the radicalized erotic reduction has marked me like a permanent scar, and has imposed upon me a new form. I eventually, over time, lost such and such other, or squandered time with her—but I will never lose what I had to become in order to love her. I keep forever within me all my acts as lover—or rather, they keep me in them and safeguard my unimpeachable dignity as lover. Those that I loved were able to disappear, but not the fact that I loved them, nor the time that I devoted to them, nor the lover that I became in order to love them. For there is never any *ex-*, only the indelible traces of others who made me a lover, a faulty and, no doubt, a finite lover, but also a permanent and irrevocable one. I will never be able to make it so that I did not attempt to love, and thus make it that I did not love.

Now let us consider, in comparison, the loves that address themselves to me without my responding to them, either because I did not know about them, or because I did not want to take them up. I nevertheless remain faithful to them, irrevocably. Of course, I may have lost all clear memory of them—in a sense, that would even be better for everyone. That doesn't change the fact that who I am now I have become only to the extent that the gazes, the advances, and even the flesh of all those who have loved me have weighed upon me, to the point of shaping me and engraving in me my true face. Whether I want it or not, their advance has made me much more than I will ever do. And it is not only a matter, with those who have loved me, of the self-esteem they have gratified me with, or of the knowledge of the world and of myself that they have opened for me, but of the fact that, by laying their gaze upon me, they introduced me into the phenomenality of the erotic "Here I am!" or at the least they opened its access to me. They made me enter, without my deciding, or even despite me and by force, into the erotic reduction, where they preceded me. I have at my disposal only one way to know what lover is finally being accomplished in me—it is enough to know whom I have loved and, above all, who has loved me. And nothing of them will ever disappear, so much so that I—the one who sums them up, receives them, loves them or does not love them, remembers them or forgets them—will still be able to act as lover. Strangely, in the most radical sense, I cannot not remain faithful even to those that I abandoned, or who abandoned me—for I owe them my status as lover, my advance, and my suspensions. Thus faithfulness also temporalizes the erotic phenomenon by rendering irrevocable to me my past as lover.

Finally, faithfulness allows the temporalization of the erotic phenomenon in the present. Indeed, there always remains a recurrent question that turns into an obsession, precisely because it seems never to receive a sure response: I say, "Here I am!"; I hear the other say, "Here I am!"; and I share a single signification with her, and yet I will never be able, by an *a priori* impossibility, to have access to her intuition or to the lived experiences of her consciousness; otherwise, my flesh, and thus my consciousness, would be merged with hers. Thus, each time that I say, "Here I am!" I pose to her and to myself, and always in vain, the question "Do you love me?" This question can only remain without an answer, since every answer that the other will give me, including affirmative responses, remains essentially doubtful. Not only because the other can intentionally lie to me (tell me what she knows is false—that she loves me), but above all because it can happen, or rather it most often happens, that the other herself does not know if she loves me or not. Henceforward, how can the oath be said and repeated? How can faithfulness be confirmed in the present? To surmount this difficulty, it is first necessary to note that the faithfulness of the other remains definitively inaccessible to the lover and that, in particular, his or her sincerity can only give a false impression: even if she wanted, the other could never prove to me, the lover, her faithfulness. There remains, then, only one route open: it is necessary that I, the lover, decide the sincerity of the other—or in other words, that I, and not the other, respond to the question "Do you love me?"

Can I take this route? Can I admit this paradox? Yes, in fact, I can perfectly well. Certainly, the other can never know if she loves me, for her sincerity deceives her as much as it leaves me distrustful; I will not expect her to attest to me what she does not know. But in all evidence I know much more about her than she does; I see, in her acts and their succession, whether everything happens as if the other loved me or not; what is more, I can lean on this *as if*, because I myself already had recourse to its paradoxical power in order to assure myself of my own amorous intuition (§ 19). Thus I assure myself of the other's behaving *as if* she loved me; and

I can do so perfectly well, for it is enough for me to measure if she behaves in my regard just *as* I would behave to her *if* I loved her, in short to compare our two *as if*s. From this point, I find myself in charge of the faithfulness of the other; I find myself its witness and its judge, for I know what an *as if* means and what it can do. And I recognize myself to be an expert in this matter, for I know from experience how to break an oath and what it costs to hold to it. Henceforward, the other will be proved faithful at each instant in which I, who know what it's all about better than anyone else, judge that she is. But I cannot decide that she is remaining faithful to me except by deciding myself to remain faithful to her—for, if I decided to become unfaithful to her, she could certainly remain faithful to me (or not), but I would no longer have to know about it or meddle with it. Thus the index of her faithfulness becomes my own faithfulness. Of course she, knowing that I decide her faithfulness in the measure that I confirm to her my own, can receive my faithfulness only by maintaining her own. From that point, just as in the radicalized erotic reduction, each receives from the other the flesh that he or she does not him- or herself have (§ 23), in a gathering of arousal that is in principle endless.

The exchange of faithfulness thus defines the only shared present of the erotic phenomenon—the lover saying to the other lover not, "I love you!" but instead giving him or her an infinitely rarer and more powerful gift, "You love me truly, I know, I assure you." The lovers give one another this present for as long as their present lasts.

§ 37. The Ultimate Anticipatory Resolution

Our lovers' present lasts for as long as we decide; and we decide by assuring the other of his or her faithfulness to the common oath, thus by anticipating him or her. Our decision thus can be resolved only by a double and reciprocal anticipation. Thus an anticipatory resolution that finally conforms to the erotic reduction is established. It is indeed a matter of a resolution, because I can only define myself as a lover in the exact measure that I come to the point of saying and then repeating the oath, which alone makes the erotic phenomenon appear (§ 21); if this resolution ceases, the erotic phenomenon disappears immediately. But it is also a matter of a resolution that is accomplished only for as long as it anticipates itself; more exactly, for as long as each lover anticipates through his or her advance (§ 18) and his or her own faithfulness (§ 36) those of the other lover, and vice versa; such an anticipation defines a temporality that is properly erotic, because it consists in the exercise of fidelity.

And yet, couldn't the lover in this way reappropriate the anticipatory resolution? It seems to belong to the phenomenality of being or more exactly of this being (that I am), wherein what is at stake is not only himself (as a being), but more radically his being, or even immediately the being of all beings. The anticipatory resolution in principle only takes place where it has meaning: beginning with the question of being and in the reduction of phenomena to their being. Moreover, by resolving myself into this being, I only anticipate my death, and the ultimate possibility (the possibility of impossibility), and thus in fact my mode of being: the possibility that surpasses actuality. Now, the possibility of death still remains the possibility of being, which is absolutely foreign to the possibility that I love or that someone loves me from out there. Why, then, risk confusion by speaking not of an ontological but of an *erotic* anticipatory resolution? Simply because, in order to be accomplished completely, the anticipatory resolution has no other choice than to pass from the ontological to the erotic. For, contrary to what is claimed, I never come to decide by anticipation by remaining in the horizon of being; the anticipatory resolution, envisaged at least in its ultimate requirements, can only be accomplished in the horizon opened by the erotic reduction. Indeed, just as I have understood for some time (§ 3) that I am only insofar as I love, or insofar as some one out there loves me, and not the inverse, so must I today admit definitively (a) that I can only truly come to a resolution and make my decision by accomplishing the oath; (b) that I can only come to a resolution in the mode of anticipation by temporalizing my oath according to faithfulness; and (c) that I only appropriate my ipseity by maintaining an oath for as long as my faithfulness will allow me.

This remains to be shown. The last resolution, and the most radical, cannot consist in being. For what can I decide, when I make my decision according to being? Would I decide to be? Clearly no, because I am and will be whether I decide it or not; and I will cease to be just as I began to be: without deciding anything about it. Nevertheless, couldn't I make a decision to die? Not really; apart from suicide's being a matter of a formal contradiction, it could be that this suicide never even results from a free decision, but instead from a constraint to which I give in because I lack the strength to make the least resolution (§ 12). Nevertheless, a better response remains: the resolution bears neither upon being, nor upon death, but upon the possibility of dying, upon death insofar as possible, which allows me to accede to my own mode of being, possibility. And one cannot contest that being toward death (the possibility of impossibility) does open my being to me as possibility; but one may contest that this possibility still depends on my free resolution, since, in the best of cases, I agree and acquiesce to what I will not in any way be able to avoid—death. Without a doubt, I ratify my possible being by resolving myself to the possibility of my impossibility, but I do not determine this (im)possibility and I decide nothing about it—not even my passage into nothing; put another way, I can resolve myself to my possibility (of the impossible, my death) by anticipating it, and subscribe to it without resisting; it is not a matter of an actual suicide, but instead of a change of style, a freer way to approach possible death; this anticipation changes nothing, neither my death nor my ipseity, nor my future. Thus, except by confusing it with a strange quietism, I will not be able to accomplish this resolution (and yet I must, for my ipseity is at stake) if I remain within the horizon of being (§ 19).

But I can accomplish it within the erotic horizon. For the lover actually makes her decision; first because she can only institute herself as lover with a radical decision, one that is unconditional and without sufficient reason: the advance (§ 18); next, because she only gives rise to her erotic phenomenon by giving and receiving the signification "Here I am!" (§ 21), which implies not only a second resolution on her part, but also a counter-resolution on the part of the other; and these two new resolutions must never cease to be repeated in order to assure the erotic phenomenon its temporality. More broadly, the lover actually accomplishes a resolution, because he attempts and must resolve himself to give to the other, first, his flesh (§ 23), and next, his faithfulness (§ 36), in short because what is at stake in his resolution is not himself, but his erotic responsibility toward the other. Thus I truly reach my decision, because under the rule of the erotic reduction (and only there), my decision bears upon the other, and not upon my *ego* alone, as in the ontological reduction. To which we add a final argument, one that is simple and primary: if the final and most radical resolution consists only of being and in being, it will ineluctably succumb to vanity, as vanity disqualifies being in the erotic reduction (§ 2); thus this resolution will no longer be able to claim itself as ultimate, or radical.

It remains that the resolution according to the question of being must be understood essentially as an anticipation; can the erotic resolution not only anticipate, but anticipate more radically than the ontological resolution? Let us start by considering a first point: the lover resolves himself par excellence and makes his decision originally, because he only decides for himself by making his decision for the other and in order to make his decision for her; now, such a decision for the other is made by the lover in principle in the mode of anticipation, and uniquely in this mode. Anticipation does not complete the resolution after the fact, rather, it defines it from its origin: right away the lover anticipates, since he declares himself without reciprocity (§ 15) and through the advance (§ 18), which frees him from the principle of reason (§ 17); anticipation also determines the eroticization of the flesh (§§ 24–25), as well as faithfulness (§ 36). This immanence of anticipation in the erotic resolution leads to the second point: anticipation clearly anticipates possibility, but a possibility that no longer plays within the limits of being, because it transgresses the limits of death. Indeed, the final anticipation does not anticipate death (the impossibility of being), but the final love—and thus, the future of the oath, insofar as it is an oath always still to come, always to come back; the future of the oath is not limited to death, and thus to the impossibility of possibility; death certainly fixes an undeniable limit to being, but absolutely does not render impossible the erotic possibility; once death is actual, there still remain for me, as lover, two possibilities. If the other is dead, I can, as lover, still love her, since I can love without reciprocity (§ 15) and even that which is not (§ 3). If I am dead, the other can still, as lover, love me for the same motives. The erotic phenomenon, as it arises through the advance that makes the lover make love, paradoxically offers death no hold—precisely because it breaks free from the horizon of being. Contrary to the anticipatory resolution in the ontological reduction, which only reaches possibility according to being (which is to say according to death, which highlights the possibility of being through the possibility of impossibility), in the erotic reduction the anticipatory resolution opens a measureless possibility—a possibility that being, and therefore death, never limits. This possibility is defined as *the impossibility of impossibility.* The erotic phenomenon, as such, has no motive to succumb to death because it does not belong to the horizon of being. Not only is love right to desire eternity, but its meaning is already found there. Thus does the lover attain a real anticipation, one that is free and truly decided—he no longer anticipates within the possibility of (the) impossibility (of the future), but in the impossibility of its impossibility. The lover, from the beginning of his advance, anticipates eternity. He does not desire it, but rather presupposes it.

However, the anticipatory resolution would have no importance if it did not allow me, in principle and in the end, to accede to my ipseity; does the erotic reduction allow the lover to arrive there? At the least, I can convince myself easily that outside of the erotic reduction my ipseity remains doubtful, or even inaccessible, since one can always substitute another ipseity for it, which would be me in the place of me. Let us first consider the transcendental reduction, in which I am insofar as I think (synthesize, constitute, deconstruct, etc.); it goes without saying that here I must think according to rationality, and thus according to the universal rules of thought; thus, the more I think correctly, the more what I think can, at least at maturity, find itself thought by any other rational mind; my thoughts can and even must become the thoughts of any old someone who thinks; thus my thoughts do not define me any more than they belong to me. If I think, perhaps I am, but I do not know who I am, nor even if I can ever become a *who*.

Let us move on to the ontological reduction, where I am insofar as I am the being in which what is at stake is being, the being of the being that I am, but also the being of all the other beings that I am not; but, even if I can put this being to work only by deciding myself absolutely and solely for it, will it for all of that confer upon me my ultimate ipseity? I have reason to doubt it, because of at least two arguments. First, this being remains the being of all beings, even and above all if only one being, like me, knows it and makes it visible; henceforward, could this being of even those beings other than me confer upon me my very own ipseity? That I must individualize myself in order to accede to it does not imply that, in return, this being permits my individualization; on the contrary, it could presuppose it without permitting it. And besides, just as every man has the vocation to exercise this function as privileged being, aren't we once again dealing with a transcendental determination, which is thus perfectly universalizable? (§ 7 and § 22). Next, and once again, if by some remote chance being accorded me an ipseity, how would it not sink under vanity (§ 3), for the same reason as did the being from which it proceeded?

On the contrary, as lover in the situation of the erotic reduction, I no longer encounter these aporiae. I know perfectly well what of me can never pass to another individual and remain indissolubly mine, more inward to me than myself: all those that I have loved as a lover, or more exactly, all my erotic lived experiences of consciousness, all my advances, all my oaths, all my climaxes and all those that I have provoked, all my instances of faithfulness and all my suspensions, all my hatreds and my first death—all of that will bear my name when I will no longer be. In fact, all of that bears my name from this moment forward, renders it honorable or contemptible, admirable or pitiable. No one can take it from me, or deliver me from it, or give it to me—I alone had to engage myself in person for it, in advance and as a lover, in order to arrive there, at that which I am as the story of a lover. And, paradoxically, I cannot trace the erotic history of this irrevocable ipseity myself—it is necessary that others tell it to me. For my ipseity is accomplished erotically, and thus beginning from "out there," from a loved (or hated) other. Not only do I experience myself as a lover only by exposing myself to this "out there" (§§ 5–6) at the risk of the advance (§ 4), but only the other confers upon me the signification of my amorous phenomenon (§ 21); she alone knows if I love her (§ 36) and if I have given her her flesh (§ 23): I do not learn, or rather, I will not learn my most proper name and identity from what I know of myself, or from what I am or from what I have decided to be, but rather from those I love (or not) and from those who love me (or not). Who am I? To this question, being has nothing to respond, nor does the being in me. Because I am insofar as I love and someone loves me, only others will be able to answer. In the end, I will receive myself from the other, just as I am born from her. Not that I must recognize myself as the other's hostage, or that an alienation holds me as the other's slave: this fear itself can only be conceived within a transcendental or ontological horizon, which presupposes precisely what we are questioning—that *I* am only concerned with *myself,* that my ipseity can be resolved in my monad, in short that I come back to myself because I proceed from myself. Now, I know, ever since the trial of vanity and the erotic reduction, that what is most inwardly my own comes upon me from elsewhere and refers back there. The lover only becomes him- or herself by being altered, and is only altered by the other, the ultimate guardian of my proper ipseity. Which, without the other, remains inaccessible to me.

§ 38. The Advent of the Third Party

Thus I will receive myself, in the end, from the other. I will receive my ipseity from the other, just as I have already received my signification in her oath, my flesh in the eroticization of her flesh, and even my own faithfulness in her declaration, "You truly love me!" But what I never cease in this way to receive from elsewhere I must still and always try to receive at the next moment, and at each new moment thereafter. In order to continue the same erotic reduction, it is necessary for us to start all over again from the beginning, unceasingly. We only love one another at the price of a continued re-creation, a continuous quasi-creation, without end or rest. We will only love one another on the condition that we endure repetition and carry the weight of the oath, like a rock that is too heavy, back up to the summit of eroticization, even and above all after each suspension, or even deception. A question thus cannot not be posed: couldn't we lovers entrust my lover's oath, which I share by giving and receiving it in the discontinuity of repetition, to a third party, who would assure it more durably than we can? A third party who, outside of our love affair and unscathed by its finitude, would assure our oath by inscribing it within a continuous duration—his or her own.

However, this third party would have no legitimacy to assure our oath, and thus our accomplishment according to the erotic reduction, if he himself did not belong to this erotic reduction; put otherwise, if he or she did not also proceed from it, and would not answer to it and thus actualize it in him- or herself. This third party, eventual witness to our oath, will have to phenomenalize our common erotic phenomenon by his or her own phenomenon—not mine, not that of the other, but precisely his or her own, a third phenomenon; in this way he or she would be able to attest to our ever-to-be-repeated visibility through the unassailable continuity of his or her own visibility; and confer upon our erotic phenomenon, always left intermittent in the oath, the stability of a durably resolved phenomenon. Henceforward, whatever may befall the first erotic phenomenon, the third party, by his or her incontestable visibility, would assure that there was a time in which our oath was phenomenalized in full daylight. We see that this third party—if he or she can be found—should be produced as a perfectly realized phenomenon, the stable visibility of which would reproduce and thus assure the unstable visibility of our oath subjected to repetition. If he or she is ever to intervene, the third party will only be produced, will only be advanced, and will only appear in erotic visibility in order to reproduce what is not unceasingly given to be seen, namely our oath and its moments of good and bad fortune. He or she will be capable of this only by remaining at the same time indissolubly tied to that to which he thus attests the phenomenality through his or her own phenomenality; he or she could only re-produce that beginning from which he or she will be produced. This third phenomenon, which re-produces in its visibility the repetitive visibility of our oath only by being produced beginning from this very oath, without ever being able to revoke it, and which comes about like an intrinsically erotic event, is called the *child*.

Such a passage from the lover, through the oath, eroticization, jealousy and faithfulness, to the child is in no way optional. Provided that we under-

stand the child as an unconditional demand of the erotic reduction, which
in no case the lover can even claim to avoid, except by suspending this reduction; and this passage has nothing arbitrary or ideological about it either, for two clear reasons. First, the passage to the child does not result
from a biological or social law, but from a phenomenological requirement:
re-production is not first of all or even essentially a matter of maintaining
the species, reinforcing the community, or enlarging the family, in short it
is not a matter of perpetuating the past in the future by iteration or accu-
mulation; this process retains its legitimacy and its role, but comes under
sociology. By contrast, according to phenomenology, the passage to the
child has the function of producing a more stable visibility of the erotic
phenomenon already accomplished by the oath and repeated by enjoyment, and thus of assuring the visibility of the lovers, as it is present and to
come. The lovers pass to the child in order to radicalize the apparition of
their own shared erotic phenomenon—not first in order to show it publicly and socially to others remaining outside of the erotic reduction, but in
order to show it to themselves and thus render *themselves visible to themselves*
beyond or despite their own intermittences. The distance between themselves and their child fills the adequate phenomenological conditions so
that at last, in this third who re-produces them because he or she is produced (comes) from them, they appear to themselves, as pure lovers and
according to the rules of the erotic reduction. Indeed, the child appears as
their first mirror, in which they contemplate their first common visibility,
since this flesh, even if they do not experience it in common, has nevertheless put their two fleshes in common, precisely in this common third,
where the child exhibits him- or herself. At the same time, this mirror is not
degraded into an idol (an invisible mirror as first visible); for, since it results
from the reciprocal oath and advance of the lovers, and thus from their im-
passible distance, the child appears to the lovers as a third party: first because his own flesh imposes a flesh that is definitively other than theirs,
confirming the principle of the inaccessibility of all flesh as such; next, because, in his own flesh, the child incarnates precisely this distance between
their two fleshes, which neither the oath nor enjoyment ever abolished, but
always confirmed. The lovers are not and never will be one with their image, nor will they make of it their idol, because it re-produces them in visibility only on the condition that it *not resemble them*.

But there is a second reason to add to the first. The passage to the child
responds to a requirement that is all the more phenomenological (not biological or social) because it can always, and must first, be understood as the

possibility of the child more than as its actuality. Indeed, for the lovers it is not first and foremost a matter of the actual child, or of that which one "has" (or believes he or she "has"), nor of that which one "wants to have"—if necessary at the price of bio-technological manipulations or socio-medical traffickings which would reduce it to the rank of a manufactured object, bought and sold; in these two cases, moreover, the obsession with possessing the thing, what one then calls "my" child, can easily go hand in hand with its being forgotten out of indifference, its instrumentalization by convenience, or even its destruction by mistreatment (physical or psychological); the actual possession of the child not only does not always prolong its possibility, but often destroys it. For lovers, on the contrary, the possibility of the child goes further than the possession of the child, and thus further than her actuality: it is a matter in fact of an unavoidable stage of the erotic reduction, and, at this moment, the first to appear to assure stability to the erotic phenomenon: the child incarnates in her flesh an oath once and forever accomplished, even if the lovers have broken it subsequently. In the child, the oath is made flesh, once and for all and irrevocably, even if the lovers are divorced from their oath. The child manifests a promise that is always already held, whether the lovers wish it or not. The child defends the oath of the lovers against the lovers themselves; she gives herself as a pledge against their separation; she interposes herself as guardian of their first advances; she projects into the future the present of the oath and, if this oath no longer lives, the child, for as long as she lives, will witness to it against the lovers. Thus the child consecrates in her flesh the lovers' faithfulness or, in her flesh, lets jealousy speak and defends against them the lovers' honor (§ 33).

Let us remain here strictly with the child as a possibility that is both required by the erotic reduction and rendered intelligible by it. The child can only be thought beginning from his possibility, because he always appears as a phenomenon given according to the advent of an event, and with a radicality that tears it from the common run of phenomena, including even given phenomena. Indeed, the child *comes forward* in this strict sense: he does not produce himself, and only re-produces the lovers by nevertheless always refusing that the least determinism (causes, decisions, manufacturing, etc.) make him come forward through the will and according to the anticipations of these very lovers. It does not depend upon lovers to become parents, even though they can; as much as I become a lover because I decide to do so, just so much is it never enough for me to decide to become a parent in order to become one; it is not enough to will and to decide "to make" a child for him to come about as a fact—first of all, because one can never "make" a child, despite all of the wills and all of the mechanisms that claim to do it; the will to beget never absolutely guarantees fertilization, any more than a will not to beget always protects against it. Apparently, even the most complex technologies designed to provoke artificial fertilization (or at least assisted fertilization, fertilizations that are in part nonnatural) do not attain, and by a significant margin, the almost absolutely certain, predictable, and flawless results obtained by technologies designed to produce industrial objects; on the contrary, the results here derive only from statistical causalities, without strict determinism and with astonishingly weak rates of success. The child is not decided upon and is not foreseen any more than he is "made": while (in principle) he proceeds entirely from us, he nevertheless does not depend exclusively on us to come or not to come. Even once conceived, his unavailability is yet marked by the delay, always uncertain, that his birth imposes upon the lovers; in any case, between the conception and the birth, they must still wait for the child; they expect his or her good will after the conception, just as they expected him or her *before* his conception; their pleasure waited while the child took his own sweet time. Even if they had decided to bring him about, the lovers still must expect the child, who at first only signals his presence by making himself be expected, and by letting himself be desired; here expectation teaches us desire, and not the other way round, as in the eroticization of the flesh, where desire provoked expectation.

This irreducible expectation imposes itself upon the lovers and proves that the appearance of the child does not depend upon their will, a condition that is never sufficient, nor even always necessary. This expectation also confers upon the phenomenon of the child the character of an *unpredictable arrival*—an arrival that is unforeseen, always uncertain even while it is hoped for with a firm hope. This unpredictable arrival implies (one could show it in detail) other characteristics: the anamorphosis, for the child surprises intentionality and demands that one regulate it after the fact according to the child's privileged point of view, and no longer according to that of the lovers; the incident, for the child comes without reason or cause, and redefines possibilities beginning from his or her accomplished fact; and finally, the event, for the child imposes him- or herself as unrepeatable, the surplus and pure actuality of a non-effect. In no case does the child perpetuate the past state of the lovers, nor does she comfort them in their intentions; rather, she breaks the planned course of their possibilities by imposing upon them the fact of her own; she arrives before them, full face, like an event come about from the outside and from nothing, neither as their offspring, nor as the fruit of their common tree, nor as the prolongation of their accomplishments; against all expectation, she arises from who knows where, or why, or by what right. In short, literally as a third party, the child invites herself over to the lovers' house; this invitee, this heir, imposes herself like the closest intruder for those without whom, nevertheless, she would not appear. The most foreign and the most intimate—it is in this way that the third party comes upon the lovers.

This advent of the child qualifies him all the more as a third party because he also imposes himself by a *facticity* that is equally out of the ordinary. Nowhere else does a phenomenon come forward with such a facticity—all the more because the child appears exactly as he comes forward: with an essence that is undecided and truly never chosen, with an unforeseen and irrevocable existence, with an unforeseeable and incorrigible future. Civil status will not give to the child the forever-lacking causes of his birth, any more than the ever-to-come knowledge of his past will give him mastery over his birth. His education will change nothing about his biological and even cultural heredity; at best, it will complete, correct, and develop his ineffaceable given. What came about will never again be able not to have come about. As for his future, it will again come upon the child as it would for anyone, under the figure of an unforeseeable event. From the outset, then, neither the lovers nor the child can appeal this shared facticity. The child, without any doubt the issue of the flesh of each of the lovers, safeguards neither the one nor the other; certainly he gives them much to see in his figure or form, but his figure nevertheless remains without a model, and the child never resembles his parents, despite what the family circle says; rather, his figure offers the phenomenon upon which the faces of the lovers are given to be seen, to be re-seen, and to be recognized more distinctly; but, if the face of the child does not repeat the sum of the two faces of origin, it nevertheless re-produces the intermittent visibility of the oath upon the visibility in progress of its new phenomenon. Chronologically, we precede the child and he proceeds from us, but phenomenologically he precedes us and we proceed from his visibility. The child's facticity renders him for us rather foreign, so that he does indeed become the third party; his facticity makes him appear to us in so very far as he remains other than us and thus offers us a fixed mirror, though one that is always changing. It could be that the child appears foreign, like the very foreignness that the lovers lacked. In this sense, and as an event in full facticity, every child comes about as a foundling.

Under the double title of the one who comes forward and of facticity, the child thus indeed imposes herself as the third party. In this way she satisfies the two requirements of her function in the erotic reduction: intrinsically tied to the oath and to the exchange of eroticized flesh, and thus to the love affair of the lovers who produce her, she remains sufficiently distant from them to attain her own visibility, stable and indisputable, and is thus able to re-produce them upon her own face. In this way she becomes the witness to her parents, the third party who confers upon the lovers the assured visibility that they themselves could not attain in the mere chaotic repetition of their erotic phenomenon.

Thus set up as third party, the child can now play the role that my extreme desire assigns to her—that of pronouncing a last judgment. Or at least, my desire may henceforward demand that she play this role. The child could, or ought to be able—as my lover's desire imagines—to excuse me from repeating the oath and the crossing of flesh, so that I am finally through with all of that. And the desire for a child can doubtless, to an extent that is undecidable but essential, be understood as a kind of desire to die—or at least, as a desire to be through with desire, to be finished with the repetition of the erotic reduction and its ceaseless, tiring demands. How does one make this end? Thanks to the very fact of the child, whose facticity and unpredictable arrival impose themselves and demand enough that we depend no longer upon our advances, nor require repetition, and thus prove that we, the lovers, have succeeded in loving one another at least for a time, at least up to this point where the child, the henceforward irrevocable third party, appeared. To make an end: to provoke the birth of the third party, who puts an end to repetition. To put an end to the questions of the erotic reduction ("Does anyone out there love me?" § 3; "Can I be the first to love?" § 16; "Do you love me?" § 36), no longer with a response that is empty because only valid for an instant ("Here I am!" § 21), but with a fact that has come forward, an event befallen, and which remains—the third flesh, definitive, of the child. In short, to be finished with the erotic reduction—"They married, had children, and lived happily ever after." Conceived in this way, the child makes manifest in her duration (during her life, beyond that of the lovers and of their repeated or stopped oaths) what the oath signified but was unable to phenomenalize durably, or manifest to others than to the lovers themselves. The child saves the lovers' oath first by making it definitively visible in her third face; next, by conferring upon it a duration longer than their own, since she can (at least hope to) survive their respective deaths and their probable infidelities. The oath makes the child possible, but only the child renders the oath actual; the parents engender the child in time, but the child fixes the lovers outside of their time. The advent of the third party—the end of the story for the lovers. End of story, end of history—last judgment.

But the desire is immediately disappointed. For this last judgment does not remain final for long; no sooner said than done, it becomes the next-to-last, ceding its place to a new possibility, a new event, or even to the possibility of another child. The last judgment does not last—precisely because the child is not finished lasting. Doubtless, as he lasts and grows, the third party in him witnesses all the more assuredly—but to what? For a time, perhaps, he witnesses to the oath of the lovers and to the exchange of their eroticized flesh; and, in so doing, he does indeed re-produce in his unquestionable phenomenon the fragile visibility of the erotic phenomenon of origin. Nevertheless, quickly, too quickly, the child third party no longer witnesses to our oath (which nevertheless made him possible), but to himself, and in time, in his time, principally, or even exclusively, to himself. If he re-produces me, I in my oath with the other, he re-produces me on his own face, in his distance from me, according to a gap as old as his time, and which time no longer ceases to increase. The child certainly re-produces the oath of the lovers on his face—but precisely for as much as his face is added to those of the lovers, is distinguished from them, and thus separates itself by consisting in its own flesh. Our oath either disappears with us or appears to us outside of us—it travels through the third party, who is himself definitively in transit. Life "continues," but it is no longer ours. The judgment has nothing final about it, time does not stop—precisely because and by virtue of the child, the third party who never stops coming forward and passing through. The re-production of the erotic phenomenon upon his face thus does not deliver the last phenomenon; it only fixes a next-to-last snapshot, already superseded by the next instant—which has already arrived, which is going to pass, which has passed.

The oath is thus found turned back on itself, once again condemned to have to repeat itself. The third party survives in time, the oath must do the same and attempt to receive another re-production—to await another end, another provisional third party.

§ 39. The Child, or the Third Party on the Point of Leaving

The child plays the role of the third party, but following a temporality such that she only comes about in transit. Once come, the third party always ends up lacking. Not by chance, nor because of a bad success, but by definition—for the child is in fact characterized by what about her escapes from her parents, the lovers. She appropriates that to which she attests, the oath, to the point of making it her own, of incarnating it, but in a new flesh, where she takes it away—and makes it disappear from the lovers' eyes. It is not a matter here of the banality that says that children always end up leaving (if not, they would become neither themselves, nor lovers), but of a more obscure sorrow: children take away with them the very oath that they have re-produced. Not only do they not remain, and not only does nothing remain of them, but nothing remains of us lovers, either. The fact, the effect, and the visibility of our oath is erased with its last stage-director —the third party.

The lacking third party falls short in several ways. First, he is lacking from the outset, from the first moment. For, when the lovers mutually eroticize their flesh, each giving the flesh that he or she does not have and receiving his or her own from the other who does not have it, when in this crossing the lovers make only a single flesh, it is clearly not a matter of their flesh, but of that of another other, of a third party. Without a doubt, each gives rise to the flesh of the other (by effacing him- or herself behind his or her advance and thereby authorizing his or her expansion), but precisely, my flesh provokes that *of the other* and the other provokes *mine,* not her own; we cross our [two] fleshes, but we do not unify them any more than we exchange them; eroticization does not mingle our flesh by making only one single flesh (§ 23), it limits itself—we are already dealing with an extreme accomplishment—to pushing each flesh to its maximal expansion in virtue of the other (§ 24), such that each flesh receives from the other what it needs to be accomplished, and thus to experience its finitude (§ 25); it is a matter of a law of the erotic reduction. Thus, if the lovers nevertheless make one single flesh, it is necessary to understand that they make another flesh than their own. This third flesh provoked by our two fleshes nevertheless does not prolong them (in eroticization, each of our fleshes is prolonged and, for that reason, has no need of any third flesh); if it does not prolong them, we must conclude that it adds itself to them; in order to add to them, it distinguishes itself from them at the outset by a definitive gap; supposing that the genetic codes of the lovers combine into another code, that is not enough to establish that their fleshes are united in themselves. The only flesh that the lovers make thus escapes them at the outset; it draws aside from them immediately and puts itself on the point of leaving even before showing itself in the light of day. Conception already accomplishes all that birth requires in order to manifest the third party; and, as birth delivers the third party with all immediacy, conception thus puts him on the point of departing. Conception is like a deception. The third party—the third flesh—only announces himself by his departure, precisely in order to abandon the lovers. The irreducible distinction between their two fleshes is repeated with the initial departure of the third flesh. Rising out of distance, the third party ratifies it without return.

There is more: the departure of the child from the lovers is not summed up in the simple distinction, as irremediable as it may seem, between their three fleshes, as if in the end it were simply a matter of safeguarding the individuality of each one. The departure of the child, and thus the escape of the only third party who could still witness to the oath, consecrates above all the impossibility of reciprocity between the lovers—or else a reciprocity that is out of phase, unendingly deferred and deferring. The advance, even redoubled here and there in the reverse sense of the unique direction of the oath, is never abolished in a stable exchange, like one would find at the end after a delay. The advance remains definitively attained, because it anticipates not so much on the other's advance (or delayed advance) as it does on itself; the lover enters in advance, like one enters into war or into religious life—by burning his ships behind him, and without hope (or the least desire) to return to the balance of exchange; he places himself forever out of balance in front of himself—without consideration of the eventual advance of the other, which in any case he cannot measure because he has no access to it. Now, if the third party must re-produce the erotic phenomenon, it is necessary that he or she witness to the advance of the lover and the imbalance of the oath, which no reciprocity will ever compensate. The child succeeds in this perfectly, because he exemplifies to the letter the impossibility of rendering gift for gift.

Indeed, the child has received from the lovers the gift of his origin, the gift in which he is, lives, and breathes, the gift that renders even being possible, and precedes it; by his own visibility, the child witnesses to the oath of the lovers and registers as a fact the eroticization of their flesh; whether he wants it or not, he is instituted as their third party for as long as he validates, by the gift that he receives and that he incarnates for a long time (what we call, for lack of a better word, life), the gift that the lovers once made to one another. And yet, will this gift, given and lasting, give back in its turn? Perhaps, or even surely, but in such a way—by yet another law of the erotic reduction—that the child will never give it back to those who gave it to him, and will always give it to the one who will not give it back to him—that is to say, his own child.

The child is no longer defined only as the gifted par excellence (the one who receives herself perfectly from what she receives), but as the one who receives the gift of origin without ever being able to give it back to its giver; and who must always give it again to a givee or recipient, who in turn will never give it back to her. She cannot repay the gift, so she puts it *in transit*—beginning with herself. Because she is defined as the third party on the point of leaving, the child definitively breaks reciprocity by diverting the return of the gift away from the giver, in order to displace it toward an unknown and still nonexistent recipient (another child, another event still to come). The child thus steals from us lovers not only the flesh that our flesh gave to her, but above all the return upon us of her testimony in favor of our oath. The child by definition abandons the lovers to themselves. Nevertheless, the lovers receive from this abandonment at least this much: they come back forever to their two advances and set aside the security-minded illusion of an external certainty; they will grow old until the end in the erotic reduction. By losing their third party through the child's departure, the lovers are condemned to remain or to become themselves—alone.

Still, does the child's departure leave the lovers absolutely without any witness to their oath? Let us consider that the child can only leave, and thus go away, because his flesh abandons the flesh of the lovers—who yet give him his flesh. How can his flesh thus rid itself of those that cross one another there and give rise to it? Because the flesh of the child, as soon as it enters into visibility, also appears in the world, like all flesh, not as flesh, but as a body. For no flesh can be seen as such—it is necessary to feel it, and each flesh can only directly feel itself. Thus, from the moment the child appears, he appears as a simple body and disappears as flesh. That said, the child simply reproduces, in the posture of the third party, what I noted in the posture of the lover: that the eroticization of my flesh always winds up ceasing (§ 26) and that my finitude brings me and the other back to the rank of bodies (§ 27). The child's departure thus confirms, without adding anything, the suspension of my eroticized flesh. His witness as third party to the oath could not last any longer than does the eroticization of flesh bound by the oath—precisely, the time of a race set to conclude as late as possible (§ 25), that is, always too soon. The child leaves in the same way as climactic enjoyment is suspended—too soon, and inevitably; for time takes back into its empire these two finitudes, which in fact form only one. Eroticization and the child thus quiet themselves with the same silence. Henceforward, the failure of the child to give testimony to our oath takes on a wholly other meaning. First because, insofar as he is lacking, the third party confirms only the finitude of all flesh and, above all, of eroticized flesh. Next, because the third party could not, as simple flesh, in any way confirm the oath, because all flesh by definition remains invisible; all that remained for him was to attempt to confirm the oath as a visible body; now, a visible body shows nothing that is flesh or an oath between two fleshes, so he can only confirm by telling that this visible body proceeds from the lovers' oath and from their eroticized flesh. The child assumes, if he so decides, the function of the third party by telling what he shows—that this body has the value of flesh, because it proceeds from an oath. The child will not be able, then, to qualify himself as the third party to the oath except by telling our name—which is equivalent to his own. He witnesses to our oath by telling his name. The lovers are born from the speech of the child. And if the child in the end must speak, it is no longer fitting to call him a child, but definitively the third party who witnesses. The child can at least, then, honor his father and mother by telling them their name—their family name; but this name, theirs, coincides with his; he honors them, then, by telling them his proper name, because this name happily remains improper to him. We keep a family name, a family likeness.

In the child's absence, I lose not so much the child (who never stops finding and re-finding himself) as I do myself—or rather, ourselves, and our oath, which goes away with him, under the cover of a thing that is apparent in the world. So the child still remains the third party for me, who witnesses to my oath, because this not-me that he becomes for me still bears within him our name—more me than I myself, me for longer than I. Without knowing where I am going, I escape too by giving myself over to the departure of the third party, to the child in transit. There, I win my name.

§ 40. The *Adieu,* or the Eschatological Third Party

I find myself in a situation in which the supposed final instance—the child as third party, who would pose the last judgment on the lovers' oath—disappears in the future under the cover of a body. The final instance, so awaited and clamored after, dissolves in the next instant to come, and then in the one that follows, and so on, until the end. Moreover, there is nothing that is more normal than this disappearance, since the sought-for third party consisted uniquely in one of my neighbors, in our first common neighbor—the child. This simple neighbor could not by definition assure the function of the last, of the ultimate, of the final point, without a second to come. I find myself, as lover, taken up again in time; we, the lovers, find ourselves subjected to repetition, exposed to the danger of being able to lose our oath at any moment—thus obliged to assure it each time once again. The amorous phenomenon thus imposes its repetition in order to hope to save itself, since no third party can sustain itself long enough to witness to it once and for all. The amorous phenomenon certainly does not lack witnesses, or third parties—but all of them are immediately on the point of departing, and only witness in the meanwhile. And because each third party in the end goes away, the next instant arrives without a witness. Repetition thus forces the erotic phenomenon to confront the plurality of possible third parties. And by right, just as the child only assures the function of the third party on the condition of leaving and departing from the role, so too does she imply her own plurality, or more exactly her ever possible proliferation, and thus her ineluctable impropriety. The child could no less claim to remain unique than she could succeed in remaining permanently a witness: caught in the repetition from which she proceeds and that she restarts, she is never born into perfect ownership of herself (it remains for her to become what she is in the mode of the unaccomplished), and above all she inscribes herself from the outset in a line that precedes and prolongs her, to the point of harboring her own identity more than she herself does. The child is multiplied or at least accepts the possibility of brothers and sisters. Like a third party always about to depart, she only witnesses against type, simply by attesting that the oath lacks a witness, is always at risk of dissipating into plurality, and thus must wear itself out in repetition. Here a redoubled danger threatens the erotic phenomenon: whether with two or the addition of a third, my union with the other would never be firmly accomplished; it would exhaust itself in pursuing without attaining anything, in endlessly repeating itself and in beginning again without hope, obsessed by the haunting memory of the same, of its lack and its return upon itself. Rather than a true other, the other would amount to the same. Which is as if to say: this is hell on earth.

What am I going to do? What am I, the lover, going to do to the other whom I claim to love in order to have us avoid this hell? All that remains is to attempt to reverse the situation: since the final instance is devalued in the next instant and its repetition, it remains to me to love otherwise—in such a way that this next instant firmly becomes a final instance. What does it mean that the next is always to be the last? That it is necessary to succeed in loving in such a way that the next instant—the one in which death might surprise me (after all, why does it not take me now, before I finish writing this sentence, or before you, reader, finish reading it?), the one in which it might freeze me in my final erotic reduction, the one in which it might engrave my final oath—that this instant, then, may, without regret, condition, and reserve, have value as the very accomplishment of my destiny as lover. So the next instant can sink into the insignificance of dissipation, and thus into repetition; or, on the contrary, it can become for the first time a last instance, in the exact measure in which I accomplish it in such a way that I am able to assert as my definitive lover's status the erotic situation in which that instant finds and fixes me. From whence there follows this precept, which is strictly speaking eschatological: love as if the next instant of your erotic reduction constituted the final instance of your oath. Or again: love now as if your next act of love were to accomplish your final possibility of loving. Or finally: love this instant as if you no longer had any other in which to love, ever. The point is to transform one instant among others—a simple insignificant *item* of repetition—into a final instance, or put another way, to render it eschatological by setting it up as the third party, which will witness forever, since no other will ever succeed it. And this can be accomplished, provided that I decide to assume the instant just to come not only as a decisive event, but as the event of the final instance—as the advent of the final instance. Which can be done, provided that I resolve myself, in this instant, to love as I would want to find myself loving (and loved) on the last day and forever, if this instant had to remain without another, and freeze my lover's face.

Within me, never has the lover anticipated so resolutely as with this decision to love in the instant as if I was loving in the final instance. Of course, it is a matter of the decision to love as it accomplishes the true anticipatory resolution: the one in which, by making love, the lover opens the very possibility of the erotic phenomenon of the other (§ 37). But it is not a matter only of anticipating in the possibility, by an anticipation of the future of the lovers and of the advent of their third party in time (§ 36 and § 38). It is a matter of anticipating the very actuality of this possibility: in effect, I love at each instant (possibility) as if this instant were to prove itself to be the final instance for making love (actuality). I no longer love only as if I were no longer to have another opportunity to make love, but in such a way and so as to make this occasion definitively the last one. Anticipation thus does not only anticipate the possibility of the oath, but also its accomplishment. I am accomplished as lover, because I am able (and this depends only upon me) to love at each instant as for eternity. The lover that I decide to become—just as much as the lover that the other becomes for me in our unique oath—accomplishes the promises of eternity without waiting, in the present instant. Or better: he does not so much promise eternity as eternalize the promise by accomplishing it (by making love) *sub specie aeternitatis,* under the aspect of eternity—more exactly, in the light of the irrevocable. The lover makes a good ending; he makes use of the power to anticipate the accomplishment and to go to the limit by loving at each instant as in the final instance; he does not need time to end to be finished with time—it is enough for him (or better, for them) to love starting from time in the final instance. The lovers do not promise one another eternity, they provoke it and give it to one another starting now. For eternity does not come as from the outside, optionally to conclude the history of the erotic reduction once time has accidentally come to completion (through death); it arises from the oath itself, like its intimate and intransigent petition, starting from the course of time (§ 22). Love willed eternity in time, and from the first instant; and it obtains it here, because it anticipates it and provokes it. Love enjoys eternity from the instant that it enjoys itself. Eternity, thus anticipated, does not bring love to a conclusion, does not recompense the oath, does not celebrate faithfulness—it satisfies the needs of erotic rationality.

Indeed, eschatological anticipation responds, according to three distinct modes, to the needs of erotic rationality. For only eternity allows us to respond to three questions that the lovers cannot avoid, and above all that they do not wish to leave unanswered. In effect, what one could call the last judgment of their love depends upon these responses: the judgment that reveals the ultimate truth of their love, still veiled up to this moment; the judgment, too, that will give witness forever to the oath; and lastly, the judgment that gives the assurance hoped for since the beginning (§§ 2–3).

The first question is expressed as follows: "In the end, whom did I truly love?" For I am perfectly able not to know, either because I imagine that I love (or rather, hesitate to love) several others at the same time, or because I believed that I loved or attempted to love several others successively, or because I am awaiting another possibility that remains anonymous. This question will clearly remain without an answer for as long as I stay in time—in the succession of instants available for a decision and disposed for repetition. It will, on the contrary, receive an answer immediately once repetition is suspended and temporal succession is stopped—for the one that I love in the final instant will appear *hic et nunc* as the one that I loved in the final instance. Not that the last one loved automatically designates the one that I love forever—but at least I will know that I love absolutely and forever when I no longer have the possibility of repetition, nor the possibility of the possibility, and accede to the impossibility of the impossibility. At the instant in which everything will be accomplished, I will at last see whom I love in the final instance—her face will arise and impose itself at the heart of the eschatological anticipation by passing into eternity. For only eternity responds to erotic reason's need for *the assurance of the present*—knowing definitively whom I love (§§ 4–6).

The second question is formulated as follows: "Will I have the strength, the intelligence, and the time to love you to the end, without remainder or regret?" For the one that I love clearly imposes herself upon me as a saturated phenomenon, whose endless and measureless intuition does not cease to overflow all of the significations that I attempt to assign to her, beginning with the first among them, "Here I am!" (§ 21). Seriously facing the face of the other, or more precisely, the face of *this* unsubstitutable other of whom I claim to be the lover (§ 22), requires that I give without end a new meaning to the intuitions that never cease coming to me, and thus that I say all the words and pronounce all the names (§ 28) I am able to mobilize, or even that I invent others, so as to accomplish the indefinite interpretation. The lover never finishes telling himself of the beloved, telling himself to the beloved, and telling the beloved to herself. The lover, in front of the intuitions that the beloved inspires in him, must deploy an endless hermeneutic, a conversation without endpoint; thus he needs a period of time without bounds in order to carry out his discourse without conclusion. Love demands eternity because it can never finish telling itself the excess within it of intuition over signification. I will only know whom I love in the final instance—by eschatological anticipation of eternity, the sole condition of its endless erotic hermeneutic. Thus, only eternity answers the need of erotic reason concerning *the assurance of a future*—being able endlessly to tell me whom I love and to make it known to her, since without me, she would not know it.

Finally, the third question asks: "How could we lose ourselves and be separated, when we were loving one another at that point?" Of course, this question does not always come up (for we do not inevitably lose one another), but nevertheless it must come up often (for we lose one another most of the time); it implies no contradiction, since erotic finitude (§ 27) entails, with the suspension (§ 26) that it indicates, the ineluctable possibility of the gap and of deception (§ 30). If this darkening is in no way invincible, it also has nothing about it that is optional, and every oath must confront it, even if every oath does not succumb to it; the oath, which allowed lovers to constitute their crossed erotic phenomenon, may have been actual, and yet have disappeared; that the suspension prevailed over the oath and denied it eternity does not, for all of that, invalidate (at least not entirely) the accomplishment of this oath. That we no longer loved one another does not imply that we did not love one another at all, or ever; but this requires discrimination between what we have accomplished and what we have missed in this ambiguous oath. Erotic reason here has the need and the right to go back over its past in order to assure it, measuring it; it must be able to re-appropriate, in a sort of retrospective counter-inquiry, its deception and its enjoyment and finish by doing them justice; in the best of cases, the lovers can recognize having performed a true oath, even if the eroticization of their flesh could not sustain it; sometimes, they can even forgive one another their mutual abandonment in the name of their first advances, which nothing, indeed, can annul. In this way, eternity satisfies the need of erotic reason regarding *the assurance of a past*—being able to tell us, in the end, how, despite everything, we still love one another.

The anticipatory resolution thus results in the eschatological anticipation—as lover, I must, we must, love as if the next instant decided, in the final instance, everything. To love requires loving without being able or willing to wait any longer to love perfectly, definitively, and forever. Loving demands that the first time already coincide with the last time. The dawn and the evening make one single twilight—the time to love does not last and is played out in an instant, a fragment, a single beat—only one heartbeat, the smallest gap, the *articulum,* separates us from eternity. We love one another *in articulo vitae,* or in other words *in articulo mortis;* death frightens the lover no more than the finish line terrorizes the runner: rather, he fears not reaching it quickly enough. Thus we have only one single instant at our disposal, one single atom of an instant, and it is now. *Nunc est amandum,* we must love now, now or never, now and forever. The instant is only given for that. The temporal tension of the flesh arousing itself, which holds itself back, for as long as it can, from releasing the "Off we go!" of climactic enjoyment (§ 25), is radicalized here by abolishing the difference even between the present instant and the final instance, between "now" and "again"—fixing the one and the other in the unique "Come!"

The time of the lovers abolishes repetition and, from the outset, settles into the end—they leave together from the moment of departure and cannot part from one another. This initial flight toward the definitive is called the farewell, the *adieu*. The lovers accomplish their oath in the *adieu*—in the passage unto God [*à Dieu*], whom they summon as their final witness, their first witness, the one who never leaves and never lies. For the first time, they say "adieu" to one another: next year in Jerusalem—next time in God. Thinking unto God [*penser à Dieu*] can be done, erotically, in this "adieu."

§ 41. Even Oneself

The *adieu* casts me into the accomplishment of my oath. Since we have made love one time, we have made it always and forever, because what was made cannot not have been made; and *this* more than anything. Once a lover, I remain so always, for it no longer depends upon me not to have loved—the other will always testify, even if I deny her, that I made myself her lover. Henceforward, I receive from the other what I do not possess of my own accord (nor she of her own accord), and that I nevertheless give to her (just as she gives it to me)—the rank of lover. Once again, after signification (§ 21) and the flesh (§ 23), climax (§ 25) and faithfulness (§ 36), each gives what he or she does not possess him- or herself, but of which nevertheless he or she has only for the other; thus each one, in his or her own shortage of self, is revealed nevertheless as more inward to the other than this other is to him- or herself. I never know, truly and assuredly, if the other loves me, when she makes love to me and makes herself my lover; but I know absolutely and establish unquestionably that, in so doing, she makes herself my lover and makes me hers; this I feel, experience, and verify once and for all. In a word, if the other, by making love to me, cannot render me loved without any doubt, she nevertheless makes of me what I alone cannot become—she makes me a lover, her lover. I cannot not establish and admit myself as a lover, from the moment that the other gives me that name by telling me that I am making love, and confers upon me the rank by letting me make it. But if the other recognizes me as her lover and allows me to experience that I am playing the part, then she validates me from the point of view of the erotic reduction. She consecrates me as lover, ratifies my claim to love, and justifies my taking part in the erotic reduction. Thus she assures me, too, that I am worthy to play the game of loving, since I play the lover well: at last, I discover myself assured. And, since only the fact that someone loves me can give this assurance (§ 2), I discover that I am lovable as a provoked lover. Loved because lovable, lovable because lover.

Beloved as a lover, will I then be able, since I experience myself as lover, at last to experience myself as beloved—and thus legitimately love myself? Of course, I couldn't go back on my radical contradiction of all love of each man for himself; each time that I claim to dispense with the other and depend upon myself alone in order to respond to the question "Does anyone love me?" I will end up, through hatred for myself, with the hatred of all for all and of each for himself (§§ 8–14). But, in these circumstances, it is no longer a matter of this suicidal autism, since here I only discover myself to be lovable for as much as the other tells me and assures me that I am acting as lover. Lovable as lover, I thus do not love myself, but rather I receive my assurance from somewhere else. I do not immediately love myself every man for himself and me for myself, but through the detour of the one who tells me that I love her, that she loves that I love her, and thus that she loves me. I discover myself lovable through the other's grace; and if I finally risk loving myself, or at least no longer hating myself (in short, if I risk forgiving myself), I dare it on the word of the other, through my confidence in her and not in me; I will surmount my hatred for myself as I would walk on water or step forward into the void—because from out there the voice of the other convinced me (or nearly) that I can do it, and that I am worth it. I love myself mediately, or rather I cease to hate myself through the other's mediation, and not through myself. This mediation nevertheless must not be understood as that of the moral law, which is supposed to make me love every man; not only can no law command love, or require one to make oneself loved; not only would such a law mask the other by lowering him or her to the rank of a simple opportunity among others to obey the law; but we are not concerned at all here with a law, because here it is precisely not a matter of a mediation between the other and me, but of a mediation by the other lover between me and my own hatred of myself. The other, under the figure of the lover, recognizes me as her lover, assures me that she can love me, and persuades me that, after all and after all the others, even I could be worthy of someone loving me from out there. Loving oneself henceforward signifies that insofar as I discover myself to be a lover, and thus lovable, I will be able to end up by *loving even myself*—I will be able to end up pardoning even myself, last of all, which is akin to pardoning the lowliest of all those lovable, the one who is most difficult to love.

This inversion of the love of myself into the love even of myself is not the result of my loving myself from this point forward any more than before (for I do not love myself as if loved by myself, I simply discover myself as the lover of the other); nor do I find myself more lovable (as myself and through myself, I can only ever hate myself); nor is it that the other at last loves me more than I love her (for I would then sink into reciprocity, which is moreover unverifiable). The inversion here results from my admitting that the other loves me more as lover than I love myself, or rather (for I in fact never love myself), that *the other loves me more than I hate myself.* In the end, I love even myself, because the other lover, through her own advance, has made me a lover, and thus lovable in her eyes and, because I believed her, lovable in my own eyes. I wind up by loving even myself, because, in the other of the oath, of the flesh, and of faithfulness, I have at last found more lover than in me; I wind up loving even myself because I have believed, seen, and experienced that I too, even I, could play the lover—make the love to her that she told to me. This time I indeed give myself over to the other, since I indeed receive myself entirely—as lover—from what I receive—her. I love even myself on the word of the other, who says she is my lover. I believe what she tells me more than what I have ever told myself.

If such a love even of oneself goes beyond the aporiae of the love of self within me, it must be due to the other—the other who discovers herself more of a lover than me and makes me become a lover by her favor. If I can finally envisage accomplishing the erotic reduction to its core by ending up no longer hating myself and, instead, loving even myself, I owe it to the other lover, and thus to her anteriority. The other thus precedes me in the role of lover, which she assumes first, contrary to what I have claimed up to this point. Inevitably, there follows the consequence that the advance is inverted, and passes from me to her. Suddenly, the center of the erotic reduction draws back in front of me and I find myself on its periphery, or at least de-centered. The reduction did not at all result from my advance. In fact, without my knowing it, it preceded my advance.

If the erotic reduction was in advance even of my advance, this means that a third and final formulation is called for. Just as it opened with the question "Does anyone out there love me?" posed by vanity (§ 3), in order next to be radicalized by the question "Can I love first?" which was imposed by the lover (§ 17); so, now that the lover's advance (§ 18) inverts itself and proceeds first from the other and no longer from me, it is necessary to think the erotic reduction beginning from the accomplished lover, beginning from the other and no longer from me, beginning from the *adieu* and not from repetition. This final swing of the center of gravity can be expressed thus: "You loved me first." Not that I can at any moment excuse myself from playing the lover by risking my own advance—without it the aporia of the love of self would perpetuate the hatred of everyone for everyone and of every man for himself; but I discover, in my impetus and in the degree to which I throw myself into it, that this very advance does not belong to me and that I do not inaugurate it, but that, instead, it was expecting me, it draws me upward and supports me, like the air gives rise to a flight, or water supports swimming. Even more, I at last comprehend that, in this advance, the other had already begun to make herself a lover well before me; that by walking blindly on the way of the erotic reduction, in fact, I had, doubtless from the outset, already found what I thought only I was searching for; or that, more exactly, what I was searching for had already found me and guided me right to it. When I was advancing bewildered in my own advance, a blind lover not knowing whom to love or how, doubtless there were other lovers, senior to me, watching me, looking after my steps, and loving me already, without my knowledge, in spite of me. In order for me to enter into the erotic reduction, it was necessary for another lover to have gone there before me, a lover who, from there, calls me there in silence.

§ 42. The One Way

Here I am, come back to the point where I started—but henceforward with the assurance that I was lacking at the beginning. I know now what I wanted to know then. I have learned that I never could have asked myself, "Does anyone out there love me?" if another did not love me first. It was necessary that I enter into the erotic reduction and that I advance under the form of the lover in order that the logic of love lead me insensibly, but ineluctably, to comprehend that another loved me well before I loved her. It was enough that I accept the possibility for it to become actual.

In fact, no one can claim, at least without lying to oneself or contradicting oneself, that no one loves him or has loved him. This is confirmed by several arguments. First, that in order to complain that no one loves me, it is necessary that I already be alive; and in order to be alive, it was necessary that others love one another (by accident or by resolution, for a moment or for eternity, how they did it matters little), such that they enjoy it and, without knowing me, give me to myself in advance; thus it was necessary that they love one another enough to make me the gift of myself from the core of my future. Next, no one can claim that nobody loves him or her if he or she does not reproach at least a possible interlocutor with the situation, which is to say if he or she does not say it to someone who can hear it. From that point, there are two solutions; either this other is already in effect listening to me and, even in a minimal sense, loves me from the present moment; or, no one is listening, or no one is listening yet. Now, even in the latter situation, I can still continue to plead my case, complain of my fate and accuse the world; and I can only do so because I judge that I am not speaking into the void, because I still believe the possibility is open that one day someone will hear me, and that one day a third party will bring me justice; in short I believe that, eschatologically, a lover, each day, will come in order to love me. Here, the future does not redeem the present with a stupid empirical illusion; rather, I challenge the present empirical indifference to my inalienable, transcendental possibility of only being insofar as I am a lover, of only being insofar as I keep at least the possibility that someone will love me (§ 3) some day, some way.

In fact, for me it is never a matter of knowing if someone loved me, loves me, or will love me, but of knowing who and when. For it always goes like this: someone already loved me, loves me, or will love me, or, more probably, all three things are happening. For me, who know myself certainly to be in at least possible debt (in fact real) to a lover (unknown or, more often, known), it is uniquely a matter of knowing if I love, whom I love, and how I love her. And, just as for knowing it, it is enough that I decide it and, in order to decide it, I only need myself; thus I am never lacking anything to make myself a lover. I love from the outset according to the impossibility of impossibility.

Doubtless these arguments may seem to be just so many paradoxes. Nevertheless, that is not enough to disqualify them, as a short view would probably not fail to conclude; for paradoxes only arise if one attempts to aim at certain phenomena starting from a point of view other than that which they ask for, or according to an intentionality that contradicts their manifestation beginning from themselves (their anamorphosis); the paradox in fact stigmatizes the figure taken by certain phenomena that are refractory to their constitution as alleged objects of a transcendental subject, of which they challenge the supposed *a priori* position. But, when he approaches erotic phenomena, the *ego* become lover no longer constitutes anything objective: no longer is any thing other than himself at stake; indeed, no things, not even the world, but only himself and his erotic reduction are at stake. The lover does not constitute erotic phenomena like new objects, annexed to the mass of those that he already knows; on the contrary, he allows himself to be taken up in their radically new visibility, exclusively reserved for those who enjoy the privilege of loving and of making themselves loved. From *this* point of view, the paradoxes fade away, or rather they appear according to their own visibility, clear and distinct in its order, with a serene, albeit conditional, evidence; indeed, the evidence of erotic phenomena only manifests itself under the condition that one accept their own logic—the logic that opens the inaugural operation of the erotic reduction. Contrary to what metaphysics has ended up claiming, love lacks neither reason nor logic; quite simply, it does not admit reason or logic other than its own, and only becomes legible beginning from there. Love is said and made one way only, its own.

Love is said and is given in only one, strictly univocal way. As soon as one multiplies it into subtle and differentiated acceptations, to the point of equivocality, one ceases to analyze it better: one dissolves it and misses it entirely. Love is defined as it is deployed—beginning from the erotic reduction, and uniquely from it; love thus admits no other variation than that found in the moments of this unique reduction. A correct thinking of love is marked by its capacity to sustain for as far as possible the essential univocality of its one way. Again, it is important not to misunderstand: this univocality is not founded in the imperial preeminence of the lover, who would hang over all that he could love to the point of indistinction, just like the unity of science grounds itself in the indifference of the *ego* toward the difference of objects leveled off by the identity of the conditions of their knowing; on the contrary, the cases of love all converge in the lover losing his primacy and, in every circumstance, exposing himself to the unique question of vanity: "Does anyone out there love me?"; beginning from which, he can undertake to traverse the figures imposed by the erotic reduction. Outside of this reduction, there is no love, and no lover. Within it, there is the one way of love.

One will nevertheless object that the concept of love remains equivocal and must remain so in order not to contradict its extreme figures. Let us examine these alleged dichotomies and see if they put into question the univocality of love. First, it is argued, how can we maintain in the same concept the drives that push me toward objects as different as money, drugs, sex, or power, and, above all, how do we assimilate these to the movement that pushes me toward the other (a man, a woman, God, etc.)? Doesn't it just make good sense here to say that it is necessary to admit a radical equivocality? To clarify the question, it is enough to come back to the criteria of the erotic reduction and to test the cases in which it can be exercised. To begin with, it appears that the question "Does anyone out there love me?" (and even less those questions that follow) cannot concern the worldly objects here listed, simply because, even if I may desire to possess them, I cannot expect from them any assurance from "out there"; in effect, possessing them excludes every elsewhere and encapsulates them in my monad, which assimilates them (or vice versa). On the contrary, the movements that push me toward the other allow me to hear the question "Does anyone out there love me?" and thus to exercise the erotic reduction, precisely because they all open out onto the irreducible alterity of the other. Here one finds no equivocality of love, but instead the strict opposition between desires for possessable worldly objects, which in no way concern love, and the one way of love, which is recognized in the exercise of the reduction and against the proof of elsewhere.

This answer nevertheless does not prevent a second objection: even inside the domain thus defined by alterity, isn't it necessary at least to distinguish between erotic love and the love of friendship, or put otherwise, to admit once again an equivocality of love? Let us return again to the criteria of the erotic reduction, and test what here allows us to pose the question "Does anyone out there love me?" One sees quickly that it is necessary to distinguish two cases. In the first case, by friendship I understand a relation of equality (or quasi-equality) between two partners, who share the same interest (pleasure, utility, virtue, etc.) for a thing of the world, which forms the third party between them; does such a relation answer to "out there"? Of course not, because it can be reversed from one to the other, and because this "out there" or elsewhere should always be able to become a *here,* contrary to the erotic "out there" (§ 5); of course not, too, because it is a matter of a reciprocal exchange of a worldly third party, which each of the partners must enjoy and possess equally; this reciprocity is thus excluded from the erotic reduction, where the lover renounces reciprocity by taking up the advance (§ 18). Such a figure of friendship, which interprets it as the reciprocal enjoyment of a worldly third party, introduces no equivocality at all into the concept of love, simply because it in no way derives from it. In the second case, one interprets friendship as the demand for an irreversible elsewhere, the friend's advance without reciprocity, and the oath as pure common signification. But, from there, it is only formally a matter of love in its original concept, even if we are not talking about the totality of its figures. In any case, this gap is not enough to introduce an opposition between love and this type of friendship, much less equivocality.

One can respond with a third objection, apparently stronger. In effect, between love and friendship there lies a gaping equivocality: friendship certainly subscribes to the erotic reduction, for as much as I ask, "Does anyone out there love me?"; friendship also leads me to play the lover, who loves first without expecting reciprocity ("Can I love first?"); but it stops in front of the radicalized erotic reduction and refuses the exchange of eroticized flesh. It even excludes this stage on good grounds: in order to protect its distinctive privilege—the ability to exercise itself at the same moment toward *several* friends—my flesh must not be received from a flesh in particular, so as not to tie itself or limit itself to any friend in particular; friendship does not ask for exclusivity; it even takes exception to it and thus opposes itself to the radicalized reduction, where I cannot (and thus must not) receive my flesh from *one* single other flesh and give hers to *one* single other. One cannot ignore such a gap—which bears upon nothing less than the exclusivity of the other and the eroticization of the flesh to the point of climactic enjoyment and suspension. But it remains to measure it with greater precision.

Let us note once again that friendship unquestionably, straightforwardly, and without any ambiguity takes the very path of the erotic reduction (vanity, elsewhere, lover, advance, oath); and thus its way truly remains that of love in its uniqueness. Nevertheless, a major difference separates them; one that plays out first over the crossing of eroticized flesh (§§ 23–24) and the passage to climactic enjoyment (§ 25), which love attains, but from which friendship abstains. Is this stopping enough to exclude friendship from the one way of love? No, it seems, and for several reasons. First, friendship, having accomplished the first stages on the path of the erotic reduction, has won citizenship on the ground, by dint of being born there; we will not contest that. And all the less because friendship does not pose the problems that the subsequent stages encounter: indeed, beginning from the crossing of flesh, each erotic phase gives rise immediately to its negative moment, inseparable and inevitable—thus the dazzling confusion of the orgasm, the automaticity of eroticization, finitude and suspension, the lie and naturalization, etc.; everything happens as if, on the erotic route, we were advancing rapidly as long as friendship could follow the lover; but the trials begin to accumulate as soon as the lover continues alone, without friendship. Thus it would be necessary to reverse the question and ask: doesn't the friend outline a shorter, yet more accomplished figure of the erotic reduction than does the lover, who carries it on further only to unfold its darkened side (at least during a long episode, §§ 29–34)?

Second, what exactly does the erotic phenomenon lack in friendship? Contrary to idle appearances, friendship does not lack the eroticization of the flesh, and it does not remain at the abstraction of the oath; in friendship, too, I can receive my flesh from the friend, who gives it to me without having it, as lover; the friend also embraces me and holds me (but also the mother and the child, the father and the son, etc.). Here, it is simply that the eroticization of flesh does not go as far as climactic enjoyment, and thus is not exposed to suspension. Neither is there any ambiguity to fear in such an eroticization of the flesh without climax: I already know that eroticization can remain free, or put another way, that the flesh can allow itself to be eroticized without the immediate touch of another flesh, through speech alone (§ 35). Indeed, it could be that friendship proceeds precisely along this way and is the first to illustrate it; the way of friendship would pass, then, directly from the crossing of my flesh with that of the other (§ 23) to free eroticization (§ 35, or even § 28), without having to traverse the involuntary finitude of suspension, or confront the confused dispute between lying and sincerity (§§ 29–34). Does the friend appear as the happy because partial lover?

Third, it could be that friendship, understood according to this privilege and this shortcut, is no longer first or only defined by its stopping during the exchange of eroticized flesh, but rather by its anticipated option in favor of free eroticization. By refusing to engage in suspension and repetition, friendship in this way breaks free in advance from its temporality, and thus from the child as the third party on the point of leaving (§ 39); nevertheless it does not accede directly to the eschatological third party (§ 40), for it does not retain the function of loving a single other, and thus of loving once and for all, and in eternity. At the least, even badly situated between the third party on the point of leaving and the eschatological third party, between the child and the *adieu,* friendship unquestionably has a footing on the erotic way, beyond suspension, naturalization, and deception. Thus friendship never leaves the erotic reduction during the journey; rather, it cuts short in order to bypass a difficult stretch and more quickly rejoin the end. If it remains within the erotic reduction, let us conclude that it does not exclude itself either from love's one way.

But precisely on this point, one will object further that there is still an equivocality, at least between ἔρως and ἀγάπη. As the precise and constant philological distinction, which could oppose them, remains to be established, let us hold to the most widely received version of their conflict: passionate love, which enjoys itself and possesses the other, would contrast with virtuous love, which gives to the other and forgets itself. Now we do not require too much attention to notice that these characteristics are exchanged from the one to the other. The lover, he or she who preeminently renounces possession and reciprocity by taking his or her advance, nevertheless does enjoy, does eroticize through speech, jealously demands, too, and sometimes runs away. But this same lover, who enjoys and possesses, nonetheless succeeds in doing so by forgetting and abandoning him- or herself first: in general and in principle by his or her advance; next, and more precisely, by eroticizing first the flesh of the other and not his or her own (he cannot do it in any case, for he does not have it); by having also to await the other giving him his own flesh; and lastly, by conferring unilaterally upon the other the faithfulness that the other cannot promise. The lover's ἔρως thus shows itself to be just as self-giving and gratuitous as the ἀγάπη from which, moreover, it is no longer distinguished. One must have a good deal of naïveté or blindness, or rather know nothing of the lover and of erotic logic, not to see that ἀγάπη possesses and consumes as much as ἔρως gives up and abandons. It is not a matter of two loves, but of two names selected among an infinity of others in order to think and to say the one love. All that is comprehended beginning from the erotic reduction is phenomenalized according to its unique logic. Whatever makes an exception to that logic does not designate some other sense of love: rather, it simply does not belong to it. The difficulty does not consist in introducing exceptions to the erotic reduction and equivocations into univocal love, but in measuring just how far love's one way extends. Clearly, beyond its sexualization, which love's one way nonetheless alone renders intelligible, even while it constitutes only one of love's figures—the sharpest, but not the strongest.

Consequently, if love is only said like it is given—in one way—and if, moreover, God names himself with the very name of love, must we conclude that God loves like we love, with the same love as us, according to the unique erotic reduction? Clearly, one may hesitate, but nevertheless we cannot avoid this conclusion. For, in fact, God does not only reveal himself through love and as love; he also reveals himself through the means, the figures, the moments, the acts, and the stages of love, the one and only love, that which we also practice. He plays the lover, like us—passing through vanity (idols), the request that one love him and the advance to love first, the oath and the face (the icon), the flesh and the enjoyment of communion, the pain of our suspension and the jealous demand, the birth of the third party in transit and the announcement of the eschatological third party, who ends up by identifying himself in the incarnated Son, up to the unilateral promulgation by him to us of our faithfulness. God practices the logic of the erotic reduction as we do, with us, according to the same rite and following the same rhythm as us, to the point where we can even ask ourselves if we do not learn it from him, and no one else. God loves in the same way as we do.

Except for an infinite difference. When God loves (and indeed he never ceases to love), he simply loves infinitely better than do we. He loves to perfection, without a fault, without an error, from beginning to end. He loves first and last. He loves like no one else. In the end, I not only discover that another was loving me before I loved, and thus that this other already played the lover before me (§ 41), but above all I discover that this first lover, from the very beginning, is named God. God's highest transcendence, the only one that does not dishonor him, belongs not to power, nor to wisdom, nor even to infinity, but to love. For love alone is enough to put all infinity, all wisdom, and all power to work.

God precedes and transcends us, but first and above all in the fact that he loves us infinitely better than we love, and than we love him. God surpasses us as the best lover.